Rogues *s*

Rogues, Rebels and Runaways

Eighteenth-Century Cape Characters

NIGEL PENN

DAVID PHILIP PUBLISHERS
Cape Town

Published 1999 in Southern Africa by
David Philip Publishers (Pty) Ltd,
208 Werdmuller Centre, Claremont 7708, South Africa,
and in Europe by Verloren Publishers, P.O. Box 1741,
1200 BS Hilversum, The Netherlands

ISBN 0-86486-386-1 (David Philip)
ISBN 90-6550-054-5 (Verloren Publishers)

Cover art by Lien Botha

Printed in South Africa by Natal Witness Commercial Printers
244 Longmarket Street, Pietermaritzburg

Contents

Acknowledgements

The chapters in this book were written over a number of years. During that time I have been advised, encouraged and inspired by more people than I can possibly mention. A special word of thanks, however, is due to my colleagues in the Department of History at the University of Cape Town. Amongst them I would like to single out Nigel Worden (who has read all the chapters in one form or another) and Patrick Harries (whose amused scepticism about my style of writing has not prevented me from benefiting from his advice). Helen Bradford kindly commented on 'Brewer Menssink' and Patricia van der Spuy made some useful suggestions to me about readings in the history of female slaves.

I would like to thank members of the Archaeology Department at UCT, for it was in their company that I experienced, at first hand, the landscape which features in the narratives in this book. John Parkington, Andy Smith, Tony Manhire and Royden Yates have been my guides on many a delightful excursion and I value their input immensely.

In the Netherlands, on a research trip made possible by UCT, I was given great assistance by Robert Ross. I thank Jaap Bosschieter for his hospitality and Anna Hesselink and Ad Biewenga for information. The staff at the Rijks Archief were extremely helpful. The bulk of my research, however, was done in the Cape Archives Depot and the Centre for African Studies Library at UCT. The staff of these institutions have been unfailingly efficient and friendly, making the labour of research a real pleasure.

Susan Newton-King and Candy Malherbe are two scholars who know more than most about the eighteenth-century Cape. Their work and enthusiasm have always been stimulating. Pippa Skotnes and Harriet

Deacon have frequently spurred me onwards by believing in my work and I am grateful to them for their faith. I would like to thank Lien Botha for designing the book cover and Russell Martin, my editor, for making the whole book possible. My final word of thanks, however, must go to Jenny Sorrell. She knows why.

Some of the chapters in this book have been published elsewhere in a slightly different form. Chapter 3 first appeared in *Social Dynamics*, 14, 1 (June 1988). Chapter 4 was first published in *Kleio*, 17 (1985) and Chapter 5 was first published in the *South African Historical Journal*, 25 (1990). Chapters 1 and 2 are published here for the first time.

Introduction

THE chapters in this book are historical narratives about men and women on the margins of eighteenth-century Cape colonial society. The characters are marginal in several senses. Firstly, in their own day, they were regarded as having transgressed the boundaries of acceptable behaviour and entered a region of criminality or rebellion on the borders of, or beyond, colonial society. They are also marginal in that they were relatively unimportant people who occupied the ordinary ranks of Cape society without, it seems, exerting any great historical influence either before or after their transgressions. Thirdly, many of them actually lived in the liminal space of the eighteenth-century Cape frontier zone, on the very fringes of colonial expansion, neither wholly European nor African, but exotic hybrids of a new society in the making. Why have I felt compelled to construct their histories?

I first became aware of the characters who form the subject of this book whilst I was undertaking research on the eighteenth-century Cape frontier zone.[1] Many of the personalities who emerged from the archival documents refused to be ignored, nor would they suffer banishment to a footnote. In keeping with the turbulent natures they displayed more than two hundred years ago, and consistent with the irrepressible qualities with which they first forced themselves into the historical record, they demanded attention. They might have been marginal but they were visible, having left better documentary evidence of their lives than many of their fellows. For all their ordinariness they were thus anomalous, the 'exceptional normal' of their day, standing out sufficiently clearly to be noticed by both their contemporaries and by historians.[2] Apart from their noticeability, however, why bother to rescue such people from the 'enormous condescension of posterity',[3] considering that their life stories have lain gathering dust in the archives for more than two hundred years? One answer would be that their stories, taken simply as stories, are intrinsically fascinating human dramas, replete with tragic twists and the odd, enjoyable, comic turn. But a more important reason is that their comparatively well-detailed lives illuminate a hitherto rather obscure period of South African history – the eighteenth century – and draw attention to the forces and processes which were shaping it.

Ask any South African school child what happened in eighteenth-century South Africa, what personalities or people existed, or whether they have any mental images of the period at all, and the answer is likely to be a blank. This state of affairs is largely the result of school textbooks which present the period as a featureless lacuna between the establishment of European settlement at the Cape in 1652 and the beginning of the frontier wars in the eastern Cape in the late 1700s. The reality is that the eighteenth century is a crucial period in South African history. It was in this century that the tiny VOC (Vereenigde Oost-Indische Compagnie) settlement at the Cape expanded into a full-blown colony, largely at the expense of the indigenous Khoisan societies. It was also in this century that the social, political and economic foundations of colonial South Africa were laid. Whilst the social formations of the Khoisan disintegrated, new societies emerged. Amongst these were the descendants of European settlers – proto-Afrikaners – imbued with a sense of their cultural distinctiveness and yet far from constituting the homogeneous, egalitarian community of later Afrikaner nationalist mythology. Alongside them were peoples of mixed descent – part European, part Khoisan and part slave – whose ambiguous, but on the whole inferior, colonial status suggested that a racially ordered society was in the process of construction in the Cape. At the very bottom of the social scale and constituting the majority of the colony's population were the slaves, whose fundamental role in South African history is only gradually being appreciated.

The stories, or microhistories,[4] which follow attempt to show how certain individuals, members of the diverse and various societies of the eighteenth-century Cape colony, fell foul of the laws of the colonial government and either suffered or sought to avoid punishment. Their struggles – whether motivated by selfishness or heroism – draw attention to those areas where the government's interests clashed with those of specific individuals. These sites of contention help us to chart both the nature and extent of colonial authority at a particular time and place. They also provide us with a fascinating amount of detail, normally so hard to come by, about ordinarily obscure eighteenth-century colonial men and women, whether slave or free, colonist or Khoi.

The institution of slavery looms large in this book. The importance of slavery does not only lie in the fact that it underpinned the Cape economy, or that slave labour generated the wealth which facilitated the emergence of predominantly white and wealthy land-owning agriculturists – the Cape gentry.[5] The institution of slavery helped to shape social attitudes towards race and labour in both the private and the public domain.[6] A great many Cape slaves, particularly females, lived, worked and slept in close proximity to their owners' families.[7] The implications of this enforced intimacy, for both owners and slaves, are explored in Chapter 1, which deals with the tortured relationships that existed within the Menssink family, the brewers at the Cape at the beginning of the eighteenth century. The chapter also deals with the economics of beer-making, the factional politics of the governorship of W.A. van der Stel, and the sexual politics which underlay a domestic situation permeated by slavery. It may be argued that the Menssink household was an exceptional one in that adultery, divorce, infanticide, necromancy and attempted murder were not typical features of most Cape families. There is some truth in this observation, but for microhistorians the value of an exceptional case, or an exceptional individual, illuminates the historical background or context, by casting a more intense light on the subject. The exception also obliges observers to reassess the relationship between the exception and the rule, between the norm and those instances or individuals that transgress or challenge the norm. In this case the story of brewer Menssink's fatal passion for Trijntje, a female slave, may be regarded as a typical piece of microhistory in which the relationship between the microscopic dimension (the individual, the family) and the larger contextual dimension (society, systems of belief, of values and representation) is the organising principle in the narration. There is also another way in which the story of brewer Menssink is a typical piece of microhistory: throughout the writing of the story I have tried to indicate that my knowledge of events is fragmentary and incomplete, and my inability to answer certain questions, because of imperfect evidence, is part of the reality of historical narrative.

The topic of slavery or, more specifically, slave resistance is one of the central themes of Chapters 2 and 5, which deal with the phenomenon of *drosters* – deserters or runaways from colonial oppression. Flight is a particular form of resistance and, at the Cape, such resistance all too often assumed a violent form. That it did so is not so much due to the fact that those who deserted were violent individuals – though many of them were – but that the system itself was intrinsically violent. In a society governed by slave owners the interests of slave masters came to dominate. Thus the legal and political climate of the day legitimised a variety of violent and oppressive measures that the state, or the master, felt obliged to inflict upon all subordinate and potentially rebellious unfree labourers. But the slaves were not simply passive victims of their masters' will. Despite arguments that, at the Cape, there was no authentic slave culture, Cape slaves did manage to impart some of their culture, some of their individuality and, indeed, some of their genes to their masters' or mistresses' families.[8] Whilst acts of slave resistance might seem to have done nothing except add to the levels of violence inherent in the slave system, it is possible to view slave desertion more positively. The *droster* gangs described in these pages acted as the matrices for the later, more sophisticated 'Oorlam' groups of the northern Cape frontier zone. Such groups, whilst shaped by colonial society, sought to maintain an independence and identity distinct from colonial society. In time they developed into powerful frontier societies which, paradoxically, pioneered colonial expansion into, and beyond, the northern Cape. At a more humble level, fugitive gangs very often represented micro-societies in which oppressed people from a variety of backgrounds – slaves, Khoi, 'Bastaard-Hottentots' and Company deserters – grouped together in units of mutual support, sharing a common consciousness of oppression and developing a tenuous form of multi-ethnic solidarity.

Droster experiences were forged in an environment in which colonial farmers increasingly sought to reduce all non-white labourers in the colony to a condition approximating slavery. There were no European slaves at the Cape and there was thus a perceptible corollation between skin colour and free or unfree status. This was a situation that particularly affected the way in which Khoikhoi and San labourers were treated. Although the government disapproved of the enslavement or maltreatment of Khoisan labourers it was frequently powerless to prevent such abuses from occurring in the distant frontier districts. A good example of this is provided in the case of Carel Buijtendag, described in Chapter 4. Buijtendag was a Bokkeveld farmer with a particularly violent disposition. It was only with the greatest of difficulty that the government's local authorities were able to curb his cruel excesses, and it is richly ironic that Buijtendag ended his days, seemingly, as a martyr to despotism.

A far more convincing martyr may be found in the figure of Estienne Barbier, the leader of an unsuccessful anti-government rebellion in 1738. Though Barbier's rebellion failed, it served to expose the corrupt practices of the Cape authorities as well as the destructive dynamics of frontier expansion. He saw himself as the champion of ordinary frontier farmers but at the same time his rebellious utterances reflected the contempt which most colonial frontiersmen felt for the indigenous Khoisan. Despite these shortcomings, Barbier remains a fascinating character whose project of resistance is, I believe, best understood as an instance of social banditry. His life, belatedly, has come to assume the lustre of mythology and has, increasingly, inspired diverse novelistic interpretations. But truth is always stranger than fiction, and historical narrative, in this case, is a form of literature more likely to approach the truth.

Though historical narrative may approach the truth it is not, of course, the truth. The reality of the past can only be partially represented and one of the ways to do so – perhaps the quintessentially human way – is to organise it into narrative structures. Historians, like other people, make sense out of reality by ordering it into story forms.[9] Narrative is, indeed, an essential and defining element of history writing and I make no apologies for attempting to make stories out of the evidence I have consulted.[10] The fact that these stories are imaginative creations whose meaning emerges from the way in which they have been constructed should not lead readers to the extreme postmodernist conclusion that history is just another form of fiction. As Hayden White points out, narrative history is a distinctive and legitimate form of discourse which bestows meaning on events but does not thereby lose touch with real events or the truth value of its factual statements.[11] Historical narratives are not, after all, completely arbitrary, since they are based on (amongst other things) documentary evidence, which has itself been subjected to critical scrutiny. The historian, moreover, unlike the novelist, feels obliged to be constrained by the evidence, and if he or she goes beyond what the evidence permits, he or she ought to admit this.

A great deal of the documentary evidence behind the narratives of this book has been drawn from the criminal records of the VOC period which are housed in the Cape Archives. Quite clearly, one cannot use this material without being sensitive to its characteristics and limitations. Despite certain problems the court records of the VOC constitute an invaluable body of evidence. Nowhere else are the voices of the oppressed and vanquished – distorted though they might be – heard so clearly. Nowhere else do slaves, Khoi, criminals and the underclasses of the Cape get to tell their stories in such detail and thereby allow historians a glimpse of their lives. This all too scanty material is the major source available to historians who might wish to construct a 'history from below' of the eighteenth-century Cape: the precious details contained in these old court cases are the raw materials most useful for the construction of thickly detailed narratives, or thick descriptions, that enable historians to apprehend the probable meanings of past events.[12]

One problem arises from the fact that the court records were often scribal summaries of complex statements rather than the word-for-word transcription of proceedings. Also, the language of the court was Dutch, whereas in the multi-lingual society of the Cape the language of the accused was quite often not Dutch, and testimonies were thus transformed by the intermediacy of a translator. It should also be noted that the evidence generated in a courtroom is bound to be influenced by its particular context.[13] Most people appearing before the court were on trial, sometimes for their lives, and their testimony was most likely to have been presented in such a way as to deny guilt or escape punishment. On the other hand, the 'free and full' confessions which resulted from the interrogation process were frequently wrung from the accused by torture, or the threat of torture, and testimonies may therefore have been shaped by what the judges wanted to hear rather than what the accused wanted to say. The characters in this book, in other words, made stories out of their own deeds or actions in order to impart a particular meaning to the events which they had experienced. By understanding the meaning that past actors gave to their lives, historians make sense of the past, and it is in the stories which people told about themselves that this meaning resides.[14] It is up to historians, however, to understand the context and conventions of these 'stories from the archives' before including them in their own historical narratives.[15] Ultimately, it is the dialogic interplay between individual texts and their context that constitutes the terrain of historical, and particularly microhistorical, explanation.[16]

With this in mind, the stories that follow cannot simply be read as stories. As historical narratives they contain information about eighteenth-century Cape society, particularly its underbelly, that forms part of the reality of this country's early colonial history. The more one contemplates this reality, the more violent it appears to be. One might argue that this impression of violence is an exaggerated one, propagated by the specific nature of the sources consulted. To this objection I can only reply that all available evidence confirms that the eighteenth-century Cape was indeed a world permeated by violence and that individual lives, however unique in certain respects, however marginal they might have been, were part of the same society. Ordinary men and women would have been fortunate to avoid becoming either a victim or a perpetrator of this violence. It is violence that links the marginal people of these pages together and it is violence that makes them our contemporaries.

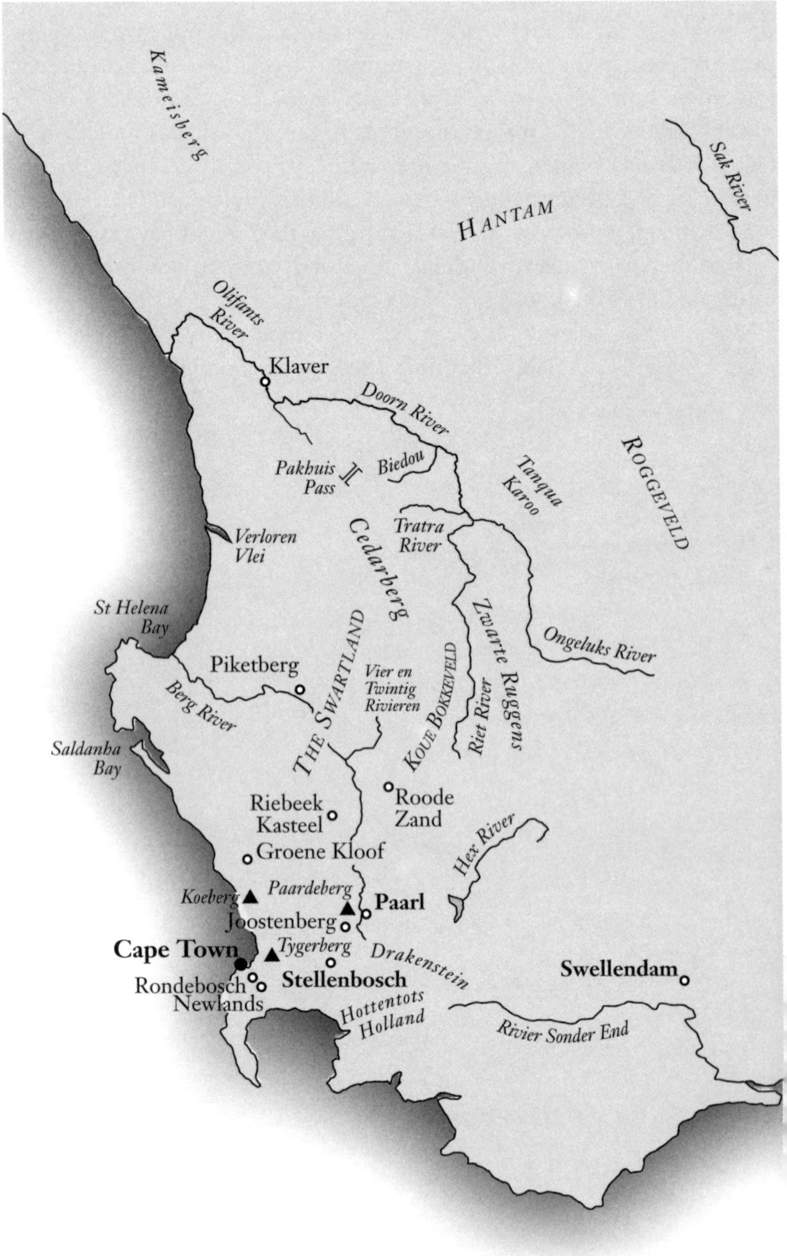

The Cape in the eighteenth century

1

The Fatal Passion of Brewer Menssink

Sex, beer and politics in a Cape family, 1694–1722

ONE evening in the year 1709 the female slave Trijntje of Madagascar stood outside her mistress's house on the corner of a Cape Town street. She was about 21 years old and had only been bought by her mistress, Elizabeth Lingelbach, two days before. It was between ten and eleven o'clock at night and Trijntje, her day's tasks done, lingered in the darkness.[1] Though new to the Lingelbach household she was not a recent arrival in the town. In 1696, as an 8-year-old girl, she had been bought at the mouth of the Maningaer River on the Madagascan coast by Andries Hummeltje, surgeon of the Dutch slaving frigate *De Soldaat*. Along with 115 other slaves she was then transported to Table Bay and there sold, for 40 rixdollars, to Mijndertsz Kruijwagen.[2] During her twelve years as a captive she had become a young woman and established a relationship with a male slave, Fredrick. Perhaps it was he for whom she waited outside her new workplace. The man who approached her, however, was not Fredrick. White and well-to-do, he wasted no time in propositioning the young woman directly. Emboldened by his considerable experience in the ungentle art of bending female slaves to his will, the man had the further advantage of being able to utilise his powerful status as a means of seduction. He could, in fact, almost claim to be the slave woman's master, for he was Willem Menssink, the Cape's foremost brewer, and the estranged husband of Trijntje's mistress.

Trijntje could not but have been aware of the nature of Menssink's relationship with her mistress. Mrs Menssink, or, to use her maiden name, Elizabeth Lingelbach, lived apart from her husband in her own house. Menssink, on the other hand, lived with his mother in another house in the Table Valley.[3] In the small world of eighteenth-century Cape Town there cannot have been many who did not know that the brewer and his wife kept separate establishments. Some, perhaps, might even have known why this was so. The truth was that Willem Menssink was not to be trusted with slave women.

Perhaps Trijntje knew this. Perhaps she did not. She was, in any event, faced with a difficult choice. Was it wise to deny such a powerful suitor his way? Would surrender to Menssink compromise her position in the Lingelbach household? What consequences might follow the acceptance, or rejection, of her mistress's husband? Flustered, she refused Menssink's advances, declaring that she was already Fredrick's lover. The disappointed brewer left without importuning her further – for the time being. The very next night, however, at about nine o'clock, Trijntje received a visit from one of Menssink's slaves. Isaac of Masulipatam[4] was in his late twenties and, as future events would demonstrate, quite familiar with the geography, both physical and social, of the Lingelbach house. Although master and mistress might live apart, their households obviously remained linked together by the surreptitious movements of their domestic slaves, who exchanged visits and information on a regular basis. It is quite possible that Isaac had acted as pander for his master before. Whatever it was he said to Trijntje had the desired effect, for the young woman was persuaded to follow him, in secret, to Menssink's house. There the amorous brewer promised her that, if she consented to his demands, neither Fredrick nor her mistress would find out. He got his way. Trijntje was rewarded with four *dubbeltjes* and a glass of corn beer. Returning guiltily to the Lingelbach household, she could not have known that she, the slave, had just made a captive of her mistress's husband. For the next four years, Willem Menssink was bound by an emotion so powerful that he would eventually disgrace himself, ruin his fortunes, and cause the death of the woman he loved. Trijntje of Madagascar had become brewer Menssink's fatal passion.

Menssink had arrived at the Cape at about the same time as Trijntje. In 1694 the Heren XVII (the rulers of the Dutch East India Company, or VOC) decided to improve the quality of beer at the Cape by sending out an experienced brewer. Their choice fell upon Rutgert Menssink of Deventer, a Dutch town on the IJssel renowned for its malt beer. Rutgert, his wife Gerbregt Berdenis, and their son, Willem, were thus shipped to the Cape at the Company's expense, arriving on the

Dregterland in 1695.[5] Willem was 30 years old at the time and, as yet, unmarried. His father was given Papenboom, a handsome property of some thirty morgen about one and a half hours' journey from the Castle, between Rondebosch and the Company's gardens at Newlands. It was plentifully supplied with water, both from the Liesbeek River and the streams which flowed from Table Mountain.[6] Here, according to Mentzel (a German visitor to the Cape during the early eighteenth century), Rutgert Menssink 'was provided with all the necessary requisites that would enable him to brew as good a beer as in his native Deventer'.[7] The Cape government, indeed, informed the Heren XVII that they had 'given' Rutgert Menssink the large boilers or brewing kettles that were required 'and further assisted him in every way'.[8] We should note, however, that at a later date the authorities declared that they had only loaned the Menssinks the brewing kettles, and that the Menssinks, for their part, would later claim that the cost of establishing the brewery had been over 20,000 guilders.[9]

Beer was the most important drink in Dutch society. As a whole the Dutch had the unenviable reputation of being a nation of drunkards, and beer was their favourite tipple – at the breakfast table as well as in the tavern. Apart from its dietary or nutritional function it served as the essential social lubricant, sealing deals between buyers and sellers, soothing and cementing relationships in homes and alehouses, and, whether consumed in informal or highly formal toasts, an important part of the rituals of social familiarity.[10] Though Dutch beer production was declining during the eighteenth century (as consumption patterns changed to accommodate beverages such as coffee, tea, wine and gin), beer remained supreme and brewing was a mainstay of the Dutch economy.[11] There were, therefore, both cultural and economic imperatives behind the Company's determination to establish beer production at the Cape. Good Dutch beer would help to make the colony properly Dutch. It would also assist in the important economic aim of restoring the health of ailing VOC sailors. A healthy brewing industry would provide employment for free burghers, revenue for the Company, and of course beer itself, the great panacea for all ills.

Earlier attempts at beer making at the Cape, in the European style, had been rather amateurish and unsuccessful.[12] Knowledge of home brewing techniques was fairly widespread amongst Dutch men and women at the Cape and a domestic production known as 'sugar beer' circulated throughout the colony. Van Riebeeck himself had made a beer, which was described as 'nothing in particular' by the Company directorate in 1658, but proper malt beer was hard to make.[13] A succession of men had preceded Rutgert Menssink in the attempt to produce a decent beer. In 1672 a certain Hendrik Evertsz Smith was given the sole lease for the brewing of malt beer for the price of 600 guilders a year. Three years later, however, the visiting commissioner Nicolaus Verburgh declared, after tasting the results, that he was unimpressed.[14] This damning judgment appears to have discouraged local endeavours until 1694 when the Company allowed Theunis Dirksz van Schalkwyk a six-year period in which to produce malt beer.[15] It is unlikely that Van Schalkwyk enjoyed much success, for the very next year the lease was taken from him and given to Rutgert Menssink. The Company had decided to apply imported expertise to the beer problem.

Part of the difficulty facing Cape brewers was to obtain satisfactory hops. Van Riebeeck had tried, and failed, to grow hops. Those who repeated his experiments also failed and hops, therefore, had to be imported in a dried form. When Rutgert Menssink and his family sailed south in the *Dregterland* they brought some hops plants with them, but these rotted on the voyage.[16] This proved to be an inauspicious omen, for, as time would tell, neither the Menssink family nor their brewing industry was to flourish at the Cape.

Once the Menssinks had been installed at Papenboom, the authorities had to decide how the brewer was to sell his beer and what price he might charge for it. Care had to be taken not to injure the interests of other parties with a stake in the beer trade. If Rutgert Menssink was allowed to sell his beer as a retailer, rather than a wholesaler, the government stood to lose a considerable amount in revenue. To begin with, they would lose 2000 guilders – the amount recently paid for the beer lease by Theunis van Schalkwyk. Other liquor leases, such as those for European beer, brandy and Cape wines, would also be prejudiced if the brewer enjoyed too many advantages. It would be absurd, argued the Council of Policy, to allow the brewer also to be a retailer, 'as the two trades are quite distinct at home, in order to prevent smuggling'. If the brewer was, at the same time, a retailer, other retailers and innkeepers would be unable to compete with the brewer's prices and would therefore close down, causing a further loss of revenue for the government. It was also feared that a great number of people who were making a living from the sale of sugar beer might 'be ruined and fall on the parish' should the colony's principal brewer be granted the right to retail beer. A resolution of July 1693 had declared that brewing was permissible to everyone, except innkeepers and retailers, and, according to the Cape authorities in 1696, 'many large families support themselves with the sale of sugar beer.'[17]

A compromise, therefore, had to be reached, and the solution was that Rutgert Menssink was permitted to sell beer to the public at 4, 5, 6 and 8 guilders a cask but not in smaller measures. The beer lease was sold to Theunis van Schalkwyk for 3400 guilders, the lessee being obliged to buy his beer from the brewer only, for 10 guilders an aum.[18] Should the brewer be unable to deliver, the lessee was to report this to the government.[19] This was an arrangement fraught with potential friction and it was not long before the imperfections of the system emerged.

By January 1697 the brewery at Papenboom was functional and Rutgert Menssink had produced his first brew of Cape malt beer. The Council of Policy ordered him to send three vats to the Netherlands, for the judgment of the Heren XVII, and three vats to the Batavian authorities for their opinion. He would be paid 36 guilders a vat. Whatever the response of these overseas tasters was, Theunis van Schalkwyk, the holder of the beer lease, was not happy with the product. He petitioned the authorities twice, on 22 January and 11 February, to complain that the beer was sour and unsaleable. Even though the Cape authorities agreed that the beer was often 'muddy and unhealthy, and hardly preservable for five days' there was probably an element of resentful rivalry in Van Schalkwyk's complaints since he claimed that, were he to be given Menssink's advantages as brewer, combined with the right to retail beer at 4 *dubbeltjes* a flask, he would pay the Company 6000 guilders for the beer lease. The Council was unmoved by this offer. Rutgert Menssink, meanwhile, declared that he could not produce a better product at that price and that he could not prevent the beer from becoming sour. By 23 February lessee and brewer had come to an agreement and the former began to retail the Menssink brew 'with apparently fair success'.[20]

The success was short-lived. The years 1696 and 1697 had been years of harvest failure and on 26 July 1698 the new brewery had to shut down because of a shortage of material. Rutgert Menssink believed, though, that he had found the reason for his beer turning sour: it was simply too hot to brew during the summer months. This did not bode well for the future and, in the meantime, Van Schalkwyk was allowed to cancel his lease, the government agreeing to refund him the difference between the cost of the lease and the money he had made from beer sales.[21]

The following year sees an ambiguity in the records, which state that Rutgert Menssink was awarded the sole right to tap Cape malt beer on condition 'that he shall provide a good article and not ask for a remission of any portion of the lease amount'.[22] And yet we also learn that the lease of Cape malt beer had been given to a certain Hendrik Mulder. Whether this means that the lease was split between the two men, with the brewer licensed to sell large quantities only, is unclear. What is certain, however, is that Mulder complained that Rutgert Menssink had been unable to supply him with sufficient beer and that he had frequently had to close his establishment as a result. Mulder was consequently awarded a *pro rata* repayment for his beer lease.[23]

Despite these rather unpromising beginnings, the brewery was obviously making some money and helping to establish the Menssinks as one of the Cape's more prosperous families. On 26 February 1696, even before the brewery went into production, Willem Menssink, the brewer's son, married Johanna Maria Tas, the youngest sister of Adam Tas.[24] The Tases ranked amongst the foremost families of the Cape and were very well connected. Adam's uncle was Henning Hüsing, one of the Cape's wealthiest men and holder of the lucrative meat lease, or *pacht*. Hüsing's wife, Maria Lindenhovius, was, in turn, an aunt of the Tases on the mother's side.[25] These family connections were to prove of vital importance to Willem Menssink, and his marriage to Johanna signalled his entry into the Cape's elite. At a later stage, with his life in ruins, it was his brother-in-law Adam Tas and his sister-in-law Sara Wilhelmina Tas, who stood by him to the end.

Apart from this advantageous marriage there were other signs that the Menssinks were moving up the social ladder. In March 1696, Willem bought a slave, Gerrit of Malabar, from Henning Hüsing for 125 rixdollars. In June 1697 Rutgert bought February of Bouton for 70 rixdollars, in March 1699 he bought Paris of Macassar for 60 rixdollars and in April 1700 he bought Susanna of Macassar for 62 rixdollars. There were clearly other slaves who were purchased by the Menssinks, for in January 1700 Rutgert was able to sell Titus of Bengal for 70 rixdollars.[26] These transactions indicate that it had not taken long for the Menssinks to acquire the capital, or credit, necessary to join the slave-owning class. Social status grew apace with slave ownership and in December 1699 Rutgert was appointed a member of the Burgher Council. Willem's status was also enhanced, as reflected in his appointment, in December 1697, to the office of church deacon and, in November 1699, to the rank of lieutenant in one of the Cape's two burgher infantry companies. His brother-in-law Adam Tas was made ensign in the other.[27]

Some time between April and August 1700 Rutgert Menssink died. He had, at least, lived long enough to see his son, Willem, and his daughter-in-law, Johanna Maria Tas, produce offspring, for on 15 February 1699 their baby daughter, Margarieta Maria Menssink, was baptised. Sadly, Johanna Maria was not to live for very much longer. We cannot say precisely why, or when, she died but Willem Menssink became a widower before the end of September 1701. Indeed, since Menssink remarried on 16 October 1701 it is likely that Johanna Maria had died at least several months before this date.[28] There is very little information about Menssink's first marriage and it is tempting to suppose – given Menssink's subsequent history – that he is unlikely to have been a faithful spouse. In contrast to this supposition, however, is the fact that the Tas family continued to count Willem as one of their number, a loyalty that would have been misplaced had Menssink dishonoured Johanna Maria.

Menssink's new wife was Elizabeth Lingelbach, daughter of David Lingelbach, a surgeon, and his wife Elizabeth Glazerus. David Lingelbach had arrived at the Cape in 1699 but his short-lived career ended with his death in 1705 or 1706.[29] Initially he must have thought that his daughter had made an excellent match, for in 1701 the prospects of Willem Menssink seemed excellent. Had he not inherited a successful brewery and was he not one of the Cape's most respectable free burghers, a fact confirmed by his reappointment as church deacon in December 1701?[30] The truth, unfortunately, was somewhat different.

In the first place the real inheritor of the brewery was not Menssink but his mother, Gerbregt Berdenis. Although under Dutch law a system of partible inheritance was applied – whereby the deceased's estate was shared equally between the surviving spouse and children – Gerbregt was the one who attempted to continue the Menssink family tradition of beer making and it was she who dealt with the day-to-day business of running the brewery. Although her son spent a considerable amount of time at the brewery, it became increasingly clear that whatever skills he possessed did not extend to the subtle art of producing potable intoxicants. There were many who doubted Gerbregt's abilities as a brewer too, but the government continued to back her for the time being. In August 1700 the Council of Policy decided that the beer licence was not to be leased but to be left to the widow Rutgert Menssink and her son for 2950 guilders since 'It was considered that last year in consequence of the failure of the harvest she had to close her stores for six months, paying her lease all the same, and been obliged to wait till December for new corn'.[31] Though the price of the lease was increased to 3000 guilders in 1701, Gerbregt and Willem were again awarded the lease for Cape malt beer, in consideration of the fact that as there was no corn their tap was closed for five months, and 'that they had through a contagious disease lost their best slaves, and also because the directors in their dispatch of 27th August 1694 had ordered the Governor and Council to help Rutgert Menssink in his first attempts and favour him further in all burgher functions'.[32]

This privileged position lasted unchallenged until 1706. Elizabeth Lingelbach, meanwhile, was learning that her new husband's façade of respectability was as dubious as his brewing skills. To her great dismay, on arrival at the brewery on the very first night of her marriage, she discovered that her husband enjoyed a 'wholly unreasonable freedom of intercourse' with the slave woman Susanna.[33] This obliged Elizabeth to request that the key to Susanna's bedroom door be handed over to her every night, a precaution which quite failed to prevent Menssink from gaining access to the slave woman during the day. According to Elizabeth, the 'sordid intercourse' between Susanna and her husband became more and more obvious. Once Elizabeth discovered them together in the attic. On another occasion she found them in a compromising situation in the dairy, whereupon Menssink pretended to hit Susanna in an attempt to allay his wife's suspicions. He was, in short, indifferent to Elizabeth and determined to satisfy his lust for his slave, calling her from her labours in order to take his pleasure.[34]

According to Elizabeth's later testimony in court, it was not only with Susanna that Menssink sinned, for she once surprised him in the stables with two other slave women. Though the stable door was locked she could hear 'ungodly activities' going on inside. She knocked loudly on the door but when her discomposed husband emerged he explained that he had followed the women into the stables in the belief that they were stealing feed, and that he had been chasing them around in order to chastise them.

Worst of all, however, was when Elizabeth woke up one night next to her husband only to discover that Susanna was lying on the other side of the bed so as to gratify Menssink's 'lascivious lust'. The outraged wife seized the slave woman by the hair and held her till she broke loose, leaving her with a head-scarf clutched in her hands. Her attempts to remonstrate with her husband were useless, for he lay still, not saying a word. In the morning further questioning provoked Menssink into a fit as he fell to the ground with 'quijl' coming from his mouth and nose, causing her to suspect that she was dealing with a form of madness ('gekheid'). Her compassion aroused, she lifted him up and, with much soft coaxing, eventually persuaded him to speak. Menssink confessed that, ever since his first wife's death, the slave woman had been coming to him. Elizabeth warned him that, if it happened again, she would tell her parents, whereupon Menssink promised her that he would rather forfeit his prospects for salvation than re-engage with the slave woman or pollute their conjugal bed.[35]

Somewhat reassured, Elizabeth attempted to resume their marriage but, only a short while later, suffered bitter disillusionment. Menssink had asked her to accompany him from the brewery to Cape Town in order to visit his mother, who was at this stage residing in town. Once there, however, he immediately pretended to have forgotten something at Newlands which neccesitated his return and he asked Elizabeth to stay and keep his mother company in his absence. A day or so later a message arrived from Menssink which stated that Susanna had given birth to a little girl. It was a full fourteen days before Menssink returned to Cape Town in order to escort his wife back to the brewery ('na buijten'), a journey which a single woman seemingly dared not undertake at that time. It was obvious to Elizabeth, both from Menssink's behaviour and the favoured treatment given to Susanna and her child, that Menssink had simply 'let the wind blow his promises away'.[36]

After this, Menssink consorted with his slave women with renewed vigour. Susanna remained his favourite, though it seems she shared her room with a male slave.[37] Menssink would wait until this slave was busy with the task of heating the water for the brewery and then, on the pretext of checking the temperature, would slip out of his own bedroom and lie with Susanna – in which circumstances Elizabeth often trapped him. She also trapped him with other slave women in a little room alongside the brewery. Menssink's response to these unwelcome interruptions was to beat his wife grievously ('seer deerlijke'), accompanying his blows with the following question: 'Weet jij nog het Caabse gebruijk niet, dat eens hier na 't oude Testament leeft' (Do you still not know the Cape custom, that here we live by the Old Testament).[38]

There are two assumptions behind this revealing remark: firstly, that the Old Testament allowed patriarchal slave-owners the right to sleep with their slave women, and secondly, that at the Cape it was customary to exercise this right. As a deacon in the church Menssink was no doubt as familiar with the Old Testament as other members of the Cape congregation. Indeed, there is evidence that he was probably better read and more thoughtful about religious matters than most. We know that he had an extensive private book collection and that the two books which were most precious to him were the Holy Bible and a book of Jewish antiquities (probably by Josephus).[39] It is possible that he saw a similarity between his position and that of Abraham in Genesis. Elizabeth Lingelbach was never to bear Menssink a child, just as, at one stage, it seemed that Sarah would never bear Abraham a child. 'And Sarah said unto Abraham, Behold now, the Lord hath restrained me from bearing: I pray thee, go in unto my maid; it may be that I may obtain children by her. And Abraham hearkened to the voice of Sarah.'[40] Though Elizabeth was never to give Menssink such an invitation, in his opinion he clearly did not need it, for the Bible's authority was sufficient. Indeed, in Menssink's reading of the Old Testament it seemed one could sleep with one's own slave women, or one's wife's slave women, even though one already had legitimate children and (since he was an unmarried widower when he first slept with Susanna) whether or not one had a wife, barren or fertile, at all.

To what extent were these views shared by Cape society at large? Were they indeed 'het Caabse gebruijk'? In the first place one should note that in all slave societies issues of sex and power are closely interrelated. As Barbara Bush explains, the root source of power in slave societies was power wielded at the most basic level over the bodies of slaves. 'In the Caribbean, white men and women alike could exercise such power over their slaves through punishment, torture and control of their physical environment. The productive body had also to be a subjected body. At a more subtle level, sexuality itself became a fundamental component of the power white men exercised over all women, black and white, and, by appropriating their womenfolk, over black men. Thus power over the body and sexual power blended together as an effective force for social control.'[41] On a mundane level, in slave societies (like the early Cape colony) where free men outnumbered free women, the men turned to female slaves for sexual satisfaction.

A wide variety of sources do attest to the prevalence of the custom whereby male Cape colonists slept with slave women. Mentzel reported that young settler males 'who, through force of circumstance, have to remain at home during these impressionable years between 16 and 21 more often than not get entangled with a handsome slave girl belonging to the household. These affairs are not regarded as very serious. The girl is sternly rebuked for her wantonness, and threatened with dire punishments if she dares to disclose who was responsible for her condition; nay, she is bribed to put the blame on some other man.'[42] Female slaves in the Company slave lodge were also subject to sexual exploitation by white male settlers who were accustomed to using the lodge as a brothel.

But despite these examples we should not conclude that such practices enjoyed either official sanction or religious approbation. The official viewpoint was that white males should be discouraged from indulging in sexual relationships with slave women and, after 1678, even marriage with a baptised, Dutch-speaking slave woman of 'full colour' (who would have to be manumitted for the ceremony) was prohibited. A *plakkaat* of the same year noted that three-quarters of the children in the Company slave lodge were half-caste and that Europeans were going about openly in the streets with slave women. Such conduct was deemed 'destructive of that respect for the European which should be the best safeguard of order in general'.[43] In 1685 Commissioner Hendrik van Reede noted that the *plakkaat* of 1678, which prohibited sexual intercourse between white men and female slaves, had been ignored and that concubinage with a slave was accepted as being lawful. Van Reede reiterated official prohibition of this practice but stipulated that female slaves who had a white father could marry whom they liked after they had been liberated, on condition that prospective grooms were upright and honourable.[44]

The church, of course, regarded all sexual relationships outside of marriage as fornication, and certainly did not condone behaviour such as Menssink's. We have this on first-hand authority, for in 1707, in sheer desperation, Elizabeth Lingelbach approached the Revd Engelbertus Franciscus le Boucq, minister of the church in Drakenstein, to act as mediator between her and her husband in an attempt at reconciliation. The attempt failed but, on being apprised of the facts of the matter, the reverend minister confided to Elizabeth that he did not know what to make of Menssink and fully supported her request to separate from her husband.[45]

This, however, was in the future, and before informing the church of her predicament, Elizabeth Lingelbach sought the assistance of her parents in changing the miserable state of her marriage. Thus, about ten months after the birth of Susanna's child, Elizabeth went to her parents' home, unable to bear her husband any longer. The question arises as to why Menssink had married Elizabeth at all since he was indifferent to her from the beginning and in no ways reliant on the institution of marriage for his sexual fulfilment. It was not because he sought a mother for his young daughter, Margarieta Maria, for the little girl was being brought up by her mother's relatives. More specifically, she was in the household of Henning Hüsing and Maria Lindenhovius in Strand Street, the residence also of her aunt, Sara Wilhelmina Tas.[46] Had Menssink married, then, for money? The Lingelbachs do not appear to have been especially wealthy. As a surgeon Elizabeth's father, David, would not have been more than comfortably well-off. His earnings were obviously not so great as to relieve his wife, Elizabeth Glazerus, from the necessity of adding to her income, for she ran a coffee house in the town. Husband and wife together earned enough money to afford several slaves and at least one or two properties in the town, but this did not mean that the Lingelbachs ranked amongst the Cape gentry. Indeed, the respectability of Elizabeth Glazerus's coffee house is somewhat questionable, for she was arrested – though subsequently released – for the illegal sale of alcoholic drink in May 1704.[47]

There is, therefore, no apparent reason for Menssink's marriage to Elizabeth Lingelbach. Despite the unhappy nature of the union her parents decided to try to salvage the relationship, for divorce was not an easy option in the early eighteenth century. The Lingelbachs spoke to their son-in-law about his sinful behaviour and he duly promised to lead a better life, stating this intention (and acknowledging his shame) in writing, in a letter to the Lingelbachs dated 3 August 1704.[48] Elizabeth returned to Menssink but she decided to insist upon his selling Susanna. He argued that, since his father had bought the slave woman for Margarieta Maria, he could not in fairness sell her. Elizabeth thereupon proposed that he send the slave to his daughter at Henning Hüsing's house but Menssink, though agreeing to do so, dragged his heels over the matter. In 1705, noticing a lapse into his old ways, Elizabeth persuaded Menssink to write out another solemn promise of good conduct. This time the brewer signed it in his own blood. But not even this measure could prevent Menssink from abandoning himself to his desires.[49]

To Elizabeth Lingelbach's distress, Menssink now began to discuss their marital problems – in a spirit of light-hearted raillery – in the presence of her mother-in-law. Topics such as divorce, and the need for men to have more than one wife as a sexual partner, received an airing. As the domestic crisis escalated, the breath of scandal also entered her mother's coffee house, since Menssink and his mother visited that establishment in order to discuss private family matters with the Lingelbachs. The death of Elizabeth's father, David Lingelbach, at some time in 1705 or 1706 seems to have afforded Menssink even greater licence to mistreat his wife. On one occasion he dragged her across the floor by her hair, on another he beat her with a sjambok, and on another he sat on her chest. Eventually Elizabeth decided that she did not dare to live with him at the isolated brewery any longer and fled to her mother in the town. She declared that she would not return to him unless he changed completely and began to behave in a decent fashion. The chances of this happening, she must have realised, were remote.[50]

Whilst these domestic dramas were being enacted, the business of beer brewing continued. It is not unreasonable to suppose that problems at the brewery contributed to the breakdown of the Menssinks' marriage. The year 1704 had been a bad one for beer due to a lack of grain and, as a consequence, Gerbregt, widow Menssink, was allowed to pay 2000 guilders instead of 3000 for the Cape beer lease.[51] The next time the lease was allocated, however, she found that the Company was far less lenient towards her. They now returned to the old conditions and stipulated that the licence for selling beer should be sold at public auction 'to see whether it will not produce more'. The brewer was to be allowed the right to bid for the lease and the lessee was 'to be bound to pay the full amount of the lease unless he can prove that he could obtain no beer through the malice of the brewer or in case the lessee be a brewer, that there was no corn, or that his machinery had become defective'. The widow Menssink and her son were also informed that they were to pay 2000 guilders for the two brewing vats which the Company had loaned them ten years before.[52]

What was the reason for this sudden loss of official favour? It is possible that the Council of Policy had received intelligence that the Menssinks, Willem in particular, were negligent brewers who deserved no special treatment. But it is far more likely that Governor Willem Adriaan van der Stel was becoming increasingly aware of a conspiracy, or protest, aimed against his administration, and led by some of Menssink's closest family and friends, most notably Henning Hüsing and Adam Tas.

The opposition to Willem Adriaan van der Stel was, in the main, centred round a group of fairly well-to-do Stellenbosch agriculturists who objected to the unfair competition they were encountering from the colony's wealthiest farmer – the Governor himself – and his cronies. Although the Governor and all other Company officials were legally forbidden to engage in farming operations, this did not deter them. In 1700 W. A. van der Stel had been granted the 400 morgen estate of Vergelegen in the Hottentots Holland (subsequently enlarged by a further 117 morgen), which he set out to transform into a productive giant. Using Company slaves and servants as though they were his own, Van der Stel constructed extensive farm buildings, planted out 500,000 vine stocks and tended over 18,000 sheep and 1000 cattle. Other Company officials followed his example, setting up large farming enterprises for themselves. Since 'they enjoyed preference in the disposal of their produce to the Company, and in the purchase of anything they required from the Company', they had a huge advantage over the ordinary free burghers.[53]

The presence of powerful and privileged competitors might not have been so bad had the Cape market been an extensive and open one. It was, however, small and closed. Colonists were required to sell their produce to the Company, or the Company's agents, at Company-determined prices. Only once the Company had met its own needs might free-burgher farmers apply for permission to sell their produce to other potential buyers – such as the crews of ships in Table Bay. It follows that Van der Stel and his favourites were in the enviable position of being able to manipulate the market to their own advantage, giving preference to their own produce and restricting the marketing opportunities of ordinary farmers.[54]

Colonists wishing to sell wheat on the market had to sell it to the Company at a fixed price. The mechanisms through which the Company regulated the marketing of meat and drink, however, were slightly more complicated and, since they have a bearing on the Menssinks, merit some attention. In order to raise revenue the Company custom was to sell the contract for supply (the *pacht*) to leaseholders (or *pacht*-holders) at a public auction. In the past the sole right to provide the Company with meat had been held by Henning Hüsing. Initially, Hüsing had been a favoured friend of the Governor, but as his wealth grew so too did his independence, and it would seem as though he and Van der Stel had a falling out. Hüsing was expected to pay considerable gifts, or *douceurs*, to

Van der Stel for the privilege of possessing the meat contract.[55] He was also, no doubt, obliged to buy much of the Governor's livestock so as to sell it to the Company (at a stipulated price), thereby acting as the outlet for the Governor's mutton and beef. The more of the Governor's meat he sold, the less he could sell of his own, and he was obviously beginning to resent these restrictions. In December 1705 the meat contract was taken away from Hüsing and given to four licensed butchers. On the face of it, it seemed fairer for the government to have several meat contractors instead of only one. But the perception in certain sections of society was that the four new men were the Governor's creatures. As Adam Tas observed: 'Now the Governor has arranged things to his own liking; he has contrived a way of disposing of his own sheep and of others of his following.'[56]

Van der Stel also moved to gain greater control over the liquor trade. The most important branch of this business in the colony was the retail of Cape wine. The right to sell wine was customarily sold at an annual auction in August. Usually, four separate *pachts* were auctioned but in 1705 the Governor arranged it so that one person might, if they could afford it, buy all four parts of the licence as one. It became clear that Van der Stel meant to have a certain Johannes Phijffer buy the consolidated *pacht* and use him to unload his own wine on the market. (By now the Governor owned one quarter of all the vines in the colony.) Phijffer was widely considered to be a rogue and a smuggler and, when he duly did become the sole concessionaire for Cape wine, a great many burghers were disgusted by the Governor's blatant manipulation of the leasing arrangements.[57] A direct source of concern to the Menssinks was that Phijffer was allowed to acquire a farm right next to their brewery, where he set up a public wine house called Wijn en Brood. This attracted a great deal of custom away from the brewery and was seen, by the Menssinks, as being a deliberate threat to their interests.[58]

The Governor was indeed concerned to bring that other branch of the Cape's drink trade – beer – under closer supervision, for it was a lucrative source of revenue and an important site of political patronage. Even though the Governor was not himself a brewer, there was no reason why his enemies should enjoy the cheap and uncontested right to sell Cape malt beer. Van der Stel obviously decided that it would be far better to auction the beer *pacht*, thereby increasing government revenue, and reward his supporters by giving them, and not the Menssinks, the right to make beer. He would make the Menssinks realise that if they opposed him or supported any opposition, they would pay for it.

Were the Menssinks really the Governor's enemies? They were definitely members of the anti-Van der Stel party by association. Menssink's daughter was growing up as one of the family in the Hüsing household whilst Menssink's brother-in-law was Adam Tas himself, who was, along with Hüsing and Jacob van der Heiden, a central figure in the organisation of opposition to the Governor. Widow Menssink was later to inform the Heren XVII that when her son had gone to petition Van der Stel for the renewal of the beer *pacht* the Governor had refused, stating that 'the children should pay for the sins of the parents'. By this he was clearly referring, so Gerbregt Menssink explained, to the fact that Hüsing was like a father to Willem since Willem had married Hüsing's niece Johanna Tas in 1696.[59] Family connections alone, therefore – and it may be seen how powerful the idea of the extended family was in early-eighteenth-century Dutch culture – were enough to implicate the Menssinks, as far as Van der Stel was concerned, in the conspiracy against him. But there is, in fact, other evidence which suggests that Menssink was indeed of the anti-Van der Stel party.

Adam Tas was a frequent visitor at the brewery and at the Menssink's townhouse, which he sometimes used as an overnight base when visiting the Cape. The two 'broeders' (for thus they referred to each other) dined, smoked and drank 'sundry glasses of beer together' in great conviviality.[60] There is no doubt that Menssink knew and shared Tas's opinions about the unfair practices of the Governor and it was not simply family solidarity that occasioned this sympathy. Menssink had himself joined the ranks of the Cape farming elite – the nursery of anti-Van der Stel opposition – with the purchase of two farms at Joostenberg in the Klapmuts area in December 1704.[61] Though he does not seem to have spent much of his own time or energy on the farms, leaving the supervision to *knechts* and the labour to slaves, at the time that rural resistance to Van der Stel was being mobilised he was the owner of Hercules Pilaar and De Waarburg.[62] These farms, of 60 morgen each, had previously belonged to the Revd Hercules van Loon, minister of the Stellenbosch church. After this rather negligent preacher committed suicide in June 1704 (apparently cutting his throat with a penknife), the farms became the property of his wife (according to Tas, a most unpleasant woman) before she sold them to Menssink.[63] As a grower of wheat and a breeder of livestock, Menssink thus had similar interests, and grievances, to the disaffected agriculturists who opposed Van der Stel and there is evidence that he played a modest part in assisting them in their cause.

In 1706, when various so-called trouble-making colonists were being interrogated about their roles in organising, or participating in, the opposition to the Governor, several made statements that incriminated Menssink. One of those who signed the memorial against W. A. van der Stel (which was sent to the Heren XVII in the Netherlands) was Pieter Meyer of Dauphine, who confessed, after eleven days in the Castle's 'Donker Gat' (Black Hole), that he had signed the memorial at the house of the brewer after being called there for that purpose by one of Menssink's slaves, and that he was encouraged to do so by Willem Menssink and Adam Tas. Another signatory, a carpenter named Daniel van Zevenhoven, claimed to have seen a seditious letter at Menssink's house in about September 1705. We can well believe that the brewery was an important centre of opposition, where people met to discuss politics over tankards of beer and to read, or compose, the circulating letters which were designed to rally the discontented.[64]

Even more incriminating was evidence that Menssink played an active role in canvassing for supporters outside the brewery walls. Hans Hendrik Hattingh, a farmer from Tijgervallei, said that he was first shown the letter of protest against the Governor when he received a visit from Menssink and Jacobus van Brakel one evening in January 1706. Van Brakel was the brother of Adam Tas's wife, Elizabeth van Brakel, and one of the foremost anti-Van der Stel agitators. On this occasion he and Menssink seem to have gone about the country districts together in a wagon – complete with a slave musician playing a fiddle – to win supporters for their cause. Hattingh was asked to sign their letter, but this he declined to do.[65] Given Menssink's close involvement in the opposition to Van der Stel, it is surprising that he was not taken in for questioning in March 1706 along with the other conspirators. We must assume that he was careful not to put his signature to anything incriminating, for otherwise he would surely have suffered imprisonment along with his brother-in-law. There were, in any event, other matters which were far closer to the brewer's heart than politics; judging from complaints received by the Council of Policy in September 1706, these matters did not include the production of decent beer.

In the liquor lease auction of 31 August 1706, Jan Mijndertsz Kruijwagen bought the *pacht* which entitled him to sell Cape malt beer in small measures. Kruijwagen, a miller, had paid 3350 guilders for this right and was anxious to recoup his expenses by retailing beer as quickly as possible. With this end in mind, he and two companions paid a visit to the house of Menssink and his mother to enquire, in a 'civil and decent manner', when he might be able to obtain some beer from them. Menssink replied in a forceful voice that he should not return until the following Monday. Kruijwagen could see that the Menssinks had some beer in the house and asked whether they could not let him have this, for an extra *stuijver* per bottle, just to help him get going. In a 'loud and brutal manner' Menssink told Kruijwagen that he could not consider doing so, nor would his mother permit it. The miller was therefore obliged to wait.[66]

On 4 September Kruijwagen drove his wagon to the brewery, bought four aums of beer from Willem Menssink for 15 guilders per aum and, without tasting the beer, set off to Cape Town with two of the aums. His plan was to supply his town taphouses with the first consignment of beer before sending the wagon back for the second two aums of beer, which would be distributed in the outlying areas. Before he picked up the second load, however, he decided to taste the Menssink brew and very quickly changed his plans. According to Kruijwagen the beer was so unpleasant ('slegt en schraal') that he immediately sent a sample to the fiscal, Johan Blesius, who was, in turn, so unfavourably impressed by the taste that he sent the messenger of the court to tap two bottles from the undelivered aums so as to allow the Council of Policy the dubious pleasure of tasting the brew for themselves. Kruijwagen also tried out the beer on certain of his customers. Fourteen of them were so revolted by the experience that they were prepared to testify to the effect that the beer was 'soo schraal en ondrinkbaar' (so thin and undrinkable) it could not be stomached, and that it was certainly not worth two 'swaar stuivers' or a *dubbeltje* a pint. Indeed, the local connoisseurs declared it to be nothing but 'spoeling of Vaderlands scharrebier' (swillings or thin beer from the fatherland), and that if such was the quality of the beer Kruijwagen proposed to serve they would not spend another penny in his establishments and would rather drink sugar beer.[67]

The Council of Policy verified that Kruijwagen was not exaggerating, for they, including Governor Van der Stel himself, sampled the offensive brew and unanimously found it to be 'zeer dun, schraal, en geensints voor de verkogte prijs a *f*15 ligt geld het aam, leeverbaar' (very meagre and thin, and by no means deliverable at the retail price of 15 guilders an aum). A further five witnesses were found who declared before the Council that they had drunk beer at Kruijwagen's taphouse and that it was 'ongelijk slegter, flaauwer en ondrinkbaarder' (far worse, weaker and undrinkable) than anything that the brewer Willem Menssink had previously produced. The Council sent Christoffel Hazenwinckel, the messenger of the court, to inform the Menssinks, both mother and son, that they would have to recompense Kruijwagen for the losses he had suffered and take care in future to supply him with good malt beer in order that the conditions of the beer *pacht* might be fulfilled.[68]

Was the Menssinks' beer really so bad or were these complaints all part of a campaign by the Van der Stel faction to discredit the Menssinks? There is certainly a possibility that there was an element of official persecution in the Council's championship of Kruijwagen against a man they believed to be an enemy. On the other hand, the Menssinks may well have decided to embarrass Kruijwagen and the administration by off-loading a substandard product on the colony. It may have been the Menssinks' way of making a political point and demonstrating to all and sundry the dangers of tampering with the *pacht* conditions.

The authorities were convinced that ultimate responsibility for the quality of Cape malt beer lay with Willem Menssink. To the amazement of both Kruijwagen and the Council, however, Hazenwinckel reported back on 11 September that Menssink had said that the whole business had nothing to do with him. His mother was the brewer. When Hazenwinckel asked Gerbregt if this was indeed the case, she replied that it was. Furthermore, she forcefully declared that it was impossible for her to deliver better beer at less than 15 guilders an aum and that she had no intention of paying Kruijwagen any damages.[69] On receipt of this intelligence the Council felt obliged to release Kruijwagen from the terms of the *pacht* and allowed him to cancel his lease with full Company compensation since, through no fault of his own, but due to the 'sheer malevolence' of the brewers he could not obtain decent beer at the agreed price. The Council also resolved, on 14 September, to summon brewer Menssink and his mother to explain themselves before the committee the next day.[70]

On 15 September the widow Menssink duly presented herself at the Castle, but without her son. On being summoned, the latter declared that he had nothing to do with brewing, that his mother was the sole brewer, and that, furthermore, he was indisposed. The Governor and Council expressed their surprise at these revelations, stating that they had always believed Willem Menssink to be the brewer since it was he who had signed the *pacht* and that he, therefore, should take responsibility.

Widow Menssink assured the Council that the brewery was hers alone and that Willem had signed the *pacht* out of obedience to her. Her son was, moreover, unpresentable, having a severely swollen face that would keep him out of circulation for at least six weeks.[71]

It is possible that, by claiming to be the real brewer, Menssink's mother was trying to protect him, but it is much more likely that she was simply telling the truth. She no doubt had far greater expertise in the business of brewing than her son did and there is nothing in the historical record to suggest that Willem had either the aptitude or the ability to become a master brewer. On the death of Rutgert Menssink the authorities would have assumed that the business – as well as the expertise – had been passed on to his son, but Gerbregt Menssink knew Willem too well to believe he could make a success of the brewery. She probably feared that the Council of Policy would baulk at the idea of a woman running the brewery and so used Willem as the front man. It is also quite likely that Willem was somewhat dominated by his mother, for, despite her age – she was 73 years old in 1706 – she was a formidable woman and, as the Council of Policy was about to discover, she could be extremely forceful and intemperate when displeased.

The Council proceeded to inform Gerbregt Menssink of Kruijwagen's complaint and asked whether she could not supply him with a better beer at 15 guilders per aum. The fury of her reply stunned them: 'That in violent anger and with flushed face resulting from simple fury and obstinacy, she had replied that what she had supplied to Kruijwagen was even better than that supplied to H. Mulder, the preceding lessee. That she could not and never would supply a better article for the price; and even for more; . . . That she did not care what became of her; that they might do to her what they liked, that she would not move a foot or bend a knee, and if the Company wished to have the brewing vats she did not care – she had 200 muids of malt on the loft which the weevil might destroy; that Kruijwagen might buy it and brew it for himself; and finally, that she had offered to take over his lease for *f*2,700.'[72]

Such an outburst did not make a favourable impression on the Council. Though Gerbregt's words contained the smart of wounded pride, Messrs Corssenaar, Van Putten and Helot (the members of the Council who were questioning her) noticed only its spiteful petulance and condemned the obstinate stubbornness of the elderly woman before them. They declared widow Menssink's statement to be a frivolous pretext to compel Kruijwagen to cede his lease to her and feared that in the future prospective lessees would hesitate to bid for the beer licence if it meant having to deal with 'deze twistgierige brouweres' (this quarrelsome breweress). They therefore decided to deliver a written protest to the Menssinks, both mother and son, informing them of the Company's intention to hold them responsible for all costs, damages and interest arising from their 'onwilligheijd en volstrekte malitie' (unwillingness and outright maliciousness) to supply reasonable beer to the *pachter* for the agreed-upon price of 15 guilders an aum. They further agreed to inform the Heren XVII of their decision. The Menssinks did not respond to the Council's written protest. Mrs Kruijwagen, accompanied by the messenger of the court, decided to visit Gerbregt Menssink and exert further pressure. She asked her whether she would be pleased to deliver good beer. In reply Gerbregt slammed the door in their faces and declared, 'I know nothing of good beer, I have nothing to do with you.'[73] In the meantime, however, the Council of Policy confiscated the large brewing kettles until such time as the Menssinks paid their debts.[74]

Beer production at the Newlands brewery came to a halt and it is surely no coincidence that about this time Elizabeth found it necessary to leave her husband because of his intolerable abuse: the brewer was venting his anger on his wife. The Company was obliged, meanwhile, to look elsewhere for its supplies of malt beer. In November 1706 it gave its consent to the request of Theunis van Schalkwyk, the man who had been ousted as brewer by the Menssinks in 1695, that he might establish a brewery of his own in the Table Valley. Van Schalkwyk was loaned a plot of land beneath Table Mountain and alongside the river, at the place where the water-pipes which brought Cape Town its water had been laid.[75] The allocation of such prime land for a brewery site is an indication of the importance the Company attached to the production of beer in the colony. The authorities must have hoped that they had found a way to obtain this beer without recourse to the Menssinks. But they had certainly not heard the last of the angry breweress and her surly son.

On 20 April 1707 Gerbregt Menssink decided to petition the Heren XVII themselves concerning her grievances.[76] The timing of her letter is extremely revealing, for on 17 April 1707 Governor Willem Adriaan van der Stel had received his letter of dismissal from the Heren XVII. These gentlemen had written their letter on 30 October 1706 but it had taken nearly half a year for their command to reach the Cape.[77] Once the news of the Governor's dismissal broke, however, it spread rapidly throughout the colony and must have encouraged the Menssinks to believe that it was a propitious moment to seek redress for the wrongs of the past. Thus it was that only three days after the Governor's dismissal (and the dismissal too of the *secunde*, the landdrost of Stellenbosch and the Revd Peter Kalde, minister of Cape Town), Gerbregt Menssink took up her pen, evidently enjoying the opportunity, which now presented itself, to injure Van der Stel's reputation still further.

Her petition was designed to convince the Heren XVII that the conditions surrounding the beer *pacht* were unfair, having been created by W. A. van der Stel contrary to the intentions and interests of the Company – which were to assist the Menssinks to make beer – in order to favour his supporters. One of these supporters, Kruijwagen, who had been awarded the beer *pacht*, was, according to Gerbregt, widely known as a thief and a housebreaker.[78] 'I mention this not to affront him,' wrote widow Menssink, 'but so that Your Excellencies may perceive how things are at present in the Cape: where rogues and thieves are favoured and preferred: and honest people are oppressed.' Her letter went on to rehearse the history of her disagreement with Kruijwagen and the Cape authorities. But the point of her petition was that she wished to sue Kruijwagen for 5200 guilders' damages, caused by the brewery having stood idle for half a year. She also requested the authorities to return the brewing kettles to her, for without them she could not make beer, and if she could not make beer she could not repay the cost of the kettles. Finally, she asked if she could be granted, for the next ten years, the right to tap Cape malt beer for the annual licence of 2000 guilders.[79]

Widow Menssink's audacious request took time to reach the Netherlands and, once there, required time for consideration. The authorities at the Cape, meanwhile, were aware that people like Hüsing, Tas and others of their party were back in favour whereas the past administration was now under critical scrutiny from above. There was an obvious need to proceed cautiously, to await for instructions from their superiors and, above all, to keep the populace supplied with beer. It should not surprise us, therefore, to learn that on 31 August 1707 Gerbregt Menssink was allowed to purchase the beer *pacht* for 2750 guilders.[80] The following year, on 30 August 1708, the beer *pacht* was granted to her again for the same amount as in 1707 'to avoid the unpleasantness which would be caused if the lease were put up publicly, as was the case in 1706 between the said widow and the lessee Jan Mijndertsz Kruijwagen regarding the supply of good beer – a dispute not yet settled by the Directors'.[81] This may be seen as a triumph for Gerbregt Menssink. The Cape authorities had probably been encouraged to treat her leniently by an alarming display of strength, early in 1708, on the part of the Hüsing faction.

On 27 December 1707 Maria Lindenhovius, wife of Henning Hüsing, was arrested and imprisoned in the Castle. Her husband was not yet back from the Netherlands, whence he had been sent – or, in the words of his wife's supporters, 'with an unheard of, very violent and more than Dionysian tyranny been snatched from her side, from his house and his property, by order of the Cape tyrants' – twenty-one months before by Governor Van der Stel, to be judged on charges of mutiny before the Heren XVII.[82] By December 1707 everyone at the Cape knew Hüsing had been found innocent and, emboldened by this knowledge, Hüsing's friends and family vigorously protested against his wife's arrest. Her crime had been that she had refused to confirm 'certain libellous expressions uttered by the Revd Engelbertus le Boucq at her house and in her presence', against the Heren XVII and the Cape's acting Governor, Jean Cornelis d'Ableing.[83]

Le Boucq was a particular thorn in the flesh of the Cape administration. According to the latter, the minister was continually 'riding, running, and trotting about; always having two slaves with him armed with heavy sticks shod with iron, and personally with a sword at his side, visiting the houses of his good friends, and not refraining, both inside and in the public streets, from uttering much malicious language against various officials and others.'[84] On this occasion Le Boucq was informed on by Maria Engelbregt, widow of the Revd Van Loon, who happened to be visiting the Hüsing household at the time. D'Ableing therefore sought to corroborate this information by forcing a confession from Maria Lindenhovius. She refused and was supported in her resistance by her friends and relatives. Twenty-seven men and women signed a memorial of protest which was presented to the Council of Policy by the wives of the burghers Claas Diepenauw, Jacob van der Heiden and Jacob de Savoije, namely Sara Tas, Abigel Vroom and Maria le Clerq. The signatories demanded the release of Maria Lindenhovius on bail and their names read like a who's who of the anti-Van der Stel faction.[85] Included amongst them, supporting his brother-in-law and his sister-in-law, was Willem Menssink. That such an unheroic figure should dare to sign an anti-government petition was a sure sign that the balance of power was shifting.

The intemperate language of the memorial is another indication that the signatories believed the power of the Cape administration to be waning: 'that therefore they felt it very severely to see her summoned under a dirty, stinking and false pretext before the Council's judgment seat, – whose members for the most part had so unjustly exiled her husband'.[86] The Council, for its part, thought the memorial to be filled with 'very sharp, calumnious and spiteful expressions against this Government, and moreover bristling with falsehood', but shifted responsibility in the matter onto the fiscal, Johan Blesius. Blesius, anxious to dissociate himself from past abuses, pronounced that although he found the memorial to be somewhat sharply worded it was not as godless or libellous as had been represented, since it should be remembered that Hüsing and others had indeed been forcibly removed from their possessions and families. At the time he himself, confessed the fiscal, to his regret had consented to this, thinking that the matter would have ended there. But now, in the light of what had happened, the memorial should not be considered so wicked after all.[87]

The Council was shocked by this disclosure, and shocked too to hear that Blesius thought that they, the Council, being partial in the matter, should leave judgment to the arrival of a new Governor, or some other eminent official from the Indies. Perversely, after delivering himself of these opinions (which the Council believed completely undermined their own authority), Blesius pronounced that he did not think Maria Lindenhovius should be released on bail since she was, after all, bound to testify to the truth.[88] Despite their general refutation and condemnation of Blesius's remarks, the Council eventually released Maria Lindenhovius after she had spent nine days in imprisonment.

The arrest of Hüsing's wife seems to have been the last repressive fling of the rump of the Van der Stel administration against members of the Hüsing–Tas party. The episode had revealed how deeply divided the Cape government now was and how cautiously they would have to proceed in the future. In these circumstances the troublesome and influential Gerbregt Menssink was allowed to re-establish her prominence in the brewing business. It is probable that Van Schalkwyk's Table Valley brewery had not lived up to expectations and that the Menssink brew, awful though it was, was indispensable to the colony's well-being. Thus, in 1709, widow Menssink was once again awarded the *pacht* for the 'tap en sleet' of Cape malt beer, without any fuss, for 2750 guilders per annum.[89] In 1710 the over-confident breweress sent her son to request the Council to grant her the lease for the following year at a reduced rate. The unwelcome response to this impertinence was that the Council unanimously resolved to increase the fee to 3000 guilders per annum.[90] A week later, however, in the face of widow Menssink's refusal to pay the higher rate (and the absence of authorisation from the Heren XVII to effect an increase), the lease was sold to her again at the old price.[91]

Ever since the dispute with Kruijwagen in 1706 the Menssinks had probably been unencumbered by the necessity of having to provide a specific licensed retailer with beer, for when such a measure was proposed, or re-proposed, by the Council in 1711 it excited the Menssinks' fierce opposition. Willem Menssink complained that if he (presumably meaning he and his mother) was required to sell his beer to a single beer retailer he would be ruined and would sooner quit the brewing business altogether. The Council no doubt recognised the threat implicit in this complaint and remembered the fiasco of 1706. They thus resolved to permit anybody to sell beer, as well as the holder of the lease and including the brewer, provided that they paid an excise before removing the beer from the brewery. In theory, therefore, the brewers could not retail beer in the brewery itself, but they could retail beer in a taphouse distinct from the brewery after having paid an excise fee.[92]

It would appear, from Willem Menssink's presence in the negotiations over the beer *pacht* in 1710 and 1711, that he was playing a greater role in the business of the brewery. It may well have been the case that his mother, now aged 78 years, was more reliant on him than before. If this was indeed the case she must have regretted it, for Willem was too distracted by other matters to be an efficient manager. Thus it was that in August 1712 Willem was called before the Council to explain why, during the last year, there had been a period of four months and eighteen days during which no malt beer had been produced, and why it was that he was seeking to be refunded for some of the cost of the beer *pacht*. Significantly, it was Willem and not his mother who was being held responsible for this failure to fulfil the *pacht* conditions. He answered that between 21 October 1711 and 8 February 1712 there had been a shortage of barley and between 10 June and 10 July 1712 a shortage of hops. The Council pointed out that, since he had been supplied with hops in May, he should surely have been able to brew beer before then. But Menssink, with a convincing display of professional competence, described how malt beer took a long time to brew and could not be rushed into maturity. He obtained a refund.

Indeed, there was little that the Company could do to put pressure on the Menssinks' beer production business, for at the public auction for the *pacht* at the end of August 1712 nobody bid against Willem Menssink and he acquired the beer *pacht* at a much cheaper price than before.[93] The declining value of the beer *pacht* may have been caused by a number of factors. Perhaps, as Willem had explained, the shortage of materials did make brewing a troublesome and risky business, in which it was not always possible to make significant profits and pay off the *pacht* fee. It is possible that a more energetic or dedicated brewer than Willem might have organised the business better but, by 1712, it seemed that prospective competitors were loath to attempt to outbid the Menssinks at the auction. We must assume that this reluctance was related to the public perception that the status and prosperity of the Menssinks now seemed assured. Their friends and family connections were back in favour and Willem himself had been appointed to the Burgher Council in December 1711.[94] His future seemed secure – but before the end of 1712 the brewer's façade of solid respectability was brought crashing down, undermined by the revelation of a spectacularly scandalous private life.

When Elizabeth Lingelbach returned to her mother's house in 1706 she had hoped that she would be free from the disturbing presence of her husband. Instead, to her alarm, she noticed how Menssink would loiter in the street outside, engaging her mother's female slaves in conversation, in this manner keeping himself informed of everything that was going on inside.[95] It was not as though he was prompted to do so by feelings of remorse or the wish to become reconciled with his wife. He seemed, rather, to want to intrude, sexually, into the very sanctum of her privacy, employing as his method the seduction (or mastery) of the female slaves who surrounded her.

The house of Elizabeth's mother was, pre-eminently, a female domain. Elizabeth's father, David, had died before she returned home and there do not, initially, seem to have been any male domestic slaves in the household. Since her mother, Elizabeth Glazerus, ran a coffee shop for a living (probably at separate premises), the two female slaves she kept at home may have helped at the shop during the day. In the evenings, though, there were usually four women and no men at the Lingelbach household. Sometimes, however, as Elizabeth discovered to her dismay, things were otherwise.

One night, hearing a noise in the attic, Elizabeth went to investigate. There she discovered her estranged husband Willem, clothed in a Japanese robe with Willemijntje, a female slave of her mother. The guilty couple were hiding, with baskets over their heads, in a cupboard. Menssink started up and chased Elizabeth down the steps. She ran into her mother's room whilst Willem made his undignified exit through the front door. What had been going on? Willemijntje confessed that Menssink 'haar al eenige tijt vleeslijke conversatie had gehoude' (had been having carnal intercourse for some time). Elizabeth must have been horrified to learn that, even in her mother's house, she was not to escape from evidence of her husband's weakness for slave women. Worse than this, he seemed determined to assert his sexual dominance under her very nose. In her frustration and humiliation all she could think of doing was trapping Menssink if he should ever dare to return to the house for Willemijntje again. The slave woman promised that she would play her part in trapping him, but this she failed to do, even though the brewer did indeed return. When Elizabeth caught Menssink with Willemijntje again, he could not be prevented from rushing from the kitchen to the 'voorhuijs' and then outside. After the failure of this plan there seemed no recourse for Elizabeth but to sell Willemijntje – 'buijten'.[96]

The gap which Willemijntje's departure left in the ranks of the Lingelbach's domestic labour force was soon filled when Elizabeth Glazerus bought a new female slave, Flora of Madagascar. Before her arrival in the household, however, Menssink made an attempt to repair his relationship with his estranged wife. First he sent his slave, Gerrit of Tutucorijn, as an emissary, bearing both verbal and written requests for reconciliation.[97] When these overtures failed, he managed to persuade the Revd Engelbertus le Boucq to act as a mediator. These negotiations too came to nothing and the minister confessed to Elizabeth that he could not understand what manner of man Menssink was. Clearly, therefore, the most outspoken representative of the Reformed church in the colony did not condone Menssink's particular interpretation of Old Testament morality. Nor, significantly, did he attempt to persuade Elizabeth to return to her husband after hearing her side of the story. Why had Menssink sought reconciliation?

Separation of married couples, or the separation of bed and board, was a situation which was recognised by Roman-Dutch law. The Roman-Dutch marriage laws observed at the begining of the eighteenth century are best consulted in the authoritative work of Henricus Brouwer, *De Jure Connubiorum*, the second edition of which was published in Delft in 1714.[98] According to Brouwer there were several legally valid reasons for separation, the foremost of these being adultery on the part of one of the spouses. Separation was also permissible if one of the partners had good grounds to fear physical assault, or mistreatment, by the other. But separation was always regarded as a temporary measure during which period the couple, with the help of the appropriate authorities, would attempt to reconcile their differences and the sinful partner would amend his or her ways.[99] In theory, if it became obvious that no reconciliation was possible and that the guilty party had no intention of reforming, divorce proceedings could begin. Menssink did not want a divorce and it was clearly up to him, as the offending spouse, to show that he was willing to attempt reconciliation. It is here that the church could play a part.

Leonard Blussé has shown, in his study of VOC Batavia in the seventeenth and eighteenth centuries, that the church had an important role to play in attempting to resolve social disputes, particularly those involving marriage.[100] When a marriage seemed about to break down, 'the first organ of social control the couple met with was the Church'.[101] The church was also clearly subordinate to the Company, employed for the purpose of keeping society in check, and often regarded as a means to achieving political goals.[102] The same may doubtless be said of Dutch colonial society at the Cape, a fact illustrated by the fate of the Revd Engelbertus le Boucq. When he tried to remove certain members from the consistories of the Cape Town and Stellenbosch churches on the grounds of corruption or 'gross irregularities' in their behaviour, the Council of Policy stepped in, deposed him from office and dispatched him to Batavia in September 1708.[103]

In keeping with Dutch social values of the late seventeenth and early eighteenth centuries, neither church nor state encouraged divorce, for marriage was the matrix, both mystical and material, from which the fundamental social institution – that of family – emerged. The laws of marriage were heavily weighted in favour of the male partner, particularly where property rights were concerned. 'De vrouw is onbekwaam' was a precept of Roman-Dutch law and a husband had the legal right to administer any property that his wife might have.[104] This applied during the state of separation too, for separation was not divorce and the bond of marriage was still held to be intact. During a period of separation a husband was expected to support his wife (or, at least, to leave her with the means whereby she could support herself) but he thereby retained his right to her property.[105] It is safe to assume that Menssink's main reason for seeking to maintain his marriage was financial. He had his eye on his wife's property or, rather, on his wife's future property. Elizabeth stood to inherit her mother's house and coffee shop. If Menssink was still married to Elizabeth when she came into her inheritance, he would be the beneficiary. But if he was divorced, nothing of the Lingelbach estate would come his way. Indeed, a divorce from Elizabeth, with him as the adulterous guilty party, would result in financial loss, and maybe even punishment and a fine. By asking for the church's mediation in his marriage he could appear to be willing to mend his ways and thus keep his marriage from ending in divorce.

Le Boucq, as we have seen, did not recommend that Elizabeth return to her husband. Neither, however, did he recommend that she instigate divorce proceedings, for divorce was regarded as a very extreme step indeed. His advice was, most probably, that she wait. By October 1707 Menssink had obviously come to the realisation that his wife was not to be won back to his side with fine words and promises, nor was she, on the other hand, about to initiate divorce proceedings. He therefore seems to have resolved to reassert his 'right' to the sexuality of the slave women of his wife's household. How else can one explain the fact that he now turned his amorous energies to Flora, the Lingelbach's new slave? Had Menssink merely wished to assuage his lust there were surely more readily available women in Cape Town – including the females of the Company slave lodge. Instead, he felt compelled to have sexual intercourse with a slave of his wife's household in his wife's home. Perhaps he sought thereby to demonstrate – to the slave woman, to his wife, and to himself – that he remained the master despite a humiliating separation, which signalled to Cape society that his wife had rejected him.

So it was that one evening in October Elizabeth Lingelbach noticed Menssink entering her yard and, upon closer investigation, found him with Flora in an 'unreasonable' and 'indecent' situation. She ran inside the house to tell her mother and, with her support, berated Menssink, forbidding him future access to the house. Menssink responded with abusive language, swearing that he would ensure that Elizabeth's mother would not live another half a year. Whether this was a curse or a threat is uncertain, but so disquieting were the effects of these fatal words that, once more, the church's mediation was sought. On 7 November the Revd Engelbertus le Boucq bore the Lingelbachs a written apology from Menssink. Though the letter has not survived it was, according to Elizabeth, well laced with wisdom and repentance. Willem asked his mother-in-law for forgiveness and claimed not to know what had come over him. Elizabeth, however, was not to be mollified. So determined was she to rid herself of her husband that she asked the Acting Governor of the Cape, Jean d'Ableing, to grant her a divorce. His advice, unfortunately, was that she should wait.[106]

In January 1708 Elizabeth's mother decided to buy a new house. Maybe it was the prospect of future property that provoked Menssink into a renewed attempt at reconciliation, for he wrote to Elizabeth to wish her good luck with the purchase. He also pleaded with her for compassion, asking her to take him back, just as Isabella had done with her Zerbino, even though (he reminded his wife piously) only Jesus Christ could forgive him.[107] Though Menssink's allusion to characters from Ariosto's *Orlando Furioso* seems to have impressed Elizabeth, she remained unmoved. Perhaps she saw no similarities between Zerbino – the 'perfect knight of whom it was said that Nature broke the mould in which he had been fashioned' – and her less than perfect husband. She could not have been unaware that in Ariosto's epic Isabella fell into the clutches of Rodomont, a pagan king, and that in order to escape his unwelcome attentions she had had to choose self-immolation. Menssink, however, appeared blind to the ironies of this sub-plot and, by portraying himself as Zerbino instead of Rodomont, provides us with further proof of his creative powers of misreading.[108]

That February Elizabeth Glazerus passed away and her daughter, Elizabeth Lingelbach, must have remembered the curse, or threat, made by Willem Menssink. As if to allay her suspicions Menssink sent messages of condolence, both verbal and written, to his estranged wife. The day after Elizabeth Glazerus's death, an event occurred whose significance was not, at first, readily apparent. A slave, Cupido, ran away from the Lingelbach household. Only several years later did Elizabeth learn that her husband had assisted the slave in his escape and arranged for an Englishman to ship him secretly out of the colony. Why? Elizabeth's speculations were not recorded in the court records but, given later developments, she probably suspected that Cupido had had a hand in her mother's death.[109] In the short term, however, Cupido's desertion may have left Elizabeth under-staffed and in the market for a new slave. In 1709 Elizabeth did indeed acquire a new slave – Trijntje of Madagascar.[110]

Given Menssink's past conduct, Elizabeth's purchase was most ill-advised. Without the support of her mother she was more vulnerable than before and her choice of domestic slaves seemed more likely to entice, rather than repel, her husband. Menssink had already demonstrated that he regarded Flora as his sexual property and it seems almost inevitable that he would seek to exert sexual dominance over 21-year-old Trijntje. Why, then, did Elizabeth surround herself with nubile women? We must assume that her options were limited. In eighteenth-century Cape Town it cannot have been easy for a single white woman to live alone; nor was it acceptable for such a woman to choose a male slave as her house-companion. Elizabeth was also a battered and betrayed woman who might have now feared the proximity of a man in the house. Perhaps, too, we should consider that the purchase of elderly, unattractive slave women would not have seemed a sound investment to the business-minded owner of a coffee house. Whatever reasons dictated her choice, she soon came to regret her purchase of Trijntje.

It is not exactly clear when Elizabeth first became aware of the fact that Menssink was sleeping with her new slave. The first seduction had taken place only two nights after Trijntje's arrival, but this was just the beginning. As the days passed Menssink became less surreptitious and Elizabeth was forced to confront renewed evidence of her husband's debaucheries. At first the brewer would send one of his slaves, either Isaac of Masulipatam or Gerrit of Tutucorijn, to summon Trijntje from her mistress's house to his side. Sometimes, however, she went of her own accord. This arrangement lasted for about two months before Elizabeth became suspicious. One night Trijntje's erstwhile lover, Fredrick the slave, had trapped her coming out of Menssink's side-gate and, in jealous anguish, he informed Elizabeth. From this moment onwards Elizabeth kept a closer watch on Trijntje and forbade her to leave the house. Next time one of Menssink's slaves tapped on the windows of the 'groote camer' (whilst Elizabeth sat in the 'voorhuijs') to summon Trijntje to his 'singneur' [*sic*], he was told by the slave woman that it was impossible and that she was no longer allowed out. A short while later Menssink himself appeared at the window and softly told Trijntje that she should expect him in the yard, for he planned to jump over the wall when it was safe to do so. That night, at about eleven o'clock, Menssink was as good as his word and the lovers enjoyed carnal intercourse in the courtyard.[111]

Several similar alfresco encounters occurred before Menssink suggested to Trijntje that, in future, they should make love inside her mistress's house. The old compulsion to sow his seed in his wife's territory had arisen. Trijntje protested that this would be impossible since she slept in the same room as Elizabeth at the foot of her bed.[112] Menssink's reply was to give the slave woman a bundled-up cloth containing a type of yellow and white dust. He told her to lay this at the foot of her mistress's mattress and that this would cause her to remain fast asleep. He added that he had used such a method, successfully, with his wife in the past. Quite what this dust, or powder, was is uncertain. But it is worth recording that when Elizabeth learnt about it later, she believed it to be made from the ground-up bones of the dead.[113]

Trijntje did as she had been told and all went well. At about one o'clock at night Menssink climbed into the house through a window which Trijntje had previously left unlocked. He lowered himself onto a chair and made his way into his wife's bedroom. There, at the foot of her bed, he and Trijntje lay as lovers through the small hours of the morning.

These nocturnal arrangements endured for about a year. Menssink's slaves Gerrit and Isaac acted as the secret go-betweens, setting up meetings for their master and alerting Trijntje to the prospect of a midnight visit. Then, one day, Menssink's faithful slaves informed him of some changes which had been made in the Lingelbach household. Elizabeth had complained to her slaves Flora and Trijntje that they were making too much noise in the night. She was not, it seems, sleeping as soundly as she used to, and was becoming increasingly aware of disturbances in the kitchen, windows opening in the 'voorhuijs' and dogs barking in the street. Once she had even discovered Trijntje in the 'voorhuijs' at night. Clearly, Elizabeth Lingelbach was becoming suspicious. Quite where Flora had been sleeping before is not recorded but she was now banished to a small room in the kitchen. Trijntje, on the other hand, was to spend her future nights in a shed in the yard.[114]

Although this arrangement was probably not as exciting for Menssink it did not impede his access to Trijntje. Flora was obviously aware of the relationship between Menssink and Trijntje, for she was now called upon to facilitate the liaison by leaving the back door unlocked on the nights when Menssink planned a visit. He would then climb through the front window, move quietly through the house, out of the back door and into the yard where Trijntje would be waiting for him in the shed. It is impossible to say what Flora thought of these proceedings. Did she feel slighted or relieved that Menssink had turned his attentions from her to Trijntje? Had Menssink, in fact, turned exclusively to Trijntje or did he allow himself the occasional indulgence with Flora? Where did Flora's primary loyalties lie? With her mistress? With Menssink? Or with her fellow countrywoman, co-captive and companion, Trijntje? It is even possible that the slave women believed Menssink, as Elizabeth's husband, had the right to command them. While Flora's thoughts are not recorded, it was she who, seemingly inadvertently, almost revealed to Elizabeth the secret of Menssink's midnight visits.

One night, when Menssink was already in Trijntje's backyard shed, Elizabeth sent Flora out to get some pepper. Hearing someone approaching, Menssink rushed to hide in the nearby cellar, which, unfortunately, happened to be flooded. Flora was most surprised to hear splashing sounds from the cellar and in her fright called out, 'O God, wat is daar!' Menssink quickly hushed her up, telling her to continue her business and not to alarm her mistress. The brewer, however, presented a miserable (and comical) sight. Sopping wet and without trousers, he stood in the water with only a Japanese robe over his shirt and a knotted scarf on his head. Back in Trijntje's shed she took off his wet garments and clothed him in her own 'cabaij' (gown), a detail which Trijntje later confessed to her mistress and which seems to have made a strong impression on both women.[115]

Shortly after this incident, perhaps noticing Trijntje's wet clothes, Elizabeth decided that the outside shed was too damp a place for the slave woman and instructed her to sleep in the 'voorhuijs'. All Trijntje now had to do to allow Menssink into the house was to unlock the window at night. On at least two occasions, however, Menssink was let in by the front door during the day and hid himself under the bed in the 'groote camer' until it was safe to emerge. It is hard to imagine that Elizabeth's suspicions were not, by this stage, thoroughly awakened and it is perhaps for this reason that Trijntje was finally ordered to sleep 'op 't solder', or in the loft above the 'voorhuijs'. This new obstacle was soon overcome. Menssink now arranged for his slaves Gerrit and Isaac to accompany him to the Lingelbach house at night, bearing a ladder. Once the ladder was propped up against the wall, the brewer quickly mounted it and entered the loft through the window, or 'dakvenster'. The slaves were then instructed to take the ladder away and to return with it some hours later, at two or three in the morning. All of this was accomplished whilst Menssink was attired in his Japanese robe and with a red scarf bound about his head.[116]

Although it is easy to see the lineaments of bedroom farce or comic opera in these proceedings, we should also be alert to the tragic dimension, lurking in the wings, ready to overwhelm the human players trapped, temporarily, inside their roles of maid, mistress or master. Sometime, somewhere in the whirligig of emotion, Trijntje became pregnant and must have realised that there were grave consequences that she would have to face. Remorselessly, relentlessly, against a background of banging windows, furtive footsteps and whispers in the night, Elizabeth Lingelbach became aware that she was mocked and deceived, betrayed and perhaps even bewitched. Sometime, somewhere, in the sweat of lust or the thrill of midnight violation, brewer Menssink became aware that he was in the grip of no ordinary passion.

It is difficult to dissect or analyse the precise nature of Menssink's passion. If his pathognomy was a mystery to his contemporaries, it is even more obscure to us. He obviously enjoyed the sexual power he was exerting, both over the slave woman and his wife, but does this mean that both women were victims of sexual exploitation? Michel Foucault reminds us that sexual power is not purely repressive, and for Barbara Bush this helps to account for the ambivalent relationships between black women and white men in slave societies. 'For white men black women were "forbidden fruit"; sexual relations between black and white could create "perpetual spirals of power and pleasure" from which white women were excluded.'[117] White women were excluded from the pleasure, that is, but not necessarily from the pain of their husbands' power. In this sense, as Elizabeth's plight clearly illustrates, white women were in a less enviable position than their slaves.[118] Conversely, in the labyrinthic 'spirals of power and pleasure', power relations could be temporarily inverted, and 'Black women, too, despite their racial and sexual inferiority could at times manipulate white men to their own advantage.'[119] Clearly, there were times when Menssink was not in control of his emotions and was dangerously addicted to Trijntje's sexual charms. Although Menssink's passion temporarily empowered the slave woman it was, in the long run, to prove fatal – if not for Menssink himself, then for Trijntje, and very nearly for Elizabeth too.

As Trijntje's belly grew (or, as the records put it, as her sins became apparent) and as Elizabeth realised that, even in the loft, her slave woman was not beyond her husband's reach, she tried to assert her authority. Next time he comes to you, Elizabeth commanded Trijntje, you must help me to trap him. Instead of doing so, however, Trijntje informed her lover that Elizabeth was more determined than ever to put an end to their liaison. Menssink's response was to encourage Trijntje to run away. He told her to pack her belongings and throw them over the wall where he would retrieve them and assist in her escape. The plan came to nothing. Elizabeth discovered, or suspected, Trijntje's intentions and had her locked in the public jail. Here she was visited by Menssink's slave Gerrit, who brought to Trijntje his master's gifts of tobacco and 'peeperkoek' (gingerbread). Gerrit assured Trijntje that Menssink had declared that if, and wherever, Elizabeth sold her he would buy her again. We must assume that this is precisely what Elizabeth feared and wished to prevent, for why else would she have endured Trijntje's troublesome presence? Menssink had not attempted to buy Willemijntje when she had been sold and his declaration in this instance was an indication of his obsession. Imprisoning Trijntje was but a temporary solution and a rather embarrassing advertisement of Elizabeth's predicament of powerlessness. When Gerrit came to visit Trijntje for the third time, the executioner, Coopman, forbade further contact and was no doubt somewhat inconvenienced by the presence of Trijntje – with her unsatisfactory and ambiguous status of would-be escaped slave and influential burgher's lover – in his prison at all. Elizabeth was thus obliged to take Trijntje back, on condition that the slave woman promised to inform her if and when Menssink next visited.

Two weeks later Elizabeth's sleep was disturbed by the sound of a clanking chain. Since her release from jail, Trijntje had been returned to the loft, but this time Elizabeth had taken the precaution of attaching a chain to her person. Making her way to Trijntje's sleeping quarters, Elizabeth was in time to see a figure climbing out of the loft window and hurrying down a ladder which had been placed beneath it. There was hardly any need to ask Trijntje who her visitor had been but the slave woman eventually admitted to the obvious – Willem Menssink was up to his old tricks.

Whether Elizabeth took any further measures at this stage to ensure Trijntje's inaccessibility to her husband is not recorded. But we do know that, according to Elizabeth, it was on this occasion that the brewer had passed on two bundles of blue linen to the slave woman. They contained within them a sort of powder and hair mixture which Menssink had told Trijntje to place in his wife's food. Fortunately, Elizabeth claimed, she had discovered these bundles hidden in the sleeves of Trijntje's 'cabaij' before they could be used. The same bundles, or their contents, were later to be shown to the court as exhibits, for although they had not been used they seem to have been a mixture similar to the sinister substance which a suspicious surgeon was later to discover in the excrement of the sickly Elizabeth.[120]

There are several possibilities to consider at this point. Perhaps Elizabeth, a surgeon's daughter, was lying about where the mixture came from in an attempt to incriminate her husband. The law stated that if one of the partners in a marriage was a murderer or poisoner, then the other partner had reasonable grounds for divorce.[121] If it seems unlikely that Elizabeth would administer unsavoury, though seemingly non-lethal, condiments of bone and hair to herself, then there is another possibility. Perhaps Trijntje had made the powder and had then lied about the provenance of the bundles, shifting the blame for the concoction from herself onto Menssink in an attempt to avoid punishment. Throughout the era of slavery at the Cape female slaves had the reputation of being either potential or actual poisoners who were likely to slip deadly substances into the food or drink of their owners or enemies. Such fears, which were multiplied if the slave woman happened to have an Eastern origin, were inevitable in a situation where slave women were employed as kitchen and domestic workers. Whether or not Trijntje was a poisoner we cannot know beyond doubt. We do know, however, that she lived in a society which was predisposed to believe that female slaves were poisoners. In this case the powder was obviously more than a pharmaceutical substance. It was, perhaps primarily, a magical substance whose power derived less from pharmacology than necromancy. This does not tell us who manufactured the potion; it merely tells us that whoever did so did not distinguish between science and magic. This does not narrow the list of suspects, for there were, in all probability, precious few people in early-eighteenth-century Cape Town who would have made such a distinction. The poisoner, or sorcerer, could quiet feasibly have been either Trijntje or Menssink, or Menssink's mother, or even Menssink's Indian slaves, Isaac and Gerrit, who so assiduously implemented their master's will. It is rather extraordinary that after discovering evidence of an attempted poisoning Elizabeth failed to notify the authorities. Perhaps she felt she would be ridiculed or disbelieved. In any event there was another substance, part magical, part natural, whose slow but mortal task was almost done. Within Trijntje's unfree womb the seed of brewer Menssink grew.

The records do not disclose the day, the month or year when Trijntje gave birth to a baby boy. Nor do they record the boy's name. He is simply refered to as 'een half slag kint . . . een jongetje' (a half-breed child . . . a young boy), born as a consequence of Menssink's 'boelagie' (mess).[122] There was no doubt as to the child's paternity. Three days after Trijntje was delivered of the child she received a midnight visitor at her bedroom window (from this it would appear that her confinement had not taken place in the loft). It was Menssink, asking to see the baby. By the soft light of a candle he examined the features of his son. What does your mistress say about the child? he asked Trijntje. She says it is a half-breed ('half-slag') child, was the reply. Even if it was the devil's, Menssink urged her, you must not say whose it is. So long as there is no evidence, you must lie to your mistress.[123]

From this exchange we may gather that Menssink, though strongly drawn to see his child, was anxious to conceal its paternity. He was, no doubt, deluding himself by imagining that his wife – and society at large – did not know who the father of the child was. But there was obviously an atmosphere of shame, of concealment, about the whole affair. Despite the remarks of visitors to the Cape in the eighteenth century concerning the prevalence of slave women giving birth to children sired by white masters, we should not believe that this was an entirely acceptable custom. Words like 'fornication' and 'adultery' retained powerful negative connotations and, when all was said and done, there was small honour to be won in siring a slave for a son.

We are not privy to all the emotions which Menssink experienced on beholding his son. We have deduced shame, from his wish to conceal his paternity, but we may also assume that feelings of tenderness and care partly informed his subsequent actions. Before leaving he gave Trijntje a gift of four shillings. He also promised to send her a bottle of beer the next day – which was duly delivered by his faithful slave Gerrit. There were some who might not have welcomed a bottle of widow Menssink's finest, but we need not doubt that Willem meant well by the gift. Less innocuous, however, was the item which accompanied the beer. Gerrit had brought along a quantity of 'kapok' with the instructions that Trijntje should put the cotton-like substance in her mistress's food.[124]

Once again we are forced to decide whose version of events is closest to the truth. Did Menssink really provide Trijntje with the means to poison his wife – and 'kapok' is surely a rather less than lethal substance – or did Trijntje herself procure the fibre? Menssink himself – and this is one of the most remarkable features of the story – was never required to give evidence before the Court of Justice. Our re-creation of events is based largely on the interrogation of Trijntje, Gerrit and Isaac, and on the testimony of Elizabeth Lingelbach. The court, in its wisdom, decided to lay the greatest burden of guilt on Trijntje, but we should not lose sight of the fact that Elizabeth had good reasons to harm both her husband and her slave woman and may have lied about certain details in order to incriminate the lovers as much as she could.

The official court version of events is that Trijntje was now consumed with hatred for both her mistress and for her own child, seeking to destroy them both. According to Elizabeth, this hatred was engendered in Trijntje after she had drunk a bottle of the beer that Menssink had sent her.[125] There is a constant suggestion in Elizabeth's testimony that a malevolent magic of charms and spells was being used against her. In this specific instance she was implying that the beer which Trijntje had drunk contained a hate-inducing poison – more so than the usual Menssink brew, that is. It is not too fanciful to see that, by pointing a suspicious finger at the beer, Elizabeth was also pointing a finger at the real brewer of the beer, Menssink's mother. Was Elizabeth, indirectly, calling her mother-in-law a witch? Who, ultimately, was responsible for the cursed circumstances in Elizabeth's home?[126]

Trijntje now began to cook 'kapok' into Elizabeth's spinach and bake it into her loaves of bread. As for the child, according to Elizabeth, a mere three weeks after its birth Trijntje left it naked, all night long, on the cold floor in the draught of the doorway. Next morning, when Elizabeth came to ask Trijntje why the child had cried so in the night, she saw the baby lying on the floor and could not repress her maternal instincts. Chiding Trijntje for her unnatural behaviour, she picked the child off the floor and re-clothed it. She also administered a dose of saffron to the boy. Shortly after this Trijntje took the saffron bottle, forced open the door of the storeroom, and threw the saffron into a tub of pickled herrings. This act of domestic sabotage was followed, again according to Elizabeth, by a campaign of 'snijs, brand en breeken' (cutting, burning and breaking) which Trijntje launched against her mistress's possessions and which left virtually nothing in the house undamaged. She also managed, by her surly, destructive behaviour, to drive away many of Elizabeth's coffee-drinking clientèle. A modern physician might, in this instance, diagnose a case of postnatal depression. But as far as Elizabeth was concerned her slave woman's ill-humour had a more obvious cause: Willem Menssink was inciting Trijntje to harm her, favouring the slave woman when she annoyed her mistress and expressing his displeasure when she did not.[127]

There is another explanation for Trijntje's behaviour. Perhaps it was a defensive reaction to the unbearable circumstances in which she now found herself. Elizabeth must have felt some anger, some jealousy, at being forced to witness and support the birth of the child that she herself could not bear – the offspring of her lying, lustful and licentious husband and her own dishonest, disloyal and dissolute slave woman. It would be quite understandable if Elizabeth had allowed herself the small satisfaction of making Trijntje's life a misery by amplifying the everyday oppressions of domestic slavery. We may sympathise with Elizabeth but we should remember that she was a coffee-shop proprietress and not a saint. Long nights of lying awake listening to the sounds of her husband making surreptitious love to her slave woman cannot have endeared Trijntje to her – or reconciled her to the presence of her husband's bastard half-caste love child (at one stage Elizabeth referred to the child as 'der mongrul') in her house.[128]

Trijntje, therefore, may have been resisting Elizabeth's attempts to torment her, by fighting back. One of the most common forms of slave resistance, observed in slave societies throughout the world, was the 'accidental' destruction of the slave-owner's property, coupled with a stubborn, sullen, uncooperative laziness in the workplace.[129] But why then, if Elizabeth was telling the truth, did Trijntje torture her own child? According to Elizabeth, Trijntje now began to stick needles into the baby's head, pins into its body, and to cut its ears with a pair of scissors when the child cried – or, indeed, in order to make the child cry. Historians have remarked that slave women in the Caribbean would not infrequently abort foetuses or commit infanticide upon their babies, either from despair or from the wish to harm their masters.[130] (A child born to a slave woman became the property of the woman's owner.) We cannot fully understand Trijntje's motives in treating her child so cruelly (if indeed she did, and Elizabeth was not lying). Perhaps she hated the infant for being the cause of her own suffering. Perhaps she hated it because her lover, Menssink, was ashamed of it. Perhaps she knew of no better way to annoy Elizabeth than to make her baby cry.

As the house filled with the screams and sobs of the innocent boy Menssink redoubled his efforts to poison his wife. This time Gerrit brought Trijntje a cloth which contained human hair and instructions from Menssink to feed this hair to Elizabeth. Trijntje duly stuffed a cabbage with the unusual filling and served it to her long-suffering mistress – with no noticeable ill-effects. The frustrated brewer then sent Gerrit to summon Trijntje to him. The young woman was able to enter Menssink's house through a side-gate – an indication that she was not as strictly confined as before – and answer his questions in person. 'Have you not been feeding your mistress the hair and kapok?' he demanded.

'Yes,' she replied. 'Why then', asked Menssink, 'is she not sick?' 'I do not know,' was the answer. Menssink then gave Trijntje two strange pips, or seeds, one white and the other yellow, with the instructions to boil them in tea-water and to make sure that Elizabeth drank the seeds after a meal. This, Menssink assured her, would cause her mistress great pain and anguish.[131]

Trijntje did as she was told. She also prepared and served additional items for her mistress's consumption – such as ground-up human bones, mysterious powders, nails and the scrapings of strange roots. The *pièce de resistance*, however, was undoubtedly a human hand, from which Gerrit, following his master's orders, had assiduously scraped the skin.[132] The hand had been cut from the corpse of some unfortunate criminal, who had been executed according to the orders of the state and left to rot on a scaffold exposed both to the elements and to the public eye. Since such executions and corpse-laden scaffolds were a common feature of eighteenth-century Cape Town, the hand of an executed felon – traditionally regarded as a particularly potent object in necromancy[133] – would not have been hard to come by.[134] Trijntje, however, was not quite sure what to do with the bloody relic and Gerrit had to advise her to bury it under the floor at the head of her mistress's bed. When Trijntje protested that the inside floor was not earthen, she was told to bury it outside, as close to her mistress's headboard as possible. Trijntje did so.

Whether or not the hidden hand exerted any magical powers is impossible to say. It is interesting to note that certain members of criminal gangs active in the Netherlands during the late seventeenth and early eighteenth centuries often carried a dead man's hand with them whilst engaged in their nefarious activities. Sometimes they would put the hand on a fire or 'place a burning candle in it in front of the bed where people were lying asleep, expecting that they would not wake up'.[135] In this instance, it seems, the hand was supposed to protect Trijntje from any harm that Elizabeth might wish to inflict upon her. The skin, meanwhile, had been saved, dried and ground up into a powder to add spice to Elizabeth's food. Remarkably, however, Elizabeth's health remained unaffected by the unpleasant new diet to which she was being, involuntarily, subjected.

Depressed by his wife's continued good health, Menssink personally visited Trijntje in order to give her a new batch of noxious powder and to impress upon her the urgency of fatal results. He confided to her that he had heard that his wife wished to divorce him. Trijntje seemed to take this news rather too calmly for Menssink's liking, so he was obliged to explain its financial implications to her. 'Why don't you hurry up and help your mistress into the next world,' he urged her, 'for then I will inherit half her estate and set you free.'[136] This prompting may well have encouraged Trijntje to be more diligent in doctoring her mistress's food, for, shortly afterwards, she was able to report a decline in Elizabeth's health – much to Menssink's delight. When Trijntje confessed that she felt a bit sorry about how bad Elizabeth was feeling, the brewer became incensed. 'Wat donder ben je nog aan haar kant, ik meende dat je aan mijn kant waart,' he complained. (Damn it, are you still on her side? I thought you were on mine.) When Elizabeth's health improved, Menssink became gloomy again and told Trijntje that she was taking much too long to kill Elizabeth. He hinted darkly that 'ik heb't al aan een gedaan, en daar heb ik niet half soo lang werk meede gehad' (I've already done one before, and it didn't take half as much trouble last time). He did not explain to Trijntje whom he meant but – if he really uttered such words – he could only have been referring to his first wife or, perhaps, Elizabeth's mother.[137]

Despite his words we should not believe that Menssink's eagerness to rid himself of his wife was entirely motivated by mercenary considerations. He seems to have retained a genuine love for Trijntje, so much so that Elizabeth's stubborn endurance prompted him to involve himself in another attempt to help Trijntje escape. About nine months after the birth of her child, with the help and advice of Menssink, Trijntje ran away. Elizabeth believed that the slave woman had stolen twenty handkerchiefs from her and this may have had something to do with precipitating her flight. For undisclosed but no doubt practical reasons, Trijntje left her child behind. At first, she hid in a rock-shelter at the foot of Lion's Head but, when darkness fell, she was led to Menssink's house by his slaves, Gerrit and Isaac. Temporarily reunited, the lovers surrendered to their passions or, as the records put it less kindly, Menssink gratified his lust. Trijntje spent the night at the house but, before dawn, returned to the shelter at Lion's Head. A precarious period of ten weeks now passed with Trijntje moving furtively from her mountain retreat to Menssink's bedroom, or from the bedroom to a small chamber of the main room in his mother's house, or from here to a shed alongside the outside lavatory in the backyard. All the time her needs were attended to by Gerrit or Isaac. Once, as Isaac led her from the rock-shelter, he could not help exclaiming to her: 'Trijntje, waar kom jy toe, weet jy wel wat je doet dat sal uijtkomen en dan ben je om hals' (Trijntje, where are you heading? You know what you're doing will lead to your death).[138]

Menssink's plan was to send Trijntje out of the country with an Englishman, the same one, it was alleged by Elizabeth, who had helped her slave Cupido to escape after her mother had died. For some reason Trijntje balked at the idea of leaving the Cape and it is not possible to say exactly why. What was it she feared losing – her mistress's house, her life of bondage, her lover, her baby? We will never know. Perhaps the unknown was ultimately more terrifying than the familiar confines of Table Valley where, hemmed in between the mountains and the sea, she knew her destiny to lie. In any event, Trijntje decided to give herself up, an action which she accomplished by returning to her previous owner, Kruijwagen.[139] Kruijwagen was no doubt somewhat embarrassed by the affair but the fact that he persuaded Elizabeth to take Trijntje back, without calling on the law to punish either her or Menssink (for harbouring a runaway slave), suggests that he was an adroit and influential mediator. Either that, or the hidden hand was working.

The death of Governor Louis van Assenburgh, an event which occurred on 28 December 1711 (and which was followed by an impressive public funeral), seems to have stimulated Menssink, with its intimations of mortality, to put renewed pressure on Trijntje to kill Elizabeth as quickly as possible.[140] In his eagerness to accomplish the act he offered to send Gerrit to finish the job, to give his wife 'een sneeden in de beck' (a gash in the mouth) or to burn down her house.[141] These remedies were not, in the event, resorted to, but we have another witness to events in the Lingelbach household about this time whose testimony suggests that Elizabeth was very lucky not to have been subjected to more overt measures of violence than poisoning.

At some stage – exactly when cannot be determined – Elizabeth had acquired a young male slave, Carel of Bengal, whose age in 1712 was 15. It is possible that Carel had been bought by Elizabeth during Trijntje's period of absconding, or when it became obvious to her that her female slaves were not to be trusted out of her sight. Carel's tasks included fetching water and wood for his mistress, jobs that took him outside the house and ones that Elizabeth may have felt could not be performed by Trijntje or Flora in case Menssink waylaid them. Menssink, however, was quick to perceive that the boy could be useful, and sent Gerrit to bring Carel to him. At first, Gerrit was unsuccessful, for Carel, no doubt forewarned by his mistress, refused to accompany him to the brewer.

Eventually Gerrit was obliged to take the reluctant boy by the hand and virtually drag him to Menssink's house. Once there, Menssink attempted to get Carel to act as a courier, to transport a packet of powder to Trijntje so that she could put it in her mistress's food. Though Carel claims to have refused to do so on the first occasion, there were to be other summonings to the Menssinks' house.[142]

Next time the boy was offered beer which, out of suspicion, he dared not drink, pouring it away when no one was watching. This mistrust of the Menssink brew must have stemmed from a deeper aversion than simple dislike of their beer and suggests that Carel was well aware that there were poisonous substances emanating from the Menssink household. If we are to believe Carel it was not always possible to refuse widow Menssink's offers of drink, and twice he was nearly poisoned as a result. Once, when he told Gerbregt that his mistress was sick, she was so pleased with this intelligence that she gave him a glass of beer. The consequence was that a terrible wringing pain shot through his entire body and head. It is possible, given the poor reputation of the Menssinks' beer, that this was the normal sensation experienced by those who drank it but, even in view of Carel's tender age, his does seem to have been an extreme reaction. A second experience was even worse and so bad that the date etched itself in Carel's memory. On Saturday, 12 November 1712 Gerrit found Carel at the water pump and and summoned him to the Menssinks' house. Here he was given a glass of beer that caused him to vomit blood.[143] Once again, one must assume that this was not the standard response to a glass of Mother Menssink's finest and, if Carel was not lying, it seems probable that the beer was poisoned. If this was indeed the case, then either the Menssinks were trying to kill Carel or, more likely, they were using him as a guinea-pig to try out their various powders and potions. The unfortunate Carel seems to have been unable to refuse the repeated summonings to the Menssinks' house and we should assume, despite his denials, that he was forced into a reluctant complicity in the plot against Elizabeth. Carel's testimony, though not completely trustworthy, does serve to alert us to the fact that Elizabeth's misgivings about the sinister influence of her mother-in-law, Gerbregt Menssink, were well founded.

One day, as Carel stood unwillingly in her house, Gerbregt Menssink introduced him to three bricklayers who happened to be drinking beer there at the time. She told Carel that he should leave his mistress's windows unlocked because the three men wanted to go and talk to

Elizabeth. For all we know, the bricklayers may have been the most amiable of sorts but, in the context of events, a 'talk' could only be construed as a euphemism masking Gerbregt's intention of wishing a rather rough and unexpected visit on Elizabeth. Since Elizabeth did not receive such a visit, we may assume either that Carel kept the windows locked on this occasion or that the bricklayers chose to honour a previous social engagement. Carel did, however, admit to leaving the loft windows unlocked, at Gerrit's request, on at least three other instances, for which Willem Menssink rewarded him with *dubbeltjes* or beer.

As it happened, the bricklayers did not lose interest in the Lingelbach household once it had been pointed out to them, and, doubtless with widow Menssink's encouragement, they probed it for weak spots. One of the bricklayers, Andries by name, gave Flora a special key which enabled her to unlock Elizabeth's chest and steal five cloths. Andries also approached Carel and told him that, with his help, he and other friends intended to break into the Lingelbach house one night and cut Elizabeth's throat. Carel's part in this would be to unlock the house and signal to the bricklayers when the coast was clear. As the appointed time drew near, Andries came across Carel in the main street. The slave was fetching water in two buckets. The bricklayer quickly improvised another plan and poured some powder into the buckets. He then accompanied Carel to the door of Elizabeth's house to ensure that the boy did not tip the water out before it reached its destination.[144] It is not known whether Elizabeth drank this particular batch of water but we do know that by November 1712 she was not a well woman.

Even though Menssink's agents were bringing him encouraging reports of Elizabeth's periods of pain and illness, this was not enough to satisfy him. At some stage, exactly when is not clear, Gerrit arrived with new supplies of 'kapok' for Trijntje. This time his instructions were that she give it to her own child. Why? According to Trijntje, Menssink wanted her to kill his son because the child was a half-caste and, sooner or later, Elizabeth would tell people that he was its father and that he would then feel ashamed.[145] The court records add that Trijntje also hated her child and, indeed, as the evidence is presented, it is hard to escape that conclusion. The slave woman would later confess that she forced 'kapok' down her child's throat with her thumbs, causing the throat to swell up and making it impossible for the little boy to swallow food. Two days later he died.[146] On learning of his son's death Menssink, according to Trijntje, pronounced the following words: 'God heeft ons gegeven;

God heeft het ons genomen' (The Lord has given; the Lord has taken away).[147]

It is hard to believe that, when the baby died, Elizabeth did not regard Trijntje with suspicion. If Trijntje's treatment of the child during its short life was anything like as cruel as Elizabeth described, then she must have wondered about the mysterious obstruction in the infant's throat. Elizabeth had even tried to feed the child herself before it died. Perhaps she voiced her suspicions. It might be that she was secretly rather pleased to be rid of the bawling reminder of her husband's infidelity. Maybe she was far more concerned about her own pains. Sometime in November a doctor was called to the Lingelbach house but when he arrived it was for Elizabeth, not for Trijntje's dead child. There does not seem to have been a post-mortem on the infant's body and the murder might have gone unremarked. But Junniaar Bronssvinkel, the surgeon who examined Elizabeth, discovered what seemed to be human hair and 'kapok' in her faeces.[148] There was no doubt that somebody had put these substances in Elizabeth's food and suspicion, naturally, fell upon Trijntje. It was not simply because she had the motive and opportunity to harm her mistress. There was also the fact that her baby had recently died in rather mysterious circumstances. The authorities therefore decided that it was time to question the young slave woman very closely. Her confession, however extracted, must have come as a terrible shock to the guardians of law and order in Cape society.

It would seem that Trijntje was arrested between 12 and 16 November 1712. On the former date Carel was still at liberty and on the later date Elizabeth Lingelbach was asked to give her testimony.[149] The other people implicated in Trijntje's confession – Carel, Gerrit and Isaac – were probably all arrested between these dates but Menssink himself was not detained until 22 November. On that date the sheriff's officer, Simon Witmond, arrested him at his mother's house on the orders of the fiscal, Willem van Putten.[150] Only on 1 December 1712 was he required to appear before the Court of Justice and answer a charge of adultery. He had already been suspended as a member of the Burgher Council. That he was not charged with anything graver than adultery at this stage may be accounted for by the fact that the Council had not yet completed its investigations and was not yet willing to believe all the aspects of Trijntje's confession. Menssink admitted that the papers in the court's possession had been written in his own hand and he was thereafter confined to his mother's house – instead of the Castle, as might have been expected.[151]

The papers in question must surely have been the letters he had written to Elizabeth some years before, in which he had promised to mend his ways and refrain from sexual activity with slave women. The fact that these letters were in the possession of the authorities suggests that Elizabeth had handed them over as evidence to the court. These letters, together with Elizabeth's testimony and the confessions of the various slaves involved in the case, would seem to have provided the court with sufficient evidence to find Menssink guilty of, at the very least, adultery and, very probably, attempted murder or incitement to murder. The extraordinary thing is that Menssink was never found guilty of anything. Even more extraordinary is that he was never asked to submit to interrogation or cross-examination, nor to give a statement in his own defence. He was never, in short, on trial before the Court of Justice. The trial which commenced on 23 February 1713 was not about Menssink's misconduct. It was about the crimes committed by Trijntje, Gerrit, Isaac and Carel. How does one account for this amazing oversight on the part of the Court of Justice?

In the first place it should be mentioned that under the Roman-Dutch law of the eighteenth-century Cape, adultery was regarded as a crime which could entail criminal prosecution. It was one of the few grounds for divorce (malicious desertion and perpetual imprisonment or banishment were the other ones), and adulterous behaviour could result in the dissolution of the marriage of the guilty party, a fine, banishment or all of these. Thus, in a case of 1708, a woman who was found guilty of adultery at the Cape was sentenced to be confined in the House of Correction at Batavia for five years and was never permitted to marry again. The marriage with her husband was dissolved and the 'co-respondent, or second accused, with whom she had committed the adultery, was sentenced to work for two years at Robben Island *ad opus publicum* and have four months' salary confiscated *pro fisco*'.[152] In 1709, when two married persons were found guilty of adultery and cohabitation with each other and having procreated children, they were each fined 70 rixdollars, both were banished from the colony, the woman was prohibited from marrying again and the marriage with her husband was declared dissolved. In 1756, when a married man committed adultery with a spinster, he was fined 100 reals and imprisoned for a month on bread and water. The woman, on the other hand, 'was ordered to stand at the church door on three consecutive Sundays with a placard on her breast on which was written the word Whore'.[153]

In all of these cases it is remarkable that the punishment meted out to the offending woman was more severe than that deemed appropriate for the offending man. Clearly, male sexual impropriety was treated with greater leniency by the law than female sexual impropriety. Race and class issues also influenced the judgment of the court, a point clearly illustrated by an affair which occurred a year after the trial of Trijntje and which was, in many ways, a negative image of Menssink's circumstances.

On 1 September 1714 Maria Mouton of Middelburg was sentenced to death for the murder of her husband, an act she had committed with the help of her lover, the slave Titus of Bengal. Maria was half-strangled, scorched, and then strangled to death. Titus was impaled alive. Upon his death his head and right hand were cut off and fixed on a pole 'beyond the limits of his late master's property'. Fortuin, a slave accomplice, had his right hand cut off and was then broken on the wheel and tied to a grating. After this his head was cut off and placed on a pole together with his hand and the head and hand of Titus. All three bodies were then left exposed to the elements. Maria's property was confiscated.[154]

One wonders whether Menssink would have been as harshly treated if Elizabeth had in fact been murdered. The terrible punishments suffered by Titus and Fortuin (and, in the case of Titus, borne with the greatest heroism imaginable)[155] were inflicted, one senses, not so much because a murder had been committed but because a slave had assisted in the killing of his master and because a white woman had given her love to a slave man.

It may be argued that adultery with a slave woman, particularly that of a master with his own slave woman, was not regarded as 'proper' adultery; and that even if Roman-Dutch law and Christian principles regarded sex between a married person and a slave as adultery, social customs at the Cape were more lenient. This may have been the case. We should note, however, that as early as the period of Jan van Riebeeck's administration, when the constable Willem Cornelis was surprised in bed with the female slave Mary, Cornelis was sentenced to pay a fine of 50 reals and was dismissed from his post.[156] It should also be remembered that Elizabeth was, ultimately, granted a divorce and that the divorce was granted on the ground of her husband's adulterous behaviour. This is not to argue that other aspects of Menssink's conduct did not influence the court in granting Elizabeth a divorce. Divorce was, after all, an extremely rare, last resort in solving the marital problems of Dutch couples in the seventeenth and eighteenth centuries and did not automatically follow the discovery of adulterous behaviour in a spouse. It is merely to state that, legally, adultery provided the ground for divorce in Elizabeth's case and that, legally, this meant that Willem was guilty of adultery.[157]

It is significant that Elizabeth only filed for divorce on 23 March 1713, after the case against Trijntje, Isaac, Gerrit and Carel had been heard and the sentences passed. From this we may conclude that the authorities wished to treat the marital problems of the Menssinks as an issue distinct from the criminal activities of the slaves, and that Elizabeth may have accepted legal advice not to confuse the two issues. The court seems to have arranged matters so that not only did Menssink not appear to be on trial for the same crimes as the slaves, he did not even appear to be in the same case as the slaves. We may thus assume that one of the state's ambitions was to maintain the social and judicial distance which existed between masters and slaves in Cape society. To place a member of the Cape's elite in the same case as criminal slaves, and to judge this member as a co-conspirator of these slaves, was obviously more than the Court of Justice could stomach. To declare them as equals before the law would be to undermine the structures of inequality which bound the Cape's colonial society together. This would be bad enough in most cases, but the scandalous details that came to light in the testimonies of Trijntje and Elizabeth had potentially devastating social consequences. If the Court of Justice placed Menssink on trial it would mean having to accept the word of slaves against the word of their master. It would also mean the public exposure of a case in which a member of the Burgher Council was prepared to murder his own wife in order to enjoy the love of a dark-skinned slave woman and inherit his wife's property.[158]

If one explanation for Menssink's absence from the court-room is that his trial would have undermined the legitimacy of the Cape's social order, there is another possibility. Perhaps Menssink was protected from the judgment of the law by his family and friends. At the time the Commander of the Cape, who was also chairman of the Court of Justice, was Willem Helot (described by Fouché as ''n deurtrapte skelm'), a long-time opponent of the Tas faction.[159] Though this individual had no reason to favour Menssink, his position as head of the Cape's government was precarious and temporary, filling the gap created by the death of Governor Van Assenburgh until the Company could appoint a new Governor (which they did in the person of De Chavonnes in March 1714). Helot was not unopposed within the Council of Policy and ended his career at the Cape in disgrace after his corrupt practices had been exposed by his colleagues.[160] It is not, therefore, implausible to suggest that the Tas–Hüsing faction, in the ascendancy since W. A. van der Stel's recall, were able to exert enough influence to keep Menssink from being tried for attempted murder. Although we shall never know for sure, we should not dismiss the notion that a bribe may have been offered and accepted, for such things were common in the venal world of the VOC's administration.

A further reason for the leniency with which Menssink was treated may be related to the indispensable contribution which the authorities still believed him to be making to the supply of malt beer. This is borne out by the response of the Council of Policy to a request from Menssink which they discussed on 13 December 1712. Menssink appealed to the Council to release him from the restrictions of his house arrest on the grounds that, whilst he was under arrest, his brewing business was suffering great damage, and that both production and sale of beer were being seriously affected. As none of his 'volk' knew enough about brewing to run the business without him, he would not be able to fulfil the requirements of his contract with the Company to supply beer. If he continued to be held under arrest, Menssink explained, he would be ruined, and since he hoped to be able to prove to the Court of Justice that he was completely innocent of the charge of adultery, this would be a most unfortunate occurrence. He therefore requested the Council to release him from arrest so that he could run the brewery, promising to make himself available to appear before the court whenever required so as to defend himself. The majority of the Council voted to allow Menssink his request, on condition that he provided sufficient security, and that he was ready to appear before the court at a moment's notice, and that he did not go too far from his home.[161] Significantly, there was no mention of Menssink's mother running the brewery in her son's absence and it may well be that she was no longer as active in the brewery as before. The Council therefore decided not to remove Menssink from society, for that would imperil the flow of beer – and beer, no matter how vile, had to keep flowing.

Trijntje, Gerrit, Isaac and Carel, therefore, faced justice without Menssink at their side, and their evidence, seemingly damning from his point of view, was never used against him – at least not in the Court of Justice. On 2 March 1713 the sentences were pronounced. Trijntje's sins, in the estimation of the court, were multiple. Firstly, there was her 'Godless intention' to poison her mistress and the 'enormity' of her actions in pursuing this goal. Secondly, there was the 'Godless and tyrannical treatment of her innocent offspring'. Thirdly, there was the adultery which she had committed with the brewer Menssink, and fourthly, the horrific acts which she had perpetrated together with her three fellow accused. These all added up to 'matters of evil and dangerous consequence which could not be tolerated in a country where justice was stressed, but as an example to others should be punished in a most rigorous way'.[162] Surgeon Bronssvinkel and the apothecary Jan Rigter had earlier assisted in the court's investigation by digging outside Elizabeth's bedroom and unearthing bones which they identified as a human hand.[163] About this, at least, Trijntje had not been lying.

Thus it was that Trijntje of Madagascar, at the age of about 25, was condemned to be taken to the place of public execution, to be bound to a pole and strangled with a cord until dead. Her body was then to be fastened to a forked post and exposed to the air and the birds of the heavens until it disintegrated.[164]

The unfortunate Gerrit of Tutucorijn, his master's faithful Hermes, was sentenced to stand beneath the gallows with the noose around his neck before being whipped and branded on his naked back. He was then to be placed in chains and condemned to labour on Robben Island for 25 years. Since Gerrit was between 40 and 50 years old at the time, this was, in effect, a life sentence. The severity of this punishment requires some explanation, for Gerrit's fellow slave, 30-year-old Isaac of Masulipatam, received a far more lenient sentence. He was to be whipped, branded and shackled but was to be banished to Robben Island for a mere three years. It would seem as though Gerrit was being heavily punished for his necromantic activities, for this is the one crime that he and Isaac did not have in common.[165] Young Carel of Bengal, Elizabeth's slave, was sentenced to be beaten on the bare back with rods. He was then to be placed in chains for two years whilst he performed his normal duties for his mistress.[166] All of these sentences were executed two days after they had been pronounced on 4 March 1713.[167]

There is no record of Menssink's feelings on that particular March Saturday. Nor, for that matter, is there any evidence of his feelings for Trijntje, Gerrit or Isaac after this date. We do not know if Menssink was present at the time and place of execution, or, afterwards, whether he ever saw the corpse of his former lover rotting on the scaffold. We cannot say that when he looked across to Robben Island he ever thought of his slaves, whipped and branded for services they had rendered him. Did he feel sorrow, guilt, bitter grief, anger or indifference? Again we do not know. All we do know for certain is that Menssink had little to rejoice in. Whilst he had been spared the ordeal of answering to the same crimes with which his and his wife's slaves had been charged, he had not emerged from the crisis unscathed.

Though uncondemned by the Court of Justice, Menssink had not escaped the taint of scandal or the censure of society. In the small world of early Cape Town the details of his affair with Trijntje must soon have become known and people would have been quick to form their own conclusions and pass their own judgments. The first sign of Menssink's decline in social status may be observed in his suspension from the rank of burgher captain and his suspension as a member of the Burgher Council.[168] This loss of social status seems to have sent signals to his creditors, who equated Menssink's fall from grace with a decline in his credit worthiness. The simultaneous intelligence that the brewer's wife was now in a strong position to obtain a divorce from her husband no doubt provided a further incentive to make claims on the Menssink estate before it suffered division. Scarcely a week after it had passed judgment on Menssink's slaves, the Court of Justice found itself considering a financial claim against the brewer and his mother. On 9 March 1713 a long-forgotten creditor, an 'onderstuursman' by the name of Arent Etman, suddenly decided to call in a debt of 21,126 Caroli guilders, 2 *stuivers* and 8 pennies which had been outstanding since 1694. He also requested interest, calculated at 4 per cent a year.[169] The timing of this action was surely not coincidental, for Etman was doubtless conscious that the fortunes of the Menssinks were on the wane. It is also possible that Etman, or his representative, seized the moment to strike because he perceived that Menssink was at his most vulnerable and that, with the brewer's political influence declining, the anticipated court-room battle would be easier. These details suggest that the Menssinks' financial situation was a lot less healthy than their social status suggested. Indeed, they may have been teetering on the brink of financial ruin for years and these circumstances could explain that Menssink had powerful monetary motives in wishing Elizabeth dead.

There is something exceptional about the rapidity of the court's decision in this case, for they decided then and there that Menssink and his mother were liable to pay the full amount claimed by Etman. The Menssinks acknowledged the debt but asked for permission to pay it off over a five-year period. Permission to do so was refused. This meant the financial ruin of the Menssinks, for in order to pay this sum, Menssink would be obliged to declare himself insolvent and to sell all his property and auction all his possessions. There seemed to be no room left for Menssink to appeal against this judgment or to delay it with legal counter-attacks. One is left with the impression that Menssink had been informed outside the court-room that if he chose to contest this ruling he would find himself before the court on a much more serious charge. The Company was, in effect, withdrawing its support from him entirely and allowing his creditors to punish him financially for crimes which ought to have been paid for in blood.

Hard on the heels of Etman's financial demands came the prospect of another court case. This time, Menssink must have been expecting it. On 23 March, Elizabeth Lingelbach asked the court for permission to divorce her husband, a request which, if granted, would have serious financial implications for Menssink.[170] Perhaps the brewer thought, as the carrion-eating birds picked Trijntje's bones clean, that the vultures were circling above him too.

Then, as if to confirm divine disapproval of recent events, a terrible outbreak of smallpox occurred at the Cape. The disease was first noted amongst the Company's slaves on 18 April 1713. By 6 May the neighbouring Khoikhoi, as well as slaves, were dying by the score. By 7 May mortality rates were so high that bodies could not be buried fast enough and lay stinking about the town. The epidemic spread into the interior, devastating the Khoikhoi but also causing deaths amongst the relatively immune settlers. Only in December did the contagion abate. It is thus no exaggeration to state that, for the last eight months of 1713, the colony seemed cursed and its inhabitants were more than usually aware of their mortality.[171] It was in these morbid circumstances that Menssink battled to hold his own.

His first response to the financial threats against him was to secure his daughter Margarieta's inheritance; the Orphan Chamber was instructed to claim 8000 guilders from his estate on her behalf. The Court of Justice was first notified of this on 30 March 1713. On 5 May Adriaan van Kervel of the Orphan Chamber reiterated to the court that, in the event of her parents' separation, Magarieta's inheritance should be protected by law. At the same time Menssink denied Elizabeth's allegations against him, and Henning Hüsing, in effect Margarieta's guardian, went on record as stating that the Menssinks' debt to Arent Etman was not as great as Etman claimed.[172] From this it may be seen that the Hüsing–Tas faction continued to support Menssink, if not for his sake alone, then for the sake of his daughter.

None of this stopped the process of the law. On 12 April 1713 David Thibault, the secretary of the Court of Justice, took an inventory of the goods of Menssink and his mother at their house in Table Valley and at the brewery in Newlands. Inventories were also made of the goods at Menssink's two Joostenberg farms – Hercules Pilaar and De Waarburg. Significantly, no attempt was made to inventorise the possessions of Menssink's wife Elizabeth in her Cape Town house. The legal niceties of the situation had, no doubt, been carefully considered by the parties involved. Although Elizabeth was in the process of filing for divorce she was, legally, still Menssink's wife and married in community of property. The law, however, did not allow a husband to appropriate the property of his estranged wife to the extent that it would compromise her ability to support herself.[173] Perhaps this ruling protected Elizabeth's property from her husband. Or perhaps it was the fact that the debt which was threatening to ruin Menssink had been incurred before he even married Elizabeth and she could not, therefore, be held accountable for it. Whatever the exact reasons, there did not seem to be an immediate danger of Elizabeth's possessions ending up under the hammer at a public auction in order to pay off her husband's debts. But for as long as the marriage endured, there was always the prospect that an insolvent Menssink could make claims on her wealth and thus every reason for Elizabeth to expedite the divorce as quickly as possible.

Her desire to proceed with the divorce received a setback on 26 October 1713 when Maria Engelbregt, the wife of Willem Helot, charged Elizabeth for a debt of 1291 guilders, outstanding since 1699, and for possession of an inheritance due to a certain Thimotheus van der Boom.[174] These demands, coming from the wife of the head of the Court of Justice and the Acting Governor, must have been a most unwelcome surprise to Elizabeth. Her first impulse was to ignore them but, after her second default in the matter, she was obliged to appear before the court. On 9 November she explained that she knew nothing about it. She was informed that the debt had been incurred by her father in 1699, before his death. Since the debt appears to have been incurred in the Netherlands, Elizabeth wanted to write to Holland for the details but she was ordered to pay without delay.[175] Quite what Maria Engelbregt's connection was with this business is uncertain. One thing, however, is clear. Maria was no friend of the Tas faction. She had been married to the minister of Stellenbosch, Van Loon, until that unfortunate man committed suicide. The farms she had been left she sold to Menssink but this did not make her a family friend. In 1705 Adam Tas described her as a 'grootse leppige wijf' who was clearly of the Van der Stel faction.[176] The fact that she married Helot in 1710 is a further indication that her sympathies lay with the anti-Tas faction. It would be difficult to state whether her actions were prompted by Helot, or whether she was hoping to injure Menssink as well as Elizabeth by resuscitating a forgotten debt.[177] Even though, legally, Maria Engelbregt may have had a case it is noteworthy that, like Etman, she chose this moment to press home her financial claims against the Menssink estate. The impression, once again, is that the public perceived the Menssinks were vulnerable and close to ruin, and this was the time to settle old debts as well as, perhaps, a few old scores.

Elizabeth may have suspected that the longer she took to meet Maria's demands, the longer it would take to get her request for divorce considered. She was thus probably 1291 guilders poorer when she next requested to be divorced from her husband, a step she took on 16 November 1713, citing adultery and desertion as her reasons. Divorce procedure deemed it necessary for both husband and wife to appear in court together in order to convince the members of the court that there was no chance of reconciliation. This step was achieved on 30 November and Menssink asked the court for copies of his wife's request for separation.[178]

In the meantime, Menssink's financial ruin continued apace. On 19 August 1713 the brewery and its contents went under the hammer. The man who made the successful bid for the brewery was Rudolph Fredrick Steenbok, the colony's future brewer. He paid 8000 guilders for Papenboom and its 30 morgen of land. He also bought some of the items at the brewery, especially those which had a specific brewing function. The total value of goods auctioned was an estimated 464 rixdollars. (There were approximately three guilders to a rixdollar.) These goods included two male slaves, Alexander of Bengal and Titus of the Coast of Coromandel – an indication of the extent to which Menssink had relied on Indian slaves at the brewery and in his household. On 28 August 1713 the Cape Town house and its contents were auctioned. The house fetched 8690 guilders and its contents about 772 rixdollars. Interestingly, it appears that quantities of malt and hops had been stored at the house rather than at the brewery. These too were bought by Steenbok.[179]

Finally, on 11 December 1713, the two farms at Joostenberg were auctioned. They were both 60 morgen in size but the most important of them was Hercules Pilaar, for it was cultivated with wheat, well timbered, and contained buildings ('huys, hok en craalen'). De Waarburg, on the other hand, was uncultivated and probably used as grazing for Menssink's livestock. All in all, Menssink, was forced to sell some 11 slaves, 1200 sheep, 190 cattle, 9 horses and 70 muids of wheat, as well as assorted tools, implements and household effects. A noticeable presence at the auction, and one who bought a lot of stock, was Jacob van der Heiden, the Company's meat contractor. The final valuation of the farms was put at 6100 guilders and the goods at 2456 rixdollars. The farms were sold on the day of the auction and the buyer signed the papers on the same day.[180] Who was the buyer?

In an extraordinary act of familial solidarity Menssink's farms had been bought by his sister-in-law, Sara Tas, the recent widow of Claas Diepenauw.[181] Sara, sister to Menssink's first wife and aunt to Menssink's daughter, clearly saw it as her duty to save Willem from ruin. She had been a buyer at the auctions of the Table Valley house and at the brewery, saving treasured family possessions and helping to pay off her brother-in-law's debts. Now, like a guardian angel, she used some of her late husband's considerable wealth to buy Hercules Pilaar and De Waarburg with the intention of settling Willem down on them as a country gentleman.[182] The farms, happily, were adjacent to one of the farms which she had just inherited from her deceased husband – D'Eensaamheit near Klapmuts. Sara arranged to lease the farms to Willem for a ten-year period at the rate of 240 guilders per annum.[183]

Sara can have had few illusions about her brother-in-law's character although she did seem to blame Elizabeth Lingelbach – whom she disliked – for much of Willem's trouble.[184] Her decision to rescue Willem was, however, motivated more by her love for his daughter, Margarieta Maria, than for Willem himself. Sara had been like a mother to Margarieta – or 'Mittjen', her term of endearment for the girl[185] – since Johanna's death, and had looked after the child in the home of her aunt, Maria Lindenhovius, the wife of Henning Hüsing. Sara had only married Diepenauw, himself a widower and eighteen years her senior, in 1707, when she was 37 years old.[186] She and Diepenauw had had no children of their own and thus Mittjen was especially dear to her. As Margarieta herself admitted, 'Tante Diepenauw' loved her as a daughter and not as a niece.[187] 'Tante Hüsing' also loved Mittjen dearly and, if necessary, the considerable wealth of the Hüsing family was at hand to secure the young girl's future.[188] In the meantime, Sara could not allow a family member, the father of her beloved Mittjen, to sink further into disgrace. Thus it was that Willem and his mother began a new life at Hercules Pilaar.

Something, then, had been salvaged from the terrible year of 1713. Thanks to the kindness of Sara Diepenauw, the Menssinks had a roof over their heads and the potential to make a living as farmers. Mittjen too had contributed, indirectly, to rescuing her father from complete poverty. Menssink's earlier request to the Court of Justice – to set aside 8000 guilders from his estate on the grounds that it was his daughter's inheritance ('die moederlike bewijs') – had fallen on the deaf ears of Willem Helot. Helot did, however, allow Menssink to set aside 600 sheep and 40 cattle from his livestock before the auction of 11 December 1713. These were reckoned to be Mittjen's because in April 1707, at a time when Henning Hüsing had been living under the threat of banishment or death, he had made a gift of 100 sheep and 12 calves to the little girl. Fortunately, documentary proof for this existed, and was presented to the court. The court calculated what the natural increase of the stock was likely to have been and allowed Menssink to retain these animals. It was therefore Mittjen's cattle and sheep that formed the basis of her father's post-1713 stock, 'waar mede beginne den landbouw bijde hand te nemen' (whereby a start was made with farming).[189] In the *opgaaf* of 1716 Menssink declared that he had 56 cattle and 600 sheep, an indication that though progress had been modest, things were not noticeably worse.[190]

It would appear that Menssink was also able to save some of his slaves from the auction, for in 1713 he had written to Helot to request certain exemptions from the sale. Menssink had offered the slave Corridon in place of the slave Aneijt, who was, the brewer explained, his daughter's. Menssink and his mother also requested to retain two slaves for themselves, Jacobin[a] or [-us] and Valentijn.[191] It cannot be stated with any certainty whether Helot allowed these requests but the names mentioned do not appear amongst the names of the slaves who were sold at the auction. Menssink clearly required labour to work his farms and although some of this may have been provided by Khoikhoi labourers it seems that he was not without slaves right from the beginning of his new life at Joostenberg.

Quite apart from the necessity of manual labour was the need for skilled supervision: it may be doubted whether the ex-brewer was capable of providing this himself. In 1713 the *knecht* in his employment was a certain Lambert Engels. In May 1714 this individual decided to go to court in order to ask that the loan which he had received from Menssink some time before, namely 1000 rixdollars, be recognised as having been granted interest-free. It is possible that Menssink, now short of cash, had been leaning on Engels for repayment of this earlier loan. It is also possible that Engels, aware of his employer's vulnerability, had decided that now was a good time to win concessions from him. Whatever the circumstances, on 24 May Engels won his case and his loan was declared to have been granted interest-free.[192] It is unlikely that Engels would have been retained as an employee after this legal victory over his boss and a 1716 document confirms that by this date a man by the name of Andries Paaster van Maagdenburg was working as Menssink's *knecht*.[193]

The same document reveals that, by 1716, Menssink owned at least four slaves, for in it Paaster explains the trouble which Menssink's slaves had been causing. One of his slaves, Benjamin, had run away but later had been recaptured. Benjamin recounted how he had encouraged another of Menssink's fugitive slaves, Jacob, to steal a cow from his master. Benjamin then pointed out to Paaster seven of Jacob's hiding-places in the bush where Jacob had managed to exist as a fugitive for four years, since 1712.[194] Two of Menssink's other slaves, Tama and Aron, corroborated Paaster's story though Aron added that Benjamin was more guilty than he admitted, having enabled Jacob to steal two muids of meal, some wheat and three guns from his master.[195]

All of these details suggest that, despite his straitened circumstances, and despite a rather high incidence of slave desertion, Menssink was by 1716 able to afford the labour services which he required in order to run his farm. His struggles in the countryside, however, initially took second place to his battles in the court-room, which occupied most of 1714. On 17 May 1714 Elizabeth Lingelbach's request to be lawfully separated from her husband was finally approved.[196] Menssink had to be officially informed of this before the request was formalised. We may assume that he was so informed, for on 24 May 1714 Elizabeth's request was indeed formalised. Menssink's response to this was that since his wife had been separated from him for ten years he could not now be legally divorced from her. He reminded the court that he was married in community of property and requested that copies of Elizabeth's divorce papers be made available to him.[197] The court appears to have been unimpressed by this litigious show of spirit. Instead they offered Menssink some sobering information. The legal representative of Arent Etman was demanding 5000 rixdollars, or 15,000 guilders, from the insolvent estate of the widow Rutgert Menssink and her son, and the court had decided to arrest 4000 rixdollars from the estate to satisfy the demand.[198] On 31 May 1714 Henning Hüsing was called in, once again, to present evidence that the Menssinks' debt was not as great as Etman claimed and on 7 June the Menssinks were allowed to put their case before the court. They admitted that they owed Etman 10,000 guilders but no more.[199] Since the court and Etman's representative now had an exact notion of how much the Menssinks' estate was worth, it is likely that some sort of compromise was reached, for on 22 June the court approved a claim by Etman's representative for 10,000 guilders against the Menssink estate.[200] Financial closure was finally achieved on 31 January 1715 when Menssink put his signature to the accounts for his insolvent estate. Thanks to the arcane arts of the Company bookkeepers the credit and debit columns had been made to balance exactly and Menssink was, in one sense of the word, free.[201]

A further, unwelcome form of freedom had been thrust on him the day before the court paid Etman his settlement of 10,000 guilders. On 21 June 1714 Elizabeth Lingelbach was finally granted a divorce from her husband. It had not been easy. On 7 June Elizabeth had had to remind the court that forty days had elapsed since her formal request for legal separation had been approved, on 24 May, and that legally the divorce should now be granted. On 14 June the court resolved to go ahead with the separation and on 21 June, 'having in vain attempted all measures to effect reconciliation between the parties', the Court of Justice granted the divorce.[202] Notwithstanding the abundant evidence of Menssink's adultery, his implication in infanticide and an attempted murder, as well as a ten-year period of separation from his wife, it had taken fifteen months from Elizabeth's first request for a divorce in March 1713 to achieve this ruling.

It would be gratifying to be able to give details of Elizabeth's response to her new freedom but, sadly, after obtaining her divorce, no further details of her life are to be found in the records. Perhaps she continued to run her coffee shop in Cape Town. If she did, she may have remarried, for a single woman of substance did not, as a rule, stay single for long in eighteenth-century Cape society. Perhaps she returned to Holland, though one would imagine it was easier for her to continue her business at the Cape – particularly with Menssink out of the way – than to begin a new life in the Netherlands.

Menssink, for his part, was obliged to live out his remaining years in the rural seclusion of Joostenberg. After his scandalous conduct such obscurity may well have been welcome to him, for there cannot have been many members of Cape society who approved of him. Despite this, he was always referred to as 'de oudburgerraad Willem Menssink', an honorific which suggests that he retained some respect for his past social status. The authorities seemed content to leave him alone even though, in October 1714, an event occurred on his farm which might have given them cause to interfere. The corpse of a slave was found by Menssink in the bushes about two musket-shots from his farmhouse. The slave, Antonij, had belonged to the farmer Andries Creugel. Antonij had been shot in the head and a knife was found on his body. Menssink informed the authorities at Stellenbosch and officials arrived at his farm to investigate. Nobody was arrested for the murder. We know that there were a lot of armed *drosters*, or runaway slaves, in the neighbourhood. Had Antonij been one of them? Had he been killed by one of them or had he been shot by Menssink himself? The investigating team expressed no opinion on the matter and do not seem to have suspected 'de oudburgerraad Willem Menssink' of foul play.[203]

It is likely that Menssink's aged mother, Gerbregt, predeceased him, for there is no mention of her in Menssink's will. The traumatic events of 1713, along with the enforced move to the country, would have been difficult even for a woman of her combative spirit and we may assume that she died shortly after 1714. If Menssink felt the death of his mother to be a loss, then at least he had the consolations of friendship available to him in the person of his brother-in-law, Adam Tas. Sara Diepenauw sold D'Eensaamheit to her brother Adam in 1714 for 4000 guilders and thereby Tas became Menssink's neighbour.[204] Tas, a widower, remarried in November 1715. His second marriage, to Johanna Kocvael of Leerdam, was not a happy one and the brothers-in-law no doubt had much in common to talk about.[205] Both Tas and Menssink were book lovers and a measure of Willem's regard for Adam may be deduced from the fact that Willem appointed Adam executor of his will.[206]

Margarieta, Menssink's daughter, did not stay in the Cape for very long. As the young girl reached a marriageable age, her aunt Sara may have decided that her prospects would be better in the Netherlands. In the Cape there would always be a taint of scandal attached to the name of Menssink and gossip might have an adverse effect on the girl's happiness. The widow Diepenauw was now a woman of means and she meant to settle a considerable sum of money on her beloved niece. The question was, Would such a girl and such a dowry not be wasted in a provincial backwater? It is possible that Sara herself was tired of Africa and anxious to spend some of her new wealth in the more congenial setting of her homeland. These resolves were doubtless reinforced by her aunt, Maria Lindenhovius, recent widow of the wealthy Henning Hüsing. Thus, in 1718, Maria Lindenhovius requested permission for herself, Sara Wilhelmina Tas, the widow of Claas Hendriksz Diepenauw, and Margarieta Maria Menssink to return to the fatherland on one of the ships of the return fleet.[207] Before she left, Margarieta drew up her will. On 1 April 1718, at the age of 19, she left everything to her father. If he should predecease her, then the nearest relative on her mother's side of the family would be the beneficiary. If she were to marry, her future husband and children would inherit.[208] Having settled her affairs, the tight-knit trio of women, bound by ties of family, affection and mutual experience, were ready to leave and it is likely that they sailed together from the Cape shortly afterwards.

At the beginning of 1721 Menssink must have received strong intimations of his mortality, for something prompted him to draw up his will in April. He was 57 years old at the time. In his will he left everything he had to his daughter, Margarieta Maria Menssink of Amsterdam. In recognition of their special relationship, Menssink left Adam Tas his favourite male slave, Valentijn, on the condition that Valentijn be given 25 guilders from the estate and that the slave should not be sold during Tas's lifetime. Menssink also left Tas all of his books – except for two which he left to his daughter. The exceptions were his Bible and the 'joodse oudheeden' (presumably Josephus' *Jewish Antiquities*).[209]

In early October 1721, Menssink died. His will was shown to the Orphan Chamber on 7 October and legal procedures to execute his last requests were commenced. News of his death, however, took a long time to reach Holland, for his daughter and sister-in-law had still not learnt of his demise by 24 April 1722. On that date the women wrote to Willem from Amsterdam, obviously oblivious of the fact that he was no longer alive. It is thanks to this ignorance that the letters have survived, for once they arrived at the Cape, the letters were placed with other papers relating to the deceased estate in the files of the Orphan Chamber.[210]

Also in the file is a letter from a brother-in-law whom Menssink had never met – Gerard Tas. Gerard was a brother of Adam Tas who had stayed in Holland with his mother and who had married Maria Gertruijd Lindenhovius, a cousin. Gerard was living in the same house as his wife (his mother, Margarieta Gertruijd Lindenhovius, was probably deceased by 1722) and two sisters, Hester Elsabe Tas and Anna Margareta Tas. To these we may add Sara Tas, the daughter of Adam Tas, who had been sent by her father to her Dutch relatives, and who may even have accompanied the widows Hüsing and Diepenauw, along with Mittjen, when they left the Cape in 1718.[211] We cannot be sure whether all of the newly arrived Cape ladies stayed in the same house as Gerard Tas but, judging by the details contained within the letters, this is likely. Even if all the family members were not under the same roof, they were extremely close to each other – both spatially and emotionally – and in close touch too with Maria Lindenhovius's brother, the Revd Gerhardus Lindenhovius of Overijssel. It was following a visit to him that Mittjen became betrothed to his son, Daniel Lindenhovius, also a clergyman, whose parish was in Overijssel. The engagement had prompted the letters to Menssink as Sara Wilhelmina Tas, the widow Diepenauw, was particularly keen to break the welcome news to her beloved Mittjen's father.[212]

There is a particular poignancy to be experienced in reading these letters, knowing that they were never seen by their intended recipient and that they were written by people who believed themselves to be addressing a still-living loved one. It is clear from the tone of these letters that the Tas–Lindenhovius network continued to regard Willem Menssink as a family member, for they address him in affectionate, inclusive terms. Sara's letter mentions earlier letters that Menssink had written to them, from which we may infer a correspondence as regular as shipping movements allowed. Sara, as Willem's sister-in-law, close contemporary (she was 52 years old in 1722) and surrogate mother of his daughter, knew him well enough to be fairly frank and intimate, yet she hints at, rather than mentions directly, the catastrophe that, but for her, would have destroyed his life.

After complaining mildly about her health (a cough and 'binnenkoortsen' having kept her from attending church) and indulging in some consoling religious platitudes (directed as much at Menssink as at herself) she proceeded to inform Willem about other members of the family. 'Moeij' Hüsing (that is, Maria Lindenhovius, widow of Henning Hüsing) was well enough to make excursions. But Willem's daughter, 'mijn Mittjen', was the main subject of her letter. According to Sara, Mittjen was a fine, modest girl, intelligent, obliging, pleasant in company, dutiful and helpful. She was shortly to leave them to get married since one could not prevent a good marriage. The future husband was a gentle, kind man who was an excellent preacher, very learned and in line for a considerable inheritance from his father and from 'Moeij' Hüsing (his aunt). Mittjen was also to inherit a considerable amount from both 'Moeij' Hüsing and from Sara herself. The couple would thus be financially very well established. In addition, Mittjen had the approval of her future father-in-law, the Revd Lindenhovius, so all in all the match seemed a great success. This was particularly gratifying, Sara continued, since ''t trouwen is tegenwoordig soo prickeleus wij souden niet durven toestaan dat sij troude om dat men hier soo veele hoort van quade houwelicken en U.E. dogter is selve oock soo beschroomt sou niet licht trouwen aan die sij nie wel kende' (Marriage is such a perilous business these days that we did not want her to marry because people here hear so much about bad marriages and your daughter is so shy that we would not lightly let her marry someone she did not know well).[213]

Reading between the lines it is not difficult to see a reference here to Menssink's own unfortunate second marriage, and Sara refers to this quite specifically further on: 'ik wenste wel dat U. E. en Broer Tas, dat geluck oock gehadt hadden in U. E. tweede trouwen maar dat is contrari uit gevallen tot U. E. en onse verdriet want een goede vrou is seer nodig in een huis en een seer swaar kruis voor die 't niet wel getroffen heeft dog nog veel beter geen vrou dan een quade vrou daar men niet mede kan leven in ruste en vrede' (I wish that you and brother Tas had both had success in your second marriages but that is not how it turned out to your and our sorrow because a good woman [wife] is really necessary in a household and a really heavy cross to bear if this is not the case, indeed rather no woman at all than a bad woman with whom one cannot live in peace and quiet).[214]

Mittjen, on the other hand, was fortunate, for she was to marry a preacher and, as a preacher's wife, could expect to live a quiet and peaceful life even though one heard about so many marriages of another sort. Sara was sad to think that Mittjen would leave her when she married, but consoled herself with the thought that she would be marrying a pious man. This was comforting because Mittjen had very few good friends in Holland. 'Elck is dog al voor sich selver en voor sijn huis darom is al best dat sij selfs een huishouden heeft en een man' (Everyone is for themselves and for their homes, therefore it is best that she has a household and a husband of her own).[215]

If Menssink had ever read these lines he may well have rejoiced in his daughter's good fortune. But he would also have reflected, as doubtless his sister-in-law intended he should, on his own imperfect marriage. It is interesting that Sara does not seem to blame Willem directly for his unhappy marriage, tactfully preferring to place the blame on his bad wife. In this she was probably reflecting Menssink's own explanation for his ill-fortune: it was not his fault but his wife's. Implausible though this may seem to be, there must have been something about Elizabeth Lingelbach that the Tases and Lindenhoviuses did not like, for how else could they have overlooked Willem's glaring faults so completely? Similarly, if Menssink could still command the loyalty of good Christians like Sara, and other family members, he could not have been as despicable as the testimony of Trijntje and Elizabeth suggests. In this respect it is unfortunate that we do not have Menssink's own testimony in the court records, for we are thus denied a more intimate glimpse into the brewer's mind. This once more raises the question as to why the authorities did not want Menssink's voice to be heard. Perhaps, after all, his biggest crime was to have loved not wisely but too well, and the government could not countenance the prospect of a prominent free burgher confessing to an unacceptable, all-consuming passion, namely a socially subversive love for a slave woman.

Sara concluded her letter by urging Willem to keep good friendship with brother Tas, pointing out that it was easier for him to visit Tas, since he was unencumbered by children, than it was for Tas to visit him. Sara also sent Willem two books by the hymnist Sluiter. Perhaps these, along with Menssink's other books, also found their way into Adam Tas's collection, which was soon to be auctioned.

Mittjen's letter to her father is less revealing than her aunt's letter.[216] It is exactly the sort of letter one would expect from the modest and dutiful young woman described by Sara. Mittjen is almost excessively respectful towards her father and her tone is one of polite formality rather than that of familial intimacy. Her news is of other family members and the most deeply felt part of the letter is when she describes the poor health of her beloved 'Moeij' Diepenauw. Sara was obviously sicker than she had implied, for her niece expresses fears that she might not recover from her illness. Mittjen is too modest to mention her marriage prospects directly but discusses some of the difficulties facing members of the preaching profession in her part of the Netherlands instead. This is the closest she gets to suggesting that her life is, in the future, to be concerned with such issues. She also mentions a visit from certain Menssink family members – 'Nicht Menssink heeft hier onlangs bij ons geweest op een koppie tee haar Broer was hier ook en de jongte Neef Oom Menssink is nog een gaauw man na zijn Jaaren' (Niece Menssink was here with us for tea, her brother was also here and also the young nephew. Uncle Menssink is still in good shape for his years).[217] The family referred to here is obviously that of one of Menssink's brothers but which one exactly cannot be stated. Mittjen concluded her letter with the strongest terms of love and respect before signing her name formally as Margarieta Maria Menssink.

Gerard Tas's letter to Menssink does not add much to our knowledge of affairs since it is largely concerned with describing the health of his wife and two young daughters. Gerard does, however, reveal that Mittjen is being troubled by headaches, a detail that neither Mittjen nor her aunt saw fit to mention.[218]

It is not easy to trace the fortunes of the Menssink family after Willem's death. Mittjen married Daniel Lindenhovius and there is evidence that in November 1722 the couple were in correspondence with the Orphan Chamber at the Cape in connection with Menssink's estate. There is no telling when Sara Tas, the widow Diepenauw and Maria Lindenhovius, the widow Hüsing, died although we do know that Sara was still alive in 1727, preparing herself to receive the orphaned sons of her brother Adam. The unfortunate Mittjen, apple of her aunt's eye, died childless and before her husband, but exactly when is unclear.[219]

Adam Tas did not long survive his friend Willem Menssink. Whilst serving as the *heemraad* for Stellenbosch he was taken ill on 1 June 1722. He prepared his will and died later in the same month at the age of 54. The likelihood is that his second wife had predeceased him, for his surviving sons had to be cared for by others. Eventually, once his estate had been settled in 1727, the boys were shipped off to Holland to join their sister Sara in the care of their aunt Sara, the kindly widow Diepenauw.[220] This remarkable woman thus proved to be the salvation of both her brother's and her brother-in-law's families. With her maternal love and material wealth she provided a stable nucleus around which less settled elements orbited. Her own life may indeed be said to have illustrated the value of the homily which she had addressed to her 'Waarder Broeder Menssink' in 1722: 'een goede vrou is seer nodig in een huis'.

2

Fugitives on the Cape Frontier

c. 1680–1770

AS THE VOC refreshment station at the Cape developed into a colony, it produced a diverse number of fugitives whose greatest desire was to remove themselves from the strictures of the colony's laws. These runaway slaves, deserted sailors, absconding soldiers, *landloopers*, vagabonds, debtors, escaped murderers, bandits, counterfeiters, thieves and assorted criminals were, in a sense, the cutting edge of colonial expansion. Of necessity they had to remain one step ahead of the colony, beyond the vanguard of the frontier farmers. In their lawless diversity these refugees and rogues constituted the outer margins of the frontier zone, the uncontrollable excrescence of the colony and, as such, their influence on the Khoisan societies of the interior was considerable.[1]

Individual fugitives would often form themselves into groups, bound together in a particular form of resistance to oppression – flight. These groups of *drosters* (from the Dutch word *drossen*, 'to run away' or 'to desert') were an integral aspect of the frontier zone. The changing nature of their composition and character is an important indicator of the transforming processes of colonial expansion. Although the immediate impact of these groups on the societies of the Cape interior was essentially destructive, in the long run they played a more positive role. From the wreckage of traditional societies arose hybrid groups, the 'Oorlams' or 'Bastaards' of later fame, and very often, at the nucleus of such a group, would be some *drosters* or their descendants.

The most common type of fugitive was the runaway slave.[2] In 1686 the Council of Policy was alarmed by the 'daily and continuous' flight of Company and private slaves who, armed with guns, sustained themselves in groups in the wilderness. It was resolved to punish recaptives with a beating with rods, the amputation of an ear and the attachment of chains to their persons. These measures were to be enforced until an improvement in circumstances was noted.[3] By October 1702, however, runaways were still so prevalent that the Company post-holders along the colony's frontier were instructed to send out a man every day to look for fugitive slaves and shoot them if necessary.[4] The situation had obviously not improved by June 1711, for on this date the punishment for recaptives was upgraded so as to cause more terror amongst the slaves and to act as a deterrent. A first offender would now not only be whipped but branded on the cheek. For a second escape attempt the punishment would include branding on the other cheek and, if a man was unlucky enough to be caught for a third time, he could expect to have his ears and nose cut off.[5] These punishments were, however, contingent on the captive's not having committed any death-deserving crimes (such as theft) during his flight. If he had done so, he could expect no mercy.

It is, perhaps, unnecessary to explain why a slave should wish to run away from a regime where such punishments were permissible. But what objectives, apart from flight, did the fugitive slave have? The mountains of the Cape interior had always beckoned enticingly to fugitives, offering a wild and elusive place of refuge seemingly removed from colonial control. There were doubtless many who imagined that they would be able to live a life of independence beyond the boundaries of the colony, trusting to their own strength and resourcefulness to survive in the wilderness. Others harboured unrealistic ambitions of returning to their countries of origin or distant lands reported to be safe havens. Several runaways, for instance, were recaptured after trying to reach Angola, Madagascar or Natal, their ignorance of geography acting as a stimulus rather than as a deterrent. Whatever their plans, however, fugitives were bound to encounter indigenous groups of people at some stage in their flight and their influence was invariably disruptive.

For the most part these *drosters* were desperate, armed and ravenous, thus posing a direct threat to the lives and livestock of the Khoikhoi. It was, in fact, extremely difficult for inexperienced and ill-equipped newcomers to survive in the Cape mountains, making it almost inevitable that the Khoikhoi would be approached. Some of the *drosters* may have had no other wish than to be accepted as new members of a protective Khoikhoi group though they were not always assured of a friendly welcome. The Company, in any event, worked hard to ensure that the neighbouring Khoikhoi would return colonial property. Groups such as the Chariguriqua, for instance, who had won the reputation of welcoming runaway slaves, were made to suffer the consequences of their misplaced generosity. The mixture of bribery and threats which were employed is well illustrated in the Council of Policy's instructions of 1696:

'The Grigriquase Hottentots lying on the other side of the Olifants River, a nation with whom the Hon. Company is not used to having the least correspondence or friendship, are accustomed to have runaway slaves of the free inhabitants amongst them who have come to them and whom they employ in their service, without anyone knowing where these fugitives hide themselves: a course of action completely contrary to the praiseworthy behaviour of other Hottentot nations, who are of a more civil disposition and loyal to the Company, and who are accustomed, whenever they apprehend a runaway slave, to deliver him up, so that he is returned to his rightful master: and that it was also thought that if the numbers of these deserted slaves increased, they might join together with the Grigriquase Hottentots, or make themselves masters of them, and attempt to surprise and ruin some of our free inhabitants who live far apart from each other. In order to prevent these threatening troubles from taking place, and also to restore these fugitives, his Excellency and the Council of Policy unanimously resolved to reinforce the aforesaid ensign [Schrijver] and his company with a sergeant, a further ten Company servants and twenty free burghers of Stellenbosch, and to dispatch the assembled company over the aforesaid Olifants River to the Grigriquase Hottentots, and without the least shedding of blood, in the most accomodating and gentlest manner, under the guise of trade or exchange, to capture the aforesaid runaway slaves who might be found with them with orders (in case of unwillingness or refusal) to take one of the aforesaid Grigriquase captains or some of their women and children as hostages to the Castle, to stay here for as long as it takes for the aforesaid Grigriquase Hottentots to return the abovementioned slaves to the Company . . .'[6]

Not all Khoikhoi needed Company prompting to discourage fugitive slaves. *Drosters* were dangerous and it was extremely risky for runaways to count on Khoikhoi support. It should be appreciated that by 1700 the Khoikhoi were themselves refugees from the colony, anxious to avoid or repel all aggressive intruders into their territory. Unfortunately for them, during the first three decades of the eighteenth century circumstances were particularly favourable for deserters. The colonial frontier petered out relatively close to Cape Town. As late as 1709 it was, indeed, still possible for fugitive slaves to skulk for days undetected in the thick bushes around the Liesbeek River and Rondebosch.[7] The dunes near Salt River and the sandy wastes of the Cape Flats also provided hiding places whilst Table Mountain itself was a domain of *drosters* well into the eighteenth century.[8] The trouble with these peri-urban retreats was that inevitably, like a moth to a candle, the fugitives would steal food from the colonists and get caught. Proximity to the town was risky but the massive mountains of the Cape Fold System rose alluringly just behind the surrounding farms of the south-western Cape. Only after 1740 did these untamed ranges fall within the colonial frontier, and to many fugitives it must have seemed as though all that stood between them and freedom was a very short journey to the horizon. At the same time the low population density of the frontier regions made it easy for runaways to move without detection. The result was that the early-eighteenth-century Cape frontier zone bristled with *drosters*, most of whom, as far as the Khoikhoi were concerned, were extremely undesirable characters.

We do not know what effect the Company's 1696 visit to the Chariguriqua had had,[9] but during the first decade of the eighteenth century the route up the west coast, beyond Groene Kloof and Saldanha Bay to the vicinity of Verloren Vlei and the Agter Piketberg, remained a favourite with deserters. The advantages of this route were that fugitives could survive by eating marine resources such as mussels and crayfish. Further progress northwards was usually unappealing because the countryside became drier and wilder. To the east runaways would have to brave the as yet unconquered Khoisan and the mountains behind the Olifants River. For this reason most *droster* groups tended to stall somewhere south of the Verloren Vlei. One group of slaves recaptured in 1707 had planned to hide in the 'ver berge' (distant mountains) and make their way to the Namaqua but they had not got very far.

Even more typical were the experiences of a group of *droster* slaves from Madagascar in 1706. This group had chosen the west coast route in an attempt to return to their home. During the course of their flight they attacked various Khoikhoi kraals in the vicinity of Saldanha Bay and abducted a Khoikhoi man by the name of Prins in the hope that he would show them the way to Madagascar. The gang then wandered as far as the Piketberg, killing two Khoikhoi at a colonial cattle-post on the Berg River before returning to the coast. Here they robbed a kraal called

Hoeties Kraal at Hoeties Baai but the occupants fought back when the slaves attempted to steal their herds and flocks. Four of the slaves were killed and another, David, was eventually captured by the post-holder at Saldanha Bay.[11]

Incidents like these help to explain why the Khoikhoi were increasingly wary of colonial fugitives and likely to receive them with violence. In January 1712 it was reported that a recaptured slave had died because 'The Hottentots beyond the mountains had beaten him most brutally; they had smashed the back of his skull, and with kieries cut his back as if it had been sliced with knives; his lips and eyes were so belaboured that there appeared hardly an hour's life in him.'[12] Of twenty or thirty slaves who escaped in October 1712, it was rumoured that eight had been killed by the Overberg Khoikhoi.[13] As more and more instances of rough treatment at the hands of the Khoikhoi became known to would-be escapees a new pattern emerged which was clearly discernible to the writer Mentzel in the 1730s:

'Towards runaway slaves belonging to the colonists, the Hottentots feel a disgust which is not only inborn, but also founded on common sense. They know very well that a runaway slave can only preserve his life by robbing them of their cattle. Therefore, if they catch one of them, they hand them over to the nearest colonist, who then takes him away and surrenders him to the authorities. But should a fugitive slave succeed in reaching the Kaffirs [the Xhosa of the eastern Cape], he would be protected against all danger, for they never give the slaves up, because they become their best fighters, more courageous than the Kaffirs themselves. They defend themselves desperately against the colonists, for fear of being caught and handed over to justice, preferring death to recapture. It is the aim of all such slaves, who band themselves together and plot to desert, to join up with the Kaffirs.'[14]

In time, as more and more Khoikhoi became absorbed within the colony and subject to the brutal exploitation of farm labour, a greater solidarity emerged between them and the slaves.[15] But this common consciousness of colonial oppression was not present in the early decades of the eighteenth century. Instead, as Mentzel explains, the cruelty of the Khoikhoi was contrasted with a rather idealistic vision of life amongst the Xhosa. These expectations may have provided inspiration for a group of twenty to thirty slaves who revolted at Groot Constantia in 1713. They made a dash for the Hottentots Holland Mountains, hoping to reach 'Caffersland', but most of them were killed or recaptured by the

Khoikhoi over the mountains.[16] We must presume that not all escapees were recaptured and that many did find succour in the distant interior. But the evidence of unsuccessful runaways suggests that the fate of such people, though obscure, was probably unpleasant.

A noteworthy feature of the early decades of the eighteenth century was that fugitive slaves often joined forces with criminals or deserters of European origin. On one level this is indicative of a common consciousness of oppression, for the treatment of Company soldiers and sailors was often worse than that of slaves.[17] But it is significant that such instances of solidarity were rare after 1740, and this is because of processes at work in the frontier zone. By 1740 the colonial boundaries had extended to the point where white deserters could find employment and shelter with outlying colonists. Frontier farmers were always happy to have white supervisors working for them, and if such men were fugitives from the law they could not demand high wages. As long as they were far enough away from the Company to avoid detection, white deserters could merge with colonial frontiersmen. Before the 1730s, however, they were often too conspicuous to do so and for this reason, finding security in numbers, they fled together with slaves.

There is an interesting episode from the years 1706–9 which illustrates some of the characteristics of the *droster* gangs of the northern frontier zone at this time. In 1706 a slave called Simon of Malabar fled to the vicinity of Vier en Twintig Rivieren where he fell in with various 'vagebonden, schelmen en gaaudieven' (vagabonds, rascals and pickpockets). In 1709, together with some other slaves who had stolen sheep, tobacco, muskets and ammunition from their masters, Simon placed himself under the supervision of two European men (one called Jan Bakker and the other known only as Jan) who undertook to lead the group to 'een ander land' (another country). The Europeans had compasses but after six weeks, somewhere over the Olifants River in ''t Cochemans land', their food supplies ran out. The group split up and the Khoikhoi attacked them, stealing their goods, smashing their guns and throwing their ammunition in the river. The survivors were later attacked by some 'Namacquas of bosjesmans' and taken prisoner before being handed over to colonial justice. Simon was hanged.[18]

The case of a group of fugitives recaptured in 1712 also provides many telling details concerning the brotherhood of *droster* communities, the insecurity of life in the frontier zone, and the limited options available to those wishing to escape to the interior. Jan Jorisz, or Snijer (as he was known to his companions), had been born in Harlingen and joined the VOC as a sailor. His was not a distinguished career. In Batavia he had been caught after deserting from his ship and handed over to the authorities for correction. For three consecutive half-days he had straddled the wooden horse of torture and then spent six months in chains. In Cape Town, in 1709, he was once more chastised for similar crimes and condemned to eight months' hard labour on Robben Island without a salary. Shortly after his release, fearing punishment for drunkenness, he deserted again and began to sleep out in the veld, living from the knapsacks of shepherds. Then, at the Koeberg farm of a man called Ten Damme, he met a slave, Benjamin of Madagascar, with whom he entered into 'brotherhood'. In the hard world that had shaped both slave and sailor, 'brotherhood' was not an abstract concept. It is not known what rituals or ceremonies the men employed to solemnise their pact but from that moment on they were bound to each other.

Although Benjamin was Ten Damme's trusted overseer, the slave was rather free with his master's goods, distributing them to Snijer as well as to other 'landloopers en vagebonden' (vagabonds, rascals and pickpockets). These other recipients of Benjamin's generosity included four slaves from neighbouring farms. They wished to escape to Natal, and Snijer, nothing loath, decided to accompany them. Benjamin gave him a musket (no doubt one of Ten Damme's), five or six bullets, a handful of powder, three loaves of bread and two knapsacks of meal. Thus equipped, Snijer and the slaves – Titus, Abel, Jonker and Abraham – set off up the coast to beyond the Piketberg where they found 'een groote valleij' (in all probability the Verloren Vlei). It was here that the group split up. Snijer and Titus returned to the fringes of the colony, where the pickings were richer, but at the Paardeberg Titus went his own way. Not long after this, Snijer was arrested and flung into the Castle's 'Donker Gat' to await trial.[19]

It seemed as though Snijer's days of roving were over. He was not alone in the dark confines, for he had two cell mates, the slaves Scipio of Coromandel (commonly known as Cupitie, and whipped and branded in 1699) and Moses of Bengal. Both slaves were under sentence of death for having stolen property whilst on the run. But, in an unprecedented occurrence, all three prisoners succeeded in escaping from the 'Donker Gat'. How this escape was effected is not recorded though it was probably the only successful escape to have been made from the colony's most notorious place of incarceration. The fugitives hastened to Snijer's 'brother' and benefactor, Benjamin of Madagascar. It was not long before they were joined by another desperate 'rondlooper', a young sailor by the name of Nicolaas Ooms, whose credentials were almost as impressive as Jan Snijer's. Ooms had previously received a public flogging in Colombo for the 'despicable wounding' of his under-helmsman and had been banished to the Cape for five years. Here he was sentenced to labour at the public works but he managed to unloosen his chains and seize a knife, threatening to kill anyone who tried to stop him. But somebody did overpower him and Ooms was returned to the chain gang. Shortly afterwards, however, he broke his bonds again and escaped into the veld. Like many other deserters he drifted between the Tijgerberg, the Paardeberg and Groene Kloof, finding shelter with shepherds, scavenging along the beach and, doubtless, slaughtering livestock.[20] Eventually his wanderings took him to Ten Damme's farm at Koeberg, where he found Snijer, Scipio and Moses. During a drinking session (with wine provided by the hospitable Benjamin) the four runaways pledged companionship ('maatschappij hebben gemaakt') and resolved 'haer fortuyn te gaan zoeken en verder veldwaart in te lopen, vagebondeeren' (to seek their fortunes and go deeper into the veld, vagabonding).[21]

Their first objective was Groene Kloof. On the way there they encountered a mounted slave who had some bread and meat on his horse. He was obliged to share his provisions. At the farm of the widow Basson they found the *knecht* Jan ter Sluijs, who was also asked for food, which he could not deny. The four pressed onwards to Petrus Tavenraat's farm where the slave Arend gave them some bread. The 'landloopers' realised that despite this they were ill provisioned for the journey which they had undertaken and resolved to steal a gun. They had seen one at Jan ter Sluijs's hut so they decided to return there, much to the *knecht*'s dismay. They greeted him with a 'Goeden avont of tabee', to which he replied: 'Tabee of niet, ik houw juiluij hier niet, of te wel juijluij moet vertrekken' (Tabee or not, I'm not having you here, you must leave).[22] But he was a lone man in the night, on the edge of the colony. Jan Snijer had a club whilst Ooms displayed his favourite weapon – a knife. Scipio slipped into the hut and found two guns: a musket and a blunderbuss. There was also ammunition. 'Men, you are using force, and violence against me,' Jan ter Sluijs complained.[23] At least, however, his life was spared and the thieves departed.

They left for the Paardeberg and found Lucas, a slave of Dirk van Schalkwyk, at his master's farm. Lucas provided food and slaughtered a sheep for them. He also gave them some tin table-board, so that they could make bullets, and showed them where Van Schalkwyk kept his gunpowder cartridges. With this extra ammunition the fugitives continued northwards, through the Swartland to the Piketberg, where they slaughtered two sheep belonging to some nearby Khoikhoi. These Khoikhoi, seeing four strangers laden with meat, guessed that they had been robbed and asked for tobacco or dagga (marijuana) in exchange. The runaways promised that they would deliver some on their return and hurried onwards. The Khoikhoi raised the hue and cry. Shortly thereafter two shots whistled over their heads and, looking behind them, they saw two Dutchmen approaching on horseback. They dropped the meat and ran but it was obvious that they would be overtaken. Ooms stopped, turned, and fired the stolen musket. Snijer discharged the blunderbuss. It misfired. In the panic of reloading Ooms jammed his musket. With bullets flying about them the fugitives continued running but it was hopeless. The two sailors eventually fell to their knees and begged their pursuers for mercy. They and the slaves were captured and taken to the Cape. All were hanged. Benjamin of Madagascar was whipped, branded and mutilated by having his nose and ears cut off. He then served six months' hard labour at the Company's works and was condemned to spend six years in chains.[24]

From these accounts it emerges that both slave and European *drosters* were capable of uniting in brotherhood and that their gangs were a danger to both Khoikhoi and colonists. Most *droster* groups were compelled to adopt a parasitic existence, preying off the societies of the frontier zone since they were unable to achieve long-term self-sufficiency by themselves. As a result their presence in any given area was soon apparent and their discovery almost inevitable. Neither Khoikhoi nor colonists felt secure with such men at large and co-operated to ensure their capture. The life of a *droster* gang was therefore overshadowed by insecurity and their situation even more vulnerable than that of their potential victims. After the smallpox epidemic of 1713 the Khoikhoi groups of the interior were weaker but the colonists were stronger, so the situation facing *drosters* was not substantially safer. Nor could *drosters* always rely on a sympathetic welcome from the slaves they might encounter on their wanderings. Not every slave was as welcoming as Benjamin of Madagascar and some could be relied upon to alert the authorities. In 1724, for instance, three Dutch vagabonds were reported to be circulating in the Riebeek Kasteel district after having stolen food from slaves at the farms.[25] The fact that all these *drosters* were white may have had some bearing on both their reception and behaviour. Nor should it be assumed that all *droster* gangs spared those from whom they extracted hospitality. Solitary hunters or stock farmers would often have had their throats cut by men who had nothing to lose by committing further crimes. In one gruesome instance, a pursuing commando shot dead three of a group of nine runaway slaves and found a human finger – from a white person – amongst their possessions![26]

Most shocking of all was a case that came to trial in December 1707. One Sunday night in the springtime of 1707 a group of ten slaves deserted their masters in Cape Town and decided to proceed to Madagascar. They had managed to steal some knives and some food before setting off. Two of the slaves were women – Marie of Madagascar (or big Marie) and Marie of Bengal (or little Marie) – who each had an infant with them. The records do not say whether any of the five males in the group were the fathers of the children. We can only state that Marie of Madagascar had shared her captivity with Augustyn of Batavia (about 21 years old) and Titus and Aaron of Cochin (about 35 and 10 years old respectively), for all four slaves had belonged to the same owner, the butcher Michael Ley. Augustyn was regarded as the leader of the group and it is very likely that Marie of Madagascar was his lover. Marie of Bengal (aged 20) was the only slave in the group to belong to the burgher Meyboom and it is possible that she had a relationship with her countryman, Antonie of Bengal (aged 30), slave of F. van der Lind. The other slaves in the group were another Aaron of Cochin (aged 25 and named big Aaron to distinguish him from little Aaron), who belonged to Matthys Wigman, and Jannetje of the Cape, a 16-year-old girl who belonged to Elias Kina.

The slaves made for the Kloof beyond Devil's Peak (either First Waterfall Ravine or Dark Gorge) and hid there for a week. They then decided to move off and had got as far as Salt River when they were diverted by the sight of the slave shepherd of Johannes Heufke. Augustyn suggested that they should kill the shepherd and steal some sheep for their sustenance. The men, accordingly, attacked the shepherd as he woke from sleep. Augustyn held his hair; big Aaron pulled his feet from under him; Titus helped to tie his hands. Augustyn then forced a rolled-up handkerchief into the doomed man's mouth to stop him from shouting and cut his throat, tearing out the larynx and throwing it on the ground. They then took a bag of money from the dead man's pocket and divided the coins between them. The sheep, however, they left, fearing discovery by some passing people.[27]

The fugitives now headed for the beach and, after a while, they journeyed northwards to Groene Kloof. Here they observed a European man in the veld with a gun over his shoulder and two dogs at his side. The four adult male slaves resolved to kill the European and, with their knives hidden in their pockets, the *droster* group approached their target. The colonist was at a disadvantage. Not only was he outnumbered but his gun was not loaded. At first, civility prevailed. The slaves asked for water and the colonist led them to a spring from which they all drank. The slaves then asked for a pipe of tobacco. This too was given. As the men smoked, the colonist tried to load his gun. Augustyn, Titus, Antonie and big Aaron took this as a signal to attack and threw themselves at the European, pinning him to the ground. Though the frightened man begged for his life, Augustyn stuffed the bloody handkerchief into his mouth and prepared to cut his throat.

At this point Jannetje cried out to Augustyn to let the man go because people were coming. The girl was not part of the group bent over the colonist, for she was standing back, horrified, with little Aaron and little Marie. Big Marie was holding down an arm whilst Antonie held down the legs. Titus sat on the victim's body whilst Augustyn and big Aaron pinned down the colonist's other arm. There were no people coming: Jannetje was lying to try to save a life. But Augustyn did not care one way or the other. 'Maski,' he told her, 'though three or four may come, I am not afraid.'[28] With that, he and big Aaron stuck their knives in the man's neck. The nameless victim kicked out desperately, dislodging Antonie from his legs and jerking his hand loose from big Marie's grasp. It was to no avail. Antonie struck him on the thighs with a cutlass; Augustyn cut his throat and then, with Aaron, ripped open his stomach and pulled out the entrails. A bloodlust seems to have descended on the murderers, for as Titus threw away the colonist's innards, Augustyn cut off the corpse's left hand and flung it away as well. The four slave men then cut off the flesh from the hips and smashed and disjointed the bones of the body using the gun-stock as a club. Augustyn repeatedly stabbed the face with his knife, until he broke the blade. The gun too was broken. The dismembered body parts were then scattered about, to the excited approval of little Aaron.

Why such barbarous behaviour? According to the later testimony of the recaptured slaves, it was to make people think that their victim had been attacked by a wild animal. It is likely, however, that darker impulses than deception were at work in the frenzied butchery of the lone colonist in the veld. What Augustyn and the others had done to the body of the European was not, after all, dissimilar to the punishments which were frequently inflicted on criminal slaves at the Cape and which would, shortly, be inflicted upon their own bodies. As the slaves rested from the murderous work, Augustyn cut and ate some 'hotnotsvy' using a bloody knife to do so.[29]

'Fie, Augustyn!' reproached Jannetje. "Why do you not wash the knife?'

'Maski,' Augustyn replied, 'I wish to drink that blood also, for then I become strong.'

The slaves continued northwards. The murders they had committed had brought them no advantage at all. At Saldanha Bay they were captured by the Company's post-holder with the help of the local Khoikhoi. They returned, as captives, to Cape Town. Jannetje confessed to the murders and the group stood trial. In the court's opinion, 'this being two frightful, cruel, unheard of, horrible and barbarous murders which make the hair of a rational being stand on end, and his entrails to shudder and freeze', the severest penalties were called for. Augustyn, Titus, big Aaron and Antonie were therefore placed on a wheel and each received eight blows to break them alive. Augustyn was then 'pinched out from four distinct parts of his body with red hot tongs'. All were then left to suffer and die. Big Marie was strangled. The bodies remained to disintegrate or provide food for the birds at the place of execution. Jannetje, little Marie and little Aaron had to stand under the gallows with the noose around their necks and behold the execution. They were then whipped and the two female slaves were branded on the cheek before being sent home in chains.[30] It is doubtful whether such spectacles served as a deterrent for very long.

During the second decade of the century *droster* gangs seemed to grow in both numbers and audacity. After the mass escape from Groot Constantia in 1713 came the flight of forty Madagascan slaves from the Company between February and April 1716. A further eleven deserted on Christmas day of that year.[31] In January 1717 a group of fifteen slaves escaped from Stellenbosch.[32] Perhaps it was they who attacked the outpost of Hans Potgieter in the Land van Waveren (the modern Tulbagh district), for he reported that fifteen slaves armed with assegais had endeavoured to surprise him at sunset. He and a companion had shot eight of them and, a week later, the local Khoikhoi had killed the rest. In May 1717 David du Buisson's farm in the Hottentots Holland was attacked by a gang of fugitive slaves. He was wounded seven or eight times and his assailants made off with his firearms, food and ammunition.[33] In May 1719 twenty runaways attacked the Swart brothers on their isolated farm in the Overberg and stole 200 sheep.[34]

No wonder that when the wife of farmer Hans Holm at Bottelary was found beaten to death with sticks and the house rifled, it led the keeper of the Company journal to lament that this was 'clear proof that this colony mainly consists of evil-disposed, head-strong slaves and the refuse of convicts'.[35] It was obviously very tempting for farm slaves to join passing *droster* gangs, especially when there were other slaves in them. In January 1713 a gang of about thirty runaway slaves arrived at the farm of J. Elivier at Vier en Twintig Rivieren and 'forced' seven other slaves to join them after they had bound the *knecht* and another servant. This gang was armed with guns and they liberated three further slaves from two neighbouring farms.[36]

The fate of all of these escapees is unknown though a steady trickle of sentences was passed on recaptured slaves year after year. In a sense the records are misleading in that they do not reveal very much about successful escapers. It would be too much to suppose that every single *droster* was either recaptured or killed by the Khoikhoi. Later evidence suggests that some *drosters* did manage to survive for a long time even without Khoikhoi assistance.[37] There must also have been some who found protection amongst the Khoikhoi after the 1690s although there is no direct evidence of this. In any event there was no let-up in the activity of *droster* gangs in the 1720s.

In 1724 the slaves of the Company's meat contractors were attacked by *drosters* (whether white or black is not stated) whilst they were herding cattle north of Groene Kloof. The drovers were bound hand and foot whilst their herd was stolen.[38] In 1725 it was thought necessary to offer a reward of 10 rixdollars for recapturing a slave, a feat which was, presumably, becoming a more dangerous and less frequent accomplishment.[39] Next year, in January 1726, the strength and size of a group of runaways in the Saldanha Bay district was sufficient for the Governor to order the landdrost of Stellenbosch to send out a commando against them. According to the reports of the post-holder at Saldanha there were more than twenty *drosters*, well supplied with guns and ammunition, causing great fear amongst the outlying farmers. The commando does not seem to have encountered the group but conflicting reports of its size, ranging from over forty to a mere six members, suggest that its membership fluctuated according to its fortunes.[40] It was probably the same group of *drosters* which was reported as being active in the area in April 1726 when the farms of the widow Ten Damme and Tobias Mostert were plundered. The membership of the group was thought to comprise both white and black vagabonds, and a reward of 10 rixdollars was offered for each one captured – dead or alive. Thirty Stellenbosch burghers were ordered to rendezvous with sixty men of the Cape burgher corps at Henrik Eksteen's farm near Saldanha Bay. It is not known what success the commando had, but the *drosters* probably disbanded as danger approached.[41]

Not all white deserters felt constrained to join the ranks of roving slaves, for not all were as desperate as Snijer and Ooms. But many soldiers and sailors of the VOC were keen to escape the murderous discipline and grinding poverty of life in the lower echelons of the Company. The expanding frontier offered such men many opportunities and, as the Company itself admitted, those who deserted were not inhibited by the thought that they would lose their pay since this was generally 'nothing in particular'.[42] There was doubtless a strong psychological impulse for freedom behind this flight to the frontier. In this respect it is instructive to read what Richard Slotkin has written about the vast frontier zone of the New World: 'The most striking quality of life in the New World was the relative absence of social restraints on human behaviour, the relative ease with which a strong man could, by mastering the law of the wilderness-jungle, impose his personal dream of self-aggrandizement on reality. In Europe all men were under authority ... [The New World] stimulated a monstrous ambition against authority, an obscene Faustian lust to satisfy nature by violating all bonds of obedience, religion and morality.'[43]

On a smaller scale the frontier zone of the northern Cape, like all frontiers of European expansion in the post-Columbian period, evoked similar emotions within the breasts of men grown tired of the confinements of their own repressive society. Few, perhaps, succeeded in surrendering totally to their 'obscene Faustian lusts' but, at the very least, the haemorrhaging of such disordered cells from the ordered body of the Company's colony posed a grave threat to political authority.

Nothing seemed to irritate the Company more than the knowledge that certain of its servants had absconded and taken up the life of a vagabond on the frontier. In 1701 it was estimated that there were no fewer than fifteen such men roaming provocatively just beyond the Company's reach, and their numbers increased year after year. Most of these deserters were well known to the authorities and their names were given to the landdrost to enable him to take steps to capture them.[44] It was most annoying, for instance, when the former overseer at the Company's post at Vissershoek, Claas Arentsz nicknamed Leegenboeten, was seen going about the countryside with a gun over his shoulder.[45] But Company officials in the frontier zone were often extremely scared or reluctant to arrest their fellows. Thus in 1725 Corporal Voetsman at Roode Zand was sternly rebuked for having chatted to the deserter Philip Kalden (who was hiding at the house of the widow of Coenraad Scheepers) without arresting him.[46] In 1730 the Governor was especially concerned to capture Pieter Holbroek, a deserted soldier who was living with a slave woman in a cave in the mountains above the farm of François du Toit. A commando was sent to catch Holbroek but he had to be shot before he would leave the cave, after which he and his lover were sent to the Castle for interrogation.[47]

Just as slaves sometimes ran away together in large groups, so too did Company soldiers desert in sizeable parties. Ten soldiers, including the ex-corporal of the Company post at Rivier Sonder End, fled into the interior in August 1727. All were recaptured.[48] In April 1729 thirteen soldiers of the garrison deserted with their arms to the Hottentots Holland Mountains and became engaged in a skirmish with the pursuing dragoons. The leader of the deserters, Jan Busch, was killed, two others were wounded and the rest captured.[49] Although both of these mass desertions ended in failure, they indicate that there were significant numbers of Company men who were desperate to exchange a life of misery for the promise of the frontier.

Company deserters were not, of course, the only white delinquents in the frontier zone and the VOC tried hard to monitor the activities of all its subjects. In theory every free colonist who went farming or hunting needed a permit or licence. The right to settle in, or indeed visit, the Cape interior was subject to Company approval. Those who did not have their own loan farm had to be registered as living with somebody who did. *Knechts* were considered to be bound by their contracts to work for their bosses on the latter's farms.[50] Single men, the 'eenloopendes', were required to 'inschryven' (register) with a particular colonist and to be registered on the lists of 'eenloopende personen'.[51] Anyone, in other words, who was not either on the Company's lists or domiciled in a registered place could be considered a vagrant or 'rondlooper' and, as such, a troublemaker.

Against such people a perpetual and largely hopeless campaign was waged. In 1687 the Council of Policy had complained that certain colonists were wandering about and living 'dan hier dan daar' without ever notifying the authorities of their whereabouts. Others were guilty of hiring out their *knechts*, even though they were on loan from the Company, to all and sundry without permission. It was also noted that some free burghers were harbouring fugitives and deserters, both free-born and slave, foreign and local. The Council therefore issued a stern warning that anyone who failed to report such people would be regarded as a traitor to the community and punished accordingly.[52]

From time to time the Company attempted to lure its deserters back with the promise of pardon. In June 1709, for instance, the Council of Policy noted that 'Many servants of the Company have deserted and fled with other offenders and Englishmen and other foreigners towards the wilderness and mountains, leading a thievish and godless life'. The Council decided to offer a pardon to all of these, excepting 'incendiaries, murderers, burglars, cattle thieves and highwaymen', as long as they reported themselves to the Castle within two months of the publication of the *plakkaat* of pardon.[53]

We must assume that such offers of amnesty had a limited appeal, for 42 years later edicts were still warning colonists against harbouring such fugitives whilst the number of 'rondloopers' had simply expanded with the frontier.[54] In 1737 landdrost Lourensz of Stellenbosch complained of the number of men in his district who were simply not where they were supposed to be and 'do not actually have any fixed abode, but wander about as vagabonds and rovers, without anyone being able to ascertain their whereabouts'.[55] Such people could not be found when it was time for the compulsory military exercises or commando duty and their absence caused great confusion in the muster-rolls. Furthermore, they committed all sorts of 'schelmstukken' (wicked deeds) and acted as a bad example to young people in the district. Lourensz named six of the chief culprits and the Council of Policy resolved to cleanse the land of these 'ledigloopers' (shiftless idlers) by forcing them to become Company sailors and banishing them from the Cape for five years.[56]

Sometimes the settler community had an interest in protecting these roving 'landloopers', who could be sponsored to undertake dangerous hunting trips or illegal bartering expeditions without implicating more respectable burghers. Most frontier farmers could use the labour of a man who was grateful for food, shelter and confidentiality. Widows, in particular, were often well disposed towards those who offered them their services.[57] There were, of course, many rogues and thieves amongst the rootless frontier colonists but, on the whole, white settlers were able to protect themselves against these undesirables far better than the Khoikhoi could.

The impact of these 'illegal' frontiersmen on the indigenous societies of the interior is a crucial issue but difficult to quantify owing to the lack of evidence. The perpetrators of evil deeds did not often leave witnesses or advertise their accomplishments. It is also debatable whether there was much to choose between lawful and unlawful European residents of the frontier zone when it came to their destructive impact. Contemporary observers, however, were in no doubt that vagabonds and freebooters were behind the various outbreaks of violence on the colony's frontiers in the early decades of the eighteenth century. In 1715 Frans van der Stel was speaking for many when he urged the government to appoint a good landdrost who would 'search for and exterminate all vagrants, who are continually wandering about the country, remain unregistered, and with some malevolent residents, impoverish the Hottentots and embitter them against our nation, by means of robbery and other atrocious acts of violence'.[58] By this date, however, much of the damage had already been done and vagrants would have had to travel far and wide to find any Khoikhoi groups to impoverish.[59] It is noteworthy that at times of frontier disturbance or Khoisan resistance there seemed to be an abatement in *droster* activity. With vengeful commandos and Khoisan raiders abroad, the frontier zone was not a safe place for fugitives.

After 1730 there were very few reports of fugitive gangs active in the areas south of the Piketberg. The colony had now expanded to the extent that it was no longer easy for refugees to evade capture within the Saldanha Bay, Groene Kloof or Stellenbosch districts. The Company post at Saldanha Bay remained, nevertheless, an important forwarding post for recaptives, as is revealed by an incident which occurred in 1732. In March that year two Company soldiers from Saldanha set out for the Cape with four fugitive slaves in their custody. The slaves managed to overpower their guards and kill them. One of the murderers was later recaptured but the rest swam across the Berg River and fled further inland.[60]

Discontented slaves might suddenly gather together, attack their masters, plunder the farmhouse and run away – as happened in the Tijgerberg in 1738[61] – but they could not stay in such a thoroughly colonised area for long. The Roode Zand was reported as still being full of fugitives, both slaves and Europeans, in 1728,[62] and runaway slaves were hiding in the caves of the Paarl Mountain as late as 1742.[63] But the main area of *droster* activity was now centred around the Piketberg and to the north in areas such as Renoster Hoek (which lies north of the Piketberg and south of the Olifants River Mountains) or the Olifants River.

This shift in focus became evident in September 1731 when a group of runaway slaves fired on a commando at Renoster Hoek and killed the burgher Samuel de Beer. Although four of the gang were captured, landdrost Lourensz was aware that there were other fugitives at large, including 'certain Europeans living at the Piketberg'.[64] A second commando was sent to deal with this menace but the *drosters* could not be found.[65] In November 1731 two fugitive slaves were shot dead whilst stealing sheep from a Piketberg farmer. Lourensz learnt from a third, who was taken captive, that the *droster* group he was after had split up because of quarrels and that they had returned from beyond the Olifants River (where they had been active) to hide around the Piketberg.[66] It is not known whether the rest of this group were ever caught. In March 1736 another commando was sent out behind the Piketberg to deal with fugitive slaves. On this occasion two slaves were apprehended and one of them was shot dead when he refused to surrender. The second escaped whilst being taken back to Stellenbosch.[67]

During the frontier war of 1739 against the Khoikhoi, it was too perilous for fugitives to roam the northern borders but shortly after fighting stopped in 1740, desertions resumed.[68] The Company was still plagued by the desertion of its employees, as can be seen from a resolution passed by the Council of Policy in 1745. Noting an increase in desertions, it ordered an increase in the punishment for offenders. A recaptured deserter would be severely whipped at the place of execution, branded and placed in irons to serve as a convict for ten years without pay. Furthermore, it was decreed that anyone convicted of harbouring or assisting a deserter would suffer the same punishment. If these measures failed to have an effect, the Council proposed to apply the same penalty as existed in Bengal, namely death.[69] In Stellenbosch, meanwhile, the landdrost and *heemraden* had decided in a resolution of 1743 to offer a reward of 10 rixdollars for slaves recaptured over the Olifants River, 6 rixdollars for slaves on the colonial side of the river and 3 rixdollars for those on the south side of the Piketberg or Hottentots Holland Mountains.[70] This revealing gradation suggests that fugitive slaves were no longer as great a threat as they had once been in the south-western Cape. They continued, however, to plague the colonists of the Piketberg and Olifants River areas for many years. In 1755, for instance, a group of fourteen runaway slaves was apprehended by *veldcorporaal* Jacob Gildenhuysen and his commando in a kloof of the Piketberg. The *drosters* would not surrender and instead brandished knobkieries and shouted loud defiance. They also had a musket, two pistols, gunpowder and a cutlass, but when the shooting started they were no match for the colonists. Five slaves were shot dead and the rest recaptured. Their numbers included a female slave, slaves from local farmers and slaves from farmers of the south-western Cape.[71]

A similar incident occurred in May 1775 near Gerrit Smit's farm, de Drooge Rijs Kloof, behind the Piketberg. Smit discovered that his barn had been broken into and that some wheat was missing. He called a friend, Gideon van Zyl, and with two servants followed the spoor of the barefoot robbers. They found four fugitive slaves hiding in a bush. The slaves all had knives and Smit ordered them to throw down their blades and approach him one by one. The four began talking in Malayan, which Smit did not understand. When they began to advance in a menacing fashion he shouted at them, in Portuguese, to get back and drop their weapons. Still they advanced. Smit told Van Zyl, who had the only other musket, to shoot one in the legs. The shot was fired. The slave fell down. But the other three shouted 'Amok! Amok! Matta garra!' and charged.[72] Van Zyl had to flee because his musket was now unloaded. Smit, though, put a bullet through the closest *droster* and killed him. The other two then chased Smit for 150 yards before returning to their original position in the bush. The two colonists reloaded and once more ordered the slaves to drop their knives. This time one of them shouted 'Bie! Bie!' and rushed at Smit. It was suicide. The slave died, shot through the body, with the knife still in his hand. The survivor told Smit that they had escaped from the Company works at Cape Town.[73]

A closer inspection of these, and other, incidents concerning fugitives in the years after 1740 reveals that the expansion of the colony would seem to have had a transformative effect on the composition of *droster* gangs.[74] From about this stage onwards whites and slaves went their separate ways. The fugitive gangs that fled beyond the Olifants River no longer contained white deserters, and the reasons for this are linked to the dynamics of frontier expansion. Between 1740 and 1770 the boundaries of the colony advanced rapidly to a point beyond which further progress became problematic. In some directions environmental conditions made pastoralism an impossibility whilst in others Khoisan or Xhosa resistance was too strong to be swept aside.[75] In these circumstances fugitives would have to be really desperate to venture into the doubly inhospitable interior and, for the most part, white deserters did not have to, since they were readily absorbed by the far-flung frontier farmers.[76] Slaves, on the other hand, could decide whether they wished to attempt the perilous journey beyond the colony's boundaries or hide out in the inaccessible mountains within the colony. Both courses were adopted and the Cedarberg range in particular served as a place of refuge for runaway slaves until well into the nineteenth century.[77]

Slaves and Company servants were not the only fugitives to flee from the colony after 1740. From this date onwards there is increasing evidence that entirely new categories of colonial subjects were moving outwards and away from the colony in an attempt to avoid economic, social and political oppression. The new fugitives were people who were described, in the discourse of the day, as 'Bastaards' or 'Bastaard-Hottentots'. Although their presence is most clearly marked in the records after 1770 their 'pre-history', shadowy though it is, deserves some attention. Not only were such people active within the frontier zone, they were, in many cases, products of the frontier zone. Indeed, some of them were doubtless themselves the descendants of colonial fugitives and frontier Khoikhoi.[78]

The word 'Bastaard' was used by contemporaries to refer to people who had been born of miscegenous relationships.[79] The term described a wide range of people of differing status and the nuances of its meaning changed with changing attitudes. Quite clearly, however, the word implied the stigma of illegitimate birth as well as the idea of racially mixed parentage. In the Cape colonial context there were three major instances of miscegenation: that of Europeans with slaves; that of Europeans with Khoikhoi; and that of slaves with Khoikhoi. The first instance was relatively rare on the Cape frontier (though fairly common in Cape Town) and the status of the resultant children varied from case to case. Some children, especially girls, might become absorbed within white society whilst other children, especially if they were dark-skinned males, might become slaves.[80] The offspring of Europeans and Khoikhoi were ostensibly free but, as a number of studies have shown, the status of 'Bastaards', though superior to that of slaves, Khoikhoi and San, declined – economically, socially and politically – throughout the eighteenth century.[81] This process was first experienced in areas of high white population density close to Cape Town where mixed marriages became less and less socially acceptable and where it became more and more difficult for 'Bastaards' to acquire loan farms.

Elphick and Shell have remarked that 'In the newly settled pastoral regions . . . considerable miscegenation, but not intermarriage, occurred'.[82] In the early phase of colonial expansion white men far outnumbered white women in the frontier zone and, indeed, in the Cape as a whole. Before the heroic childbearing efforts of white women succeeded, several generations down the line, in rectifying the sexual imbalance within white society, white frontiersmen struggled to find white wives. Biological imperatives, however, combined with the unmonitored freedom of the frontier zone to promote sexual conduct and sexual relationships that would have been censured in the more settled areas of the colony. Whilst 'civilised' observers of white Cape society displayed a prurient revulsion when describing the sexual charms of Khoikhoi women, white frontiesmen had fewer qualms. They slept with Khoikhoi women but, for the most part, declined to marry them. According to Elphick and Shell, very few marriages at the Cape church (and none at Stellenbosch, which was the magisterial seat of the northern frontier zone) were obviously mixed marriages and it does indeed seem that the majority of 'Bastaards' were born out of wedlock.[83]

This state of affairs was partly due to the paucity of churches in the northern Cape frontier zone. It was only after Commissioner Gustaaf van Imhoff visited the outlying districts of the Cape in 1743 that a decision was made to establish a church in the Swartland and a church between Roode Zand and Vier en Twintig Rivieren. Van Imhoff had been shocked by the 'sorgeloosheijd en onweetenheijd' (carelessness and ignorance) of a large number of frontier farmers concerning religious matters, and remarked of the region 'that it seems to be more like a collection of blind heathens than a colony of Europeans and Christians'.[84]

A lack of churches might certainly have contributed, as Van Imhoff feared, to the barbarisation of frontier farmers and a careless attitude towards the sacrament of marriage. But the qualification ought perhaps to be made that it was *Christian* intermarriage that did not occur. In 1738 Willem van Wyk 'took to wife, Hottentot fashion a near relative of the chief, conducting himself in the manner and clothing himself at the time as a Hottentot';[85] later evidence from Namaqualand suggests that white colonists were adopting Khoikhoi wedding customs in the 1770s.[86] It seems that although some of the frontier colonists saw little reason to marry, in a Christian fashion, the Khoikhoi women with whom they slept, they were somewhat more punctilious about providing a Christian baptism for the offspring of such relationships. The christening book of the Swartland church (the most north-westerly congregation in the colony for most of the eighteenth century) has a special section – 'Gedoopte Bastaarts 1752–1769' – and many of the names there are typical Dutch surnames.[87] One may assume that these 'Gedoopte Bastaarts' enjoyed a status in society superior to that of unbaptised 'Bastaards', Khoikhoi or slaves but the very fact that their names were recorded separately is evidence of discrimination. Their precise status no doubt depended on the details of their family background and the social climate of the district into which they were born. Favoured children of respected colonists probably passed unobtrusively into the ranks of colonial society, suffering no discrimination on account of their mixed blood. But others were not so fortunate.

Hinrich Lichtenstein, an observer at the Cape between 1803 and 1806, commented on the difference between the attitudes of colonists towards the 'Bastaards' in the mid-eighteenth century and at the end of the century. He recognised that the crucial test was whether or not they were allowed to obtain and retain property. Initially, he noted, a 'Bastaard' might acquire property after having worked as a farm overseer and, on the death of the master, the servant 'would often assume his name; and not infrequently sought himself some little spot, to which he retired with all belonging to him, and gained a subsistence for himself and his family by the breeding of cattle'.[88] 'Bastaards' who succeeded in possessing farms of this sort did not, apparently, attach the same importance to legitimising their claims by the prompt payment of loan-farm rental; or perhaps it was because their claims were not readily recognised by the authorities. Whatever the reasons were, however, it would seem as though 'Bastaards' ended up with the least desirable, often unregisterable, land within the colony or else with land outside the colony. As Lichtenstein observed: 'The white children of the colonists did not hesitate to make use of the right of the strongest to drive their half-yellow relations out of the places where they had fixed their abodes. These Bastaard Hottentots were then obliged to seek an asylum in more remote parts, till at length, driven from the Sak River as they had been before from the Bokkeveld, nothing remained for them but to retreat to the Orange River.'[89]

The availability of land did not become a crucial issue until the 1770s. Before this date the expansion of the frontier, coupled with the low population density and the relatively weak demographic presence of adult male 'Bastaards', served to mask the fact that, once the frontier began to close, racial criteria would help to determine access to farms.

The offspring of slaves and Khoikhoi were known as 'Bastaard-Hottentots' and, in certain quarters, were thought to constitute a category of unfree labour from a fairly early stage. In 1721, for instance, some free burghers of the Stellenbosch district had written to the government to ask for permission to bind in service, for a certain number of years, the children of slave and Khoikhoi unions.[90] The issue seems to have lain dormant until 1775 when the landdrost and *heemraden* of Stellenbosch decreed that 'Bastaard-Hottentot' children should be bound to serve their masters until the age of 25.[91] But this early interest in the matter is probably indicative of both common attitudes and common practice, at least in the more thoroughly colonised areas of the south-western Cape. The trend was towards a decline in the status of 'Bastaard-Hottentots' and, ultimately, that of 'Bastaards' too. Though this process was delayed on the open frontier, individuals of mixed racial descent could not have been oblivious of the increasing and encompassing forms of discrimination practised against their kind within the colony. Eventually they would be faced by a choice: to stay within the colony and accept their declining status, or to move beyond the colony and assert their independence.

Like the *drosters* who had preceded them, the 'Bastaard' or 'Bastaard-Hottentot' individuals who decided to move beyond the colony often gathered together in groups. These, in turn, formed the nucleus of societies which later became known as Oorlams.[92] To some extent the Oorlams were larger, more successful versions of *droster* gangs. They were composed of the same motley collection of colonial fugitives but were distinguished by their having achieved a measure of political independence, economic viability, social cohesion and military capability which enabled them to secure themselves in a region beyond the reach of colonial commandos. Although there were runaway slaves amongst them, it would be erroneous to think of these groups as maroon communities, for the adherence of many Khoikhoi, San and 'Bastaard-Hottentot' members gave them a strongly indigenous component.[93]

The word 'Oorlam' is, perhaps, preferable to the pejorative terms which it replaced but its usage was not as widespread or common as recent research would suggest. Until the late eighteenth century it was somewhat of a floating signifier and its meaning only began to solidify once the groups which it denoted themselves acquired a more stable identity.[94] An 1805 definition of the word has it that Oorlams are 'Hottentots who come from the upper country [i.e. beyond the frontier] and are born and bred with the farmers; most of whom understand and speak the low Dutch language'.[95] The paradox of this definition is obvious: Oorlams are people living outside the colony but possessing attributes acquired inside the colony. The historian De Bruyn states, more generally, that the term refers to 'all Khoikhoi and Basters who took up employment with whites and acquired European skills . . . particularly a knowledge of the use of horses and firearms'.[96]

Such knowledge could only be obtained through contact with the colonists and was often dearly bought. Quite apart from the essential skills of marksmanship and horsemanship was the necessity of acquiring gunpowder, muskets, horses and all the other commodities that were highly prized: tobacco, brandy, hats and clothes of European style. From their contact with the hunters and robbers of the open frontier, the proto-Oorlams learnt how to dispose of ivory, hides and stolen livestock. From their labour with white stock farmers they learnt both low Dutch and the value of organisation along the lines of the commando system. Belatedly, some learnt the rudiments of Christianity, thinking that its possession would preserve them from the status-reducing threats of the closing frontier. And, ultimately, many learnt that the best they could aspire to was a marginal position.

Oorlam identity, as well as the status of 'Bastaards' and 'Bastaard-Hottentots', evolved slowly. It would be quite wrong to believe that either the categories or conditions of their existence were formalised in the first half of the eighteenth century. The fluid nature of both racial attitudes and identities in the northern Cape frontier zone at this time is well illustrated by the events surrounding the disappearance of one Jacob Nortje in 1749. Nortje's name was registered in the roll of 'eenloop-endes', and the man for whom he worked was a certain Willem Odendaal.[97] In February 1749 a Khoikhoi named Andries came across Nortje, whom the records describe as a burgher, on the farm Matroose

Craal. He was surprised to see that Nortje had taken off his Dutch clothes and donned a Khoikhoi kaross and cap in their place. In response to Andries's questions Nortje eventually confessed to having shot his *baas*, Odendaal, by accident; he had then thrown away his musket and clothes, and obtained Khoikhoi clothes from Knapkoek, a Khoikhoi hunter of the Haegel Kraal. Thus attired, Nortje left Andries, saying that he was on his way to the Piketberg.[98]

Not long after this Daniel Bokkelenberg, who owned the farm Het Cruijs behind the Piketberg, told some of his neighbours that it seemed as though a runaway 'jong' (slave) of David Malan was hiding on the farm of Abraham Mouton and pretending to be a 'Bastaard-Hottentot' called Claas. Bokkelenberg and two others went secretly to Mouton's farm one night and took the suspicious character captive. The prisoner then confounded them by claiming to be Jacob Nortje and neither a 'jong' nor a 'Bastaard-Hottentot'. He explained that he had shot Odendaal in the back of the neck by accident whilst the two of them had been stalking an eland. Odendaal's widow, Magdalena le Roux, was subsequently able to confirm that Nortje (whom she described as a 'landbouwer', or agriculturist) and Odendaal had indeed gone out hunting together, barefoot and friendly, but that the two horses had returned later without their riders. Upon investigation, the body of Odendaal was discovered with a bullet wound in the neck.[99]

Nortje's strange behaviour suggests that the death of Odendaal was indeed accidental and that it had triggered a series of complex psychological responses within him. It would seem, to put it mildly, that the trauma of the event had induced a profound identity crisis within a person whose sense of self-identity was already insecure. It is obvious from the responses of the various people who encountered Nortje that he had the official status of a burgher, albeit of the low-class, 'eenloopende' variety. It is also clear that he did not look quite white, being able to pass himself off as a 'Bastaard-Hottentot' and being mistaken for a slave. We cannot know whether these aspects of his appearance bothered Nortje but we can speculate that they did when we consider his response to killing Odendaal. To kill a fellow human is to break powerful taboos and often places the killer in a liminal state, both socially and psychologically. The killer is in a state of impurity and social alienation. Only the performance of cleansing rituals, akin to those of rites of passage, can reintegrate the individual into his society and restore his psychic equilibrium.[100] It is significant that Nortje's first response to killing Odendaal was to divest himself of his clothes, thereby attempting to cleanse himself of the deed but also in order to divest himself of the colonial identity which he had transgressed. He then adopted one of the many other identities close to hand in the frontier zone – that of a Khoikhoi. Later he both took and was given further frontier identities, and it was only on being captured that he seemed to re-accept his status as burgher, perhaps so as to stave off punishment. In the event, Nortje managed to break the chains which had been put around his neck and escape from the cellar where he had been locked up. He was not found again and we may suppose that he continued to live as a fugitive, in the liminal state of the frontier zone, under his multiple identities.

This evidence suggests that it is extremely difficult to generalise about racial categories and identities in an open frontier situation. In 1749 the status of someone like Nortje was, even to himself, unclear. By the 1770s, however, as the colonial frontier ceased to expand and processes of closure intensified, more and more 'Bastaards' and 'Bastaard-Hottentots' began to leave the colony in order to avoid the inferior status which was being forced upon them by white colonists. It should be noted that in taking the positive step of fleeing the colony these non-white fugitives began to establish, for themselves, a common Oorlam identity. In time their ranks would be augmented by numbers of other frontier fugitives, both *droster* gangs (which, as we have noted, included fewer and fewer European members) and refugee Khoikhoi.

Fugitives were, as we have already stated, the true pioneers of the colonial frontier. They were always in search of the outer limits of the colony in order to pass beyond them. In so doing, paradoxically, they served only to extend the colonial frontier, for they, unwittingly, took the colony with them. It is, perhaps, a moot point whether their impact on Khoisan societies was more or less devastating than that of the trekboers on their heels. Ultimately, both trekboers and fugitives were part of the same frontier zone. It is for this reason that one should not make too great a distinction between them.

Although it has been convenient for the purposes of our discussion to treat the subject of fugitives within the frontier zone separately from that of frontier farmers or other officially authorised colonial frontiersmen, this should not be interpreted as endorsing Guelke's view that 'there were two different frontiers at the Cape inhabited by two different kinds of European settler'.[101] The 'fugitive frontier' is certainly not the same as Guelke's 'frontier of inclusion', nor does the frontier of colonial farmers correspond to his 'frontier of exclusion'. However one chooses to describe the processes and peoples of the Cape colony's frontier zone, and whatever concepts one uses to enhance one's understanding of events, it is not helpful to construct mutually exclusive principles of binary opposition. There is no sense in Guelke's idea that there was a frontier of 'exclusion' – pioneered by a fragment of south-western Cape society that was primarily white, middle class, orthodox and dedicated to the maintenance of an exclusivist European way of life – and a frontier of 'inclusion' – pioneered by single white men who hunted, traded and tended livestock, did not settle and who constituted a community involved in the 'blending of cultures and people within an informal social framework'.[102] In the first place it draws attention away from the non-European frontiersmen, and -women, suggesting that their role was a reactive, rather than an active, one. What about the *drosters* and 'Bastaards' of the frontier zone? Secondly, it implies that the contradictory impulses which he describes could not both be present (along with other 'obscene Faustian lusts' or pious Calvinistic, capitalist values) simultaneously in the body of one individual. There was nothing to prevent today's murderous cross-cultural robber-rapist from becoming tomorrow's white-wived, prosperous farmer.

In the inchoate flux of an open frontier zone individual identities, cultural certainties, political strength and economic fortunes fluctuated wildly. It was only as the frontier began to close that these shifting values began to crystallise. In the Cape's northern frontier zone processes of closure only began to occur once the frontier ceased to expand.[103]

3

Estienne Barbier

An eighteenth-century Cape social bandit

On the night of 24 March 1738 Estienne Barbier, a sergeant of the VOC, escaped from the Cape Town Castle (where he had been under arrest) and disappeared. The authorities presumed that he had managed to stow away on the ship *'t Huys de Marquette* in Table Bay and hence make his way back to Holland. Though annoyed by his escape, they cannot have been sorry to be rid of the troublesome soldier who had had the audacity to accuse several of his superiors of corruption. It must have come as an unpleasant surprise to them, therefore, when nearly a year later, on Sunday 1 March 1739, Estienne Barbier appeared at the head of a group of armed and mounted men to read a seditious statement to the congregation of the church of Drakenstein as they came from their devotions. Having read his 'avis of great importance' – whose language was as rude as its message was subversive – Barbier compounded his crime by nailing the paper to the church door, an expressly forbidden act since the government had reserved this particular channel of communication for itself. No sooner had the authorities learnt of Barbier's return and digested his message than they proclaimed him to be an outlaw (*vogel-vry* in the Dutch) wanted dead or alive. This proclamation too was affixed to the church door at Drakenstein but, on 16 March, Barbier tore it down – another crime. It is some indication of Barbier's local popularity that he was able to do so without being apprehended. An even greater indication of popularity, however, was that despite every effort on the government's part to arrest him, Barbier stayed free until 9 September 1739. Though the authorities managed to defuse the burgher rebellion he led – which coincided with the most serious outbreak of Khoisan resistance in the colony's history – they could not threaten or bribe Barbier's rural supporters into betraying him. Eventually he gave himself up, foolishly believing that because his cause was just he would be pardoned. Instead, with a gruesome excess of state terror, he was barbarously executed. His right hand and his head were cut off, his body was quartered and the sections displayed, impaled, next to the busiest roads of the colony.[1]

More than 250 years later it is time to re-examine the unsuccessful rebellion of Estienne Barbier. There are several good reasons why we should do so. Though the bare outlines of Barbier's rebellion are to be found in various histories of the Cape under VOC rule, the rebellion has not received the type of analysis that its importance merits.[2] Those who have shown the most interest in Barbier have been scholars whose chief concern was to analyse his language – the broken Dutch of a French speaker in the early eighteenth century.[3] The best of these studies, Professor Roy Pheiffer's, is far more than a linguistic one, being in addition an invaluable work of history. The fact remains, however, that Barbier and his rebellion should be revisited, particularly in the light of current trends in the writing of African history.

A recent collection of essays on banditry, rebellion and social protest in Africa is testimony to a widespread scholarly interest in such phenomena – as well as an indication that there is a need for further research.[4] This is especially true of Eric Hobsbawm's concept of social banditry, the applicability of which to the African historical experience has been rigorously questioned by Ralph Austen.[5] It is the intention of this chapter to use some of the insights developed by Austen to show that in the person of Estienne Barbier, we have the first genuine southern African (and perhaps even African) social bandit.[6] Though this chapter will, no doubt, not be entirely free of the Hobsbawmian heresy of adding to bandit mythology (for Barbier's life and death, treated purely as a dramatic narrative, deserve to join similar examples of bandit folklore), its purpose is not simply to tell an intrinsically fascinating tale.

There are three historical phenomena which a study of Barbier's rebellion helps to illuminate. These are the nature of the early-eighteenth-century colonial state; the existence of class struggle in the remote rural areas of the western Cape; and the pressures and processes behind the expansion of the Cape's frontier. Before proceeding to a consideration of these topics, though, we should explain what social banditry is and suggest reasons for its importance.

According to Eric Hobsbawm, social banditry is a primitive form of social protest which is 'a universal and virtually unchanging phenomenon . . . little more than endemic peasant protest against oppression and poverty: a cry for vengeance on the rich and the oppressors, a vague dream of some curb upon them, a righting of individual wrongs. Its ambitions are modest: a traditional world in which men are justly dealt with, not a new and perfect world.'[7] The 'ideal' bandit is someone who does something which is regarded as criminal by the state or the local rulers, but who is not considered to be a criminal, or to have acted against local conventions, by the population. He is protected by the people, though he is frequently a lone wolf living on the margins of society. If he forms a band of followers, this band is usually small and held together only by his personal magnetism. If he robs, he is usually obliged to conform to the Robin Hood stereotype since 'there is more to take from the rich than from the poor, and if he takes from the poor or becomes an "illegitimate" killer, he forfeits his most powerful asset, public aid and sympathy'.[8] When he can he is free-handed with his gains. As a social protest movement banditry is 'inefficient in every way', being incapable of effective guerrilla organisation and archaic in siding with doomed archaic forces. Though it occurs amongst peasant societies which 'know rich and poor, powerful and weak, rulers and ruled', these societies remain 'profoundly and tenaciously traditional, and pre-capitalist in structure'.[9]

These then are the broad patterns of social banditry. Part of Hobsbawm's interest in the phenomenon stems from the universality of these patterns. But underlying these forms is the deeper significance of content. What does social banditry represent? For Hobsbawm it is a predominantly rural response to the process of being broken into modern society. It is a form of primitive rebellion against the world of capitalism, which 'comes to them from outside, insidiously, by the operation of economic forces which they do not understand and over which they have no control, or brazenly by conquest, revolutions and fundamental changes of law whose consequences they may not understand, even when they have helped to bring them about.'[10]

Hobsbawm has not been without his critics, and his theory of social banditry has been severely qualified or modified by several writers.[11] Blok, for instance, points out that Hobsbawm has exaggerated the element of social protest in banditry as well as obscuring the ties which link the bandits to other groups.[12] Austen, in particular, believes that

Hobsbawm has minimised the role played by the state in defining social banditry. Without a state, to put it crudely, there can be no social banditry. This is of particular relevance to the African historical experience – about which Hobsbawm had nothing to say[13] – because it was not always necessary for deviant groups to enter the category of criminals opposed to a general political authority. As Austen says, 'for criminals to become social heroes – or more significantly, for heroes to become criminals – there must not only be poor classes who resent the rich, but also a political system claiming hegemony over both the rich and the poor.'[14] Austen's point is that in Africa – as opposed to Europe and Asia, from which Hobsbawm draws most of his examples – the states were usually too weak to define and delimit criminality.

A further related problem is that in Africa the coming of the modern capitalist world (against which social banditry is rebellion) frequently coincided with the arrival of the colonial frontier. Austen cautions: 'We need to make a distinction between frontiers within a given social system, and the situation of "interpenetration between two previously distinct societies," which is the African colonial frontier. The former gave rise to banditry as one means of contesting the values that were to be deployed in controlling economic and political life. The latter produces "primary resistance" in which no institutions or repertoire of values are shared between the two sides.'[15]

As we shall see, Barbier's rebellion qualifies as social banditry by meeting both of Austen's requirements. Though the wider context of the rebellion was indeed the African colonial frontier, Barbier deliberately placed himself within (or on the margins of) the social system of Cape colonial society and against the general political authority of the capitalist VOC.

There is, however, one further set of objections to Hobsbawm's concept of social banditry which has to be considered before it can be imported into an African context. These objections centre around the two preconditions which Hobsbawm sees as being necessary for the existence of social banditry; a social environment constituted by a traditional peasantry; and a 'pre-capitalist' or 'pre-industrial' social environment. O'Malley, who identifies and dismisses these two preconditions, rightly draws our attention to the vagueness of Hobsbawm's use of the term 'peasantry'.[16] For Hobsbawm peasant types can range from the communal peasantry of mid-nineteenth-century Russia to the French peasantry 'who operate in a framework of bourgeois institutions and law, especially property law, most likely as individual commodity producers, possibly shading over to commercial farmers'.[17] Such a broad definition of peasantry, as O'Malley notes, clearly permits the penetration of a capitalist productive order. It is, therefore, extremely difficult to talk about a 'traditional peasantry' when the matrix of social banditry is precisely that period of the peasantry's history in which it is being 'modernised' or transformed. Rather than defining the support base of social banditry as being a 'traditional peasantry', it is more accurate to state that 'social banditry presumes as one of its conditions of existence chronic class struggle which permeates the social and geographical terrain of the bandit'. In order for this 'chronic class struggle' to support social banditry, it has to be manifested in a 'unified conflict consciousness among direct producers' – 'be they all peasants, or an admixture of sharecroppers, labourers, small-scale cash croppers or whatever'.[18]

Corrigan, however, has noted that this unified conflict consciousness need not necessarily be determined by common class membership since 'particular producers in specific situations embody social relations and think thoughts about their experiences of labouring with others against enemies natural and human'.[19] These are important and useful distinctions to make, for it would be very difficult to describe Barbier's rural supporters as being 'peasants', still less as 'traditional peasants'. Moreover, their communal unity was, as we shall see, as much a product of class conflict as it was of conflict with the Khoisan. Though they thought of themselves as being of the rural poor, they certainly did not wish to make common cause with the even worse-off Khoisan.

There is one final point to make about Hobsbawm's stricture that social banditry occurs within essentially 'pre-capitalist' or 'pre-industrial' (also vague terms) societies. What Hobsbawm is really trying to draw our attention to, O'Malley insists, is that social banditry occurs in societies where 'more effective mechanisms for articulating social protest' are lacking. He is arguing that only with the emergence of modern capitalism does one find the rise of institutionalised movements representing the interests of direct producers.[20] It is certainly worth bearing this point in mind, for as we turn to a more detailed consideration of Barbier's rebellion, it is obvious that nothing propelled him into his short career as a social bandit more strongly than the refusal of the authorities to listen to his complaints.

Estienne Barbier was born in the village of Bazoches near Orleans in 1699. By 1734 he had joined the Dutch East India Company as a soldier, for he sailed from Zealand in June 1734, arriving at the Cape in October of the same year.[21] In June 1735 he appeared on the muster-roll as a sergeant, a very rapid and desirable promotion, for the life of a common soldier at the Cape could be one of great hardship, characterised by brutal punishments and grinding poverty.

How had Barbier achieved this promotion? According to Mentzel, our chief source of information on Barbier's career as a Company soldier – apart from what can be gleaned from archival documents – Barbier was a turbulent fellow who was promoted so as to silence him. He had made it known that he was skilled at constructing fortifications and was therefore entrusted with the building of a small redoubt for six cannon. Upon the satisfactory completion of this task he was promoted to the rank of corporal in charge of the redoubt with six men under his command. His subsequent promotion to sergeant, again according to Mentzel, came about because he had caused rumours to be spread that he was acting as a spy for the directors of the Company in order to watch the actions of officials and discreetly report on them.

This, at least, was Mentzel's explanation and it is as well to check his credentials before accepting his story. Mentzel is best known for his *Geographical and Topographical Description* of the Cape in the eighteenth century though he was also the author of a biography of Rudolf Siegfried Allemann. It is in this latter work, first published in 1784, that his account of Barbier is to be found.[22] Allemann was to become captain of the military forces and commander of the Castle at the Cape in 1740. In the process of rising to this position he became the patron of Mentzel and the sworn enemy of Barbier. One can expect, therefore, Mentzel's account to be biased in favour of his patron and against Barbier. It was, indeed, the feud between Barbier and Allemann which led to the former's initial imprisonment. Barbier had accused Allemann of embezzlement but the charges did not stick. On being ordered to offer a public apology to Allemann, Barbier refused and suffered incarceration in the Castle's 'Donker Gat'. Despite Mentzel's bias in recounting the affair, his comments on the social, political and economic circumstances prevalent at the Cape at this time are invaluable. He experienced, at first hand, the same conditions as his hero and his hero's enemy, for all three men – Mentzel, Allemann and Barbier – began their careers at the Cape in the early eighteenth century as Company soldiers. Though their careers took very different paths thereafter, they all originally shared the same milieu.

Another invaluable contribution which Mentzel is able to make is that he takes great delight in recalling the exact workings of the Cape system. Like Robinson Crusoe he waxes most lyrical when presenting a balance sheet. In this he typifies the capitalist spirit of the VOC as well as the predominant ethos of the times, but his enthusiasm leads him, despite himself, into describing corrupt practices from which his hero is obviously not exempt. Since one of the concerns of this chapter is to consider the characteristics of the colonial state in the early-eighteenth-century Cape, and since it was against this institution that Barbier rebelled, these details are not unimportant. It becomes clear from a close reading of Mentzel that it was customary for those in authority at the Cape to extract as many perquisites and advantages from their offices as possible. What was at issue was not whether such practices were illegal – they were – but whether the right people were being bought off. This was something which Allemann, Mentzel and the various officials of eighteenth-century society understood very well. It was not something, however, which Barbier found acceptable, and by raising his voice against the system he fell foul of it.

Barbier's principal duty after his promotion was to guard the convicts ('bandieten') at the Chavonnes Battery. He was later to be accused of having freed a runaway slave, Rosette, after she had spent the night in his room. Another accusation was that he had sold drink to the convicts, not being averse to a drink himself since he once had to be carried to his battery dead drunk by the Ratelwag.[23] In the light of Barbier's subsequent career it is tempting to see some sympathy for the underdog behind these exhibitions of human frailty. But it was Barbier's behaviour on the Sunday evening of 5 May 1737 that first incurred official displeasure. On that night Barbier, equipped with a flask of wine and in a drunken state, sat himself down in the presence of two fellow sergeants in the Castle in order to continue drinking in company. Earlier he had made a point of offering the common soldiers on watch some wine, but not Corporal Courthym, characterising him and other corporals as thieves. Whether it was his companions' unconvivial attitude (they told Barbier that he had had enough to drink and should go to bed) or the loosening effects of the wine is not clear, but Barbier began to divest himself of certain deep-rooted resentments. Sergeants G.L. Kok and Van Hagen, as well as Corporal Courthym, who was present, heard him mutter 'All thieves' and then, more forcefully, 'My lord Allemann is a scoundrel and a blackguard, I have told him so to his face in the presence of Panhart and I will prove it'. Barbier was not to be dissuaded from his estimation of

Allemann despite the objections of his listeners, who happened to fall under Lieutenant Allemann's command, and added, before being led off to bed, that anyone who held a contrary viewpoint was also 'a scoundrel, and a blackguard'.[24] The incident could not be hushed up and was reported to De Grandpreez, secretary of the Council of Justice. On 7 May 1737 Barbier was placed under civil arrest facing charges of having slandered Lieutenant Rudolf Siegfried Allemann, and on 5 September the case began.[25]

By 12 September the Council had heard Allemann's evidence and gave Barbier the opportunity to support his public defamation of Allemann. This Barbier did, in writing, on 26 September. The main charges Barbier levelled against Allemann were that he had cheated soldiers by depriving them of a portion of their *pasgeld* and that he had been selling Company firewood to certain burghers.[26] *Pasgeld*, or *diensgeld*, was the money which was paid by those soldiers who were able to earn money by practising a trade, to those who were not so fortunate. Since the salaries paid to soldiers at the Cape were not sufficient for them to exist on, they were obliged to supplement their income by accepting non-military employment. Quite obviously not everyone could be exempted from sentry duty, so the custom was for the *pasgangers* to pay 9 guilders 12 *stuivers* monthly, to be divided amongst the rest of them.[27] Barbier alleged that Allemann chose not to record all the men who were away as *pasgangers* in order to divert their *pasgeld* into his own pocket and had even instructed him (Barbier) to ignore two or three passes. With regard to Allemann's illegal sale of firewood, Barbier was able to produce statements from seven burghers who swore that Allemann had sold them wood, bast or reeds.[28]

These statements, upon which Barbier pinned a great deal, were held over on 24 October pending consideration. The accusations concerning the *pasgeld*, however, were, it seems, effortlessly shrugged off by Allemann, who 'expressed amazement that Barbier had attempted no defence, and had merely made a number of foolish charges against him that he was unable to support with the testimony of any witnesses'. He said, further, that 'he did not intend to trouble about them as they were obviously false. Further, was it likely that he would so far confide in an inferior as to speak in such a confidential manner with a man he never saw outside of military circles or in the course of duty?'[29]

Though Barbier believed that his evidence concerning Allemann's sale of wood from the Company's *buijten-posten*, or cattle outposts (of which

Allemann was *commissarius*, or inspector) was incontrovertible, he was, in fact, on very shaky ground. In the first place, notwithstanding Company orders which prohibited Company officials from taking part in private trade, the practice was so widespread at the Cape that it was considered to be a perquisite rather than a peculation. This was especially true of the post of inspector of the *buijten-posten*. Mentzel estimated that Allemann made at least 40 guilders a month out of his position.[30] Allemann defended his actions by arguing that 'The Governor De la Fontaine, Adriaan van Kervel and Mijnheer Van den Henghel all were aware of what he was doing, and that it was in a way allowed as a reward for his trouble as Country Commissioner'. Indeed, according to Mentzel, Allemann was within an ace of proving that not only had Governors Van Noot and Van Assenburgh acted in the same way, but so had the present independent fiscal (Van den Henghel) and present Governor (Swellengrebel) when they had held the post. With such illustrious examples to appeal to in mitigation, Allemann was hardly likely to be condemned for his actions.[31]

A second reason why Barbier's case against Allemann was not investigated with greater vigour was that Allemann was a very good personal friend of the fiscal, Daniël van den Henghel. In fact it was during Barbier's trial, on 20 September, that Van den Henghel became, for a short time, Governor of the Cape. The circumstances of his appointment illustrate the corrupt and venal world of Cape politics at its worst. There is a sense in which Barbier's charges of official thieving came at a particularly delicate time since they coincided with an extremely unsettled period in the Cape's administration. There were no fewer than four changes of Governor between August 1737 and April 1739. De la Fontaine retired in August 1737 to be succeeded by the *secunde*, Adriaan van Kervel. Van Kervel died on 16 September 1737, and an ungraceful struggle for the governorship ensued between Van den Henghel and Swellengrebel, the *secunde*. Ordinarily Swellengrebel should have become Governor, by virtue of his being the *secunde*, but Van den Henghel objected to this on the grounds that he, as senior upper-merchant, had a better claim. To an overbearing and dictatorial disposition Van den Henghel could add the claim that he was an educated Netherlander instead of being a simple Cape-born product like Swellengrebel. He could also offer bribes to prospective followers from the notoriously fat pickings of the fiscal office as well as the promise of even greater rewards in the future. Swellengrebel, however, was worth a fortune, for his father was a wealthy German immigrant. In the short term, though, it was Van den Henghel's bullying that won the day, for he convinced the Council of Policy to submit the question to the drawing of lots. He won. But in April 1739 the Heren XVII appointed Swellengrebel in his place, prompted, it was rumoured, by a handsome present.[32]

With all this jockeying for position it might seem as though Barbier could have found some powerful allies. But since his evidence was injurious to all, he was an embarrassment to all. There was, however, political capital to be made of the influential Allemann, who was badly in need of a powerful friend. His guilt was widely acknowledged publicly and in order to escape further humiliations he became a fervent supporter of Van den Henghel, making him a present of his own riding horse, the only snow-white horse in the Cape.[33] The new Governor responded by increasing the legal pressure on Barbier in order to crush him and suppress his accusations.

The government's counter-attack came on 21 November 1737 when Sergeant Godfried Lodewijk Kok accused Barbier of making slanderous statements against him. These statements had arisen from Barbier's response to Kok's account of the night of 5 May. Barbier had announced, on 31 October, that Kok was not an honourable man since he had stolen sheep from the widow Elizabeth Joubert. It took until 12 December for Barbier to collect and present his evidence – a seemingly clear-cut indictment of Kok – but the Council of Justice was not impressed. Instead they decided against Barbier and instructed him to acknowledge Kok as an honourable man. This was too much for Barbier, who had been gradually worn down by his loss of freedom and the expense and futility of the legal process. The records describe that 'The above sentence had no sooner been read when the accused Estienne Barbier said in the most offensive and brusque manner, "If I am ordered to do so, I cannot do it; the fellow is a rogue who had robbed his master. I request that my statement be maintained." He then raised his voice and with his hand indicating the entire Council said in an evil manner: "Now I see how it is here," without ceasing to speak and gesticulating violently with his hands. But since he spoke very angrily and mumbled one could not understand what he was saying.'[34]

For this insolent and aggressive outburst Barbier was locked in the 'Donker Gat' for twenty-one days on bread and water. It was an experience which haunted him for the rest of his brief life. Whilst he starved in prison, Kok's evidence was accepted as admissible and the case of

Allemann *vs* Barbier was decided in the former's favour. Barbier was ordered to apologise to Allemann and beg his forgiveness in a humiliating public ceremony – as well as paying the legal costs.[35] Despite his recent experiences Barbier did not consider this possible, and as soon as he emerged from his cell, he appealed against the sentence. It was his last recourse to the law. This time he proposed to appeal over the heads of the Cape officials to Batavia even though his official request to do so had to go through the local Council of Justice. Permission was granted but there was one final snag. Copies of the court proceedings had to be sent to Batavia and Barbier had to pay for this expense. The cost, it transpired, was 32 rixdollars and 3 shillings – a great deal of money for someone like Barbier who had already had to sell his watch and clothes. Barbier, however, agreed to pay this to the secretary of the Council of Justice, De Grandpreez, from his forthcoming pay. By the time payment fell due, on 21 February, Barbier had had a chance to read the copies and was shocked to see that they did not reflect the word-by-word proceedings of the court. He realised De Grandpreez's censored version of the proceedings would not win him justice if the papers ever reached Batavia, and announced that he intended laying a charge against the secretary. This, however, was impossible without the permission of the Council of Justice and Barbier at last realised that he had exhausted all legal channels.[36]

In a long letter which Barbier wrote over a year later to Governor Swellengrebel, he mentioned there was a French saying which helped to explain his next move: 'La faim, fait sortir le loup hoors du Bois' – 'de honger jaagh de wolf uijt de Bosch' (Hunger drives the wolf from the forest). As Barbier slipped out of the Castle on the night of 24 March 1738, anything must indeed have seemed preferable to the dark thickets of the law.

It would appear that Barbier's first intention was to board a ship and leave the Cape. On the night of his escape he met, by pre-arrangement, with a certain Nic Wijs behind the Castle. It is not known who Wijs, a 'drummer', was but he too must have wanted to leave the Cape quickly and surreptitiously. The two men took a boat alongside the ship *'t Huys de Marquette* but they were probably already being sought. At any rate Barbier returned to the shore alone, leaving Wijs aboard, where he was subsequently arrested. Barbier made his way to the farm De Roode Blom on the outskirts of town and from there to Isak Nieuwout's farm in the Tijgerberg. The next stage of his flight took him to Drakenstein, where he spent a night at the farm of the widow of Lowies Leriche. Finally he reached Orleans, the farm of the widow 'Silje', or Celliers, where he was to stay until February 1739.[37]

Perhaps Barbier might have been content to dwell in rustic obscurity with a widow who spoke his mother tongue. But towards the end of February a group of ten or twelve armed men rode by the farm filled with resentment towards the government. Barbier, who heard that 'they wished to raise a rebellion', offered them his services.[38] There was still something deep within him that hated the idea of government corruption and injustice. Although their grievances were rooted in rural issues, which Barbier had not previously been concerned with, he was quick to make their cause his own by acting as their spokesman. His literacy and leadership soon placed him at the head of these rural rebels. His career as a social bandit had begun.[39] But who were his followers and what cause was he championing?

The core of Barbier's followers came from a group of colonists who had made an illegal trip to the Orange River in 1738. It was illegal because the colonists went with ten wagons laden with trade goods for the purpose of bartering cattle from the Great and Little Namaqua. Such commerce was contrary to Company policy. It is likely that the sponsors of this illegal expedition included wealthy men with connections in the northern frontier zone – men like the partners Jan Valck and Jürgen Hanekom – since Willem van Wyk, a member of the expedition, was superintendent at Valck's farms in the Sandveld. The other colonists in the party were Lodewyk Putter, Hendrik Ras, Matthys Willemsz, Jacob Swart, Frans Campher, Andries van der Walde, Sybrand van Dyk, Augustus Lourens and Jan Gous.[40] They were a closely related group of men who were assisted and accompanied by their Khoisan servants.[41]

After successfully bartering some cattle from the Little Namaqua, the expedition left these in the safe-keeping of a servant, Jantje, and proceeded to the land of the Great Namaqua across the 'Groot' or Orange River. Here they stayed for a month at the kraal of Gal, a chief of the Great Namaqua. This expedition is notable not so much because it was illegal but because it is the first recorded expedition of Europeans to the Orange River.[42] Other Europeans, in search of ivory, had certainly preceded them here (indeed, they were joined by a certain Pieter de Bruyn, who had been out hunting elephant before them),[43] but none had left a record, nor had they so baleful an influence as Van Wyk and his fellows.

During their stay at Gal's kraal, the colonists occupied themselves with bartering cattle from their hosts whilst Willem van Wyk 'took to wife, Hottentot fashion, a near relative of the chief, conducting himself in this matter and clothing himself at the time as a Hottentot'.[44] This act of amity would appear to have been a ruse on Van Wyk's part, however, for when the time came for their departure, the colonists slipped secretly away and instructed their servants to return to the kraal, attack the Great Namaqua, and carry off their cattle. This order the servants were willing to obey since their masters promised them a share of the loot and provided them with firearms for the occasion. In the subsequent surprise attack at dawn, seven of the Great Namaqua, including Captain Gal, were killed and their cattle driven away. The expedition then returned to the Piketberg area but stopped along the way to attack the kraal of Arisie, a captain of the Little Namaqua. Arisie's wife was shot, her baby wounded, and another member of the kraal killed. In both of these attacks the 'Hottentot Keyser', described as living with the farmer Hendrik Kruger, was prominent. So too was the 'Hottentot Claas Kok' who was, in all probability, an ancestor of the family that would later become famous throughout the frontier zone.[45]

On returning to the vicinity of the Piketberg, the colonists failed to honour the agreement which they had reached with their Khoisan servants. Instead of compensating theit numerous employees with cattle, they hid some of the stolen livestock in secret kloofs and redistributed the rest amongst friendly neighbours (whose numbers doubtless contained some sponsors of the expedition). The cheated servants, led by Swartbooij and Titus (Khoisan servants of Jan Valck), went to report the matter to the authorities at the Cape. Their story was corroborated and amplified by the evidence of Plato, Vulcanus and Arisie, captains of the Little Namaqua, as well as by Captain Gaaren, son of the late Captain Gal of the Great Namaqua, who, having survived the attack on his father's kraal, had journeyed all the way to Cape Town to seek justice.[46]

The reason why some sort of governmental response was imperative was not so much the need to punish thieves and murderers – though the colonists could obviously not be allowed to flout Company regulations with impunity – as it was the need to try to quell an outbreak of Khoisan attacks on the colony's north-western frontier. These attacks, which should be seen in the broader context of Khoisan resistance to colonial penetration, intensified after the expedition of 1738.[47] Indeed, the Khoisan resistance of 1738 and 1739 grew to assume the proportions of an anti-colonial war and was, in many cases, led by the frustrated servants of the Orange River raiders. In early 1739, before the events got out of hand, in an attempt to prevent the frontier war from escalating, the colonial authorities decided to confiscate any cattle which the colonists may have stolen from the Khoisan and return them to their rightful owners. The decision to attempt to placate the Khoisan was partly an acknowledgement that the colonists had caused the disturbances in the first place, but it was also the result of the realisation that it would be very difficult to send a commando so far to the north. What the authorities could not have foreseen was that their attempts to confiscate cattle from the colonists would spark off a burgher rebellion with Barbier at the fore.

In January 1739 the deputy landdrost of Stellenbosch, Carel Christoffel Counitz, was authorised to confiscate any cattle that he thought had been acquired illegally and to command the offenders to appear before the Council of Justice. His task could not have been an easy one, for the stolen cattle had been mixed amongst the herds of a number of people in order to make identification more difficult. Counitz undoubtedly made some mistakes but he had a pretty shrewd idea as to the identity of the offenders, aided no doubt by the confessions of Matthys Willemsz and Pieter de Bruyn, both of whom had been involved in the 1738 expedition and who had been under arrest in the Castle 'for a considerable time'.

Willemsz and De Bruyn had revealed that well over a thousand cattle had been taken from the Namaqua, and in the light of this figure the 279 cattle confiscated by Counitz do not seem to be an excessive amount. At a later date the government was to receive a complaint from the farmers Hendrik Kruger (whose servants had participated in the attacks on the Namaqua and who was Van Wyk's brother-in-law), Sybrand van Dyk, Hendrik Ras and Arnoldus Basson (Van Dyk and Ras had been part of the expedition). They complained that Counitz had taken not only the 'bartered' cattle, but also a large number belonging to themselves and to other people. A subsequent thorough investigation by Lourensz, the landdrost of Stellenbosch, into Counitz's behaviour did not reveal that Counitz had erred greatly in executing his instructions. The case of the memorialists was also seriously weakened by the injudicious claims of Sybrand van Dyk, who maintained that 88 of his own cattle had been confiscated even though the landdrost well knew that 'the said Van Dyk never possessed eight head, to say nothing of eighty-eight; and if he did have them he must most certainly, like his comrades, have stolen and bartered them from the Hottentots'.[48]

The way in which their cattle had been acquired was, however, of less importance to many of the colonists than the fact that Counitz, with Khoi assistants, was busy confiscating them. On 24 January Counitz was obliged to report to Lourensz that certain residents and agriculturists were refusing to obey his orders. As yet this disobedience was fairly inchoate but, with Barbier's intervention, the colonists began to articulate their grievances. On 24 or 25 February Barbier met with nine or ten of the angriest men on the farm of Johannes Ras near 'de Paerl'. Here he helped them to compose and write a letter of complaint to Swellengrebel, President of the Council of Justice. Though Barbier did not sign the letter (significantly, only two out of nine signatories could write – the rest made crosses), he later confessed to having written it at the request of those present. The letter was a sharp attack on landdrost Lourensz, accusing him of having stolen the cattle of the undersigned and asking that Swellengrebel order Lourensz to return the livestock. A remarkable feature of the letter was the inclusion of quasi-legal Latin terms, which Barbier had obviously picked up during the course of his long series of litigations. Such language was quite beyond the comprehension of the illiterate farmers whom Barbier now represented but by using it he must have enhanced his prestige greatly and encouraged them to believe the law was on their side. Johannes Ras was dispatched to deliver the letter to the relevant authorities at the Cape.[49]

His reception there was less than cordial. Van den Henghel, the Governor, was tempted to arrest him whilst Swellengrebel advised him to take the matter to the landdrost of Stellenbosch. Since it was precisely that person against whom the complaint was lodged, this did not appear to Ras, Barbier or their companions to be the best course to adopt. Instead they resolved to emulate the founder of the Reformed religion and nail their grievances to the church door.[50]

Among those who accompanied Barbier to the church were some who had been involved in the expedition to the Orange River and some who resented the government's recent actions. Though Barbier had written the document, he had not been without advisers, and it represented a significant departure from the letter sent to Swellengrebel, for its list of grievances was far more comprehensive and it did not confine itself to the question of the confiscated cattle. Indeed, it may be taken as a fair reflection of the issues that were causing resentment amongst colonists on the Cape frontier.[51] The 'avis' was aimed at the 'Afrikaner brothers' and its first complaint concerned the issue of the payment of 24 rixdollars per annum for a loan farm. According to Barbier and his constituents, this payment was ruining the farmers. Furthermore, they questioned its legality since its institution had never been announced by public edict (*plakkaat*), and they disputed the obligation to put down a deposit on leasing a farm. The people held responsible for these evils were the 'rulers' and the 'principal ruler'. Barbier took care to distinguish between 'the Lords seventeen' (whose laws were just) and the 'Roguish and damned wilfulness of our rulers'. In this he was conforming to the essentially reformist ideals of primitive social protest, seeking to restore the traditional order. This order, he believed, was expressed in the Company regulations of 20 October 1687, which instructed officials at the Cape to provide prospective farmers with as much land as they could use and to equip them with the necessary items to start farming.

Times had changed. According to Barbier, the Governor was now a protector of 'Scoundrels, idlers, and whip-branded thieves', as well as a participant in robberies against honest free burghers. What rankled in particular was that the Governor and the landdrost (described as the 'King of the rogues') chose to believe the words of 'unbaptised hottentots, who know nothing of salvation or damnation' and stole the cattle of the colonists so as to distribute them amongst their 'hottentot cronies'. This had encouraged the Khoisan to believe that they now had more rights than the colonists, and the subsequent spate of robberies was thus a direct result of the government's interference. 'And in addition the hottentots wish to violate the worthy Christian women: Saying that they have nothing to fear: alleging that the landdrost shall listen to them rather than to the Christian people.'[52]

After this attack on the government's pro-Khoisan policies, the 'avis' returned to the theme of the great difficulty experienced by aspirant farmers in making a beginning. Soldiers and sailors who were discharged from Company service with the intention of working for someone else as a *knecht* or leasing their own farm were obliged (or else their employers were) to pay a fee to the Governor. The best part of their labours was then spent in paying back to the Governor the interest on the money they had borrowed. Hundreds of young men and women (according to Barbier) found themselves unable to contemplate marriage, either because they had no prospects of being able to afford a farm or because they would have to re-pay too much to the Governor. The document went on to list some of the corrupt trading practices of the Governor and his officials, and it concluded by urging the colonists to cease paying deposits or rent for their loan farms; to cease paying money to obtain *knechts;* and to submit a list of all claims against the government for forwarding to Holland so that they could be reimbursed and the 'roguish acts of our land' exposed.[53]

Whilst it is difficult to prove that the government was insisting on 'deposits' or percentages of money over and above the rental of 24 rixdollars per annum, it is highly likely that in this, as in everything else, the administration was corrupt.[54] What is not in contention is that young men were finding it difficult to acquire loan farms and become independent farmers (though it is doubtful whether the marriage rate diminished as a result).[55] It is significant that none of the colonists who went on the expedition to the Orange River, or who rode with Barbier to the Drakenstein church, had loan farms.[56] This was not only because of the cost of the rental but because of the other costs involved in farming (hence the attraction of stealing Khoi cattle). A further stumbling block to aspirant farmers was that it was very difficult for newcomers to relax the tight control which the Company exercised over the meat market through the agency of monopolies granted to the privileged few. Though Barbier did not attack this elite in his 'avis' there is a constant implicit criticism of those who worked hand in glove with corrupt officials, and in some of his subsequent statements this criticism became far more explicit.[57]

For the time being, however, Barbier's message was quite subversive enough. The government was informed of the events outside the church as well as of the identity of the instigators and the content of their proclamation by J.M. Friek, messenger of the court in Paarl.[58] Realising that with such a programme Barbier would be able to command a great deal of support, they decided to act as swiftly and tactfully as possible in order to nip the revolt in the bud. The first step was to declare Barbier an outlaw and issue instructions for his apprehension – dead or alive. The second step was to try to separate Barbier from his followers by issuing the latter a pardon if they abandoned him and gave themselves up within a month.[59] No sooner had this announcement been pinned to the church door in Paarl than Barbier himself tore it down.

He and his followers had been hiding out in the Piketberg since 1 March but had returned to Paarl, armed, on 16 March. They had received notice that the *heemraden* of Stellenbosch wished to discuss things with them and decided to risk an encounter.[60] The first *heemraden* they met were Theunis Boota and Charl Marais. These gentlemen suggested that the meeting take place the next day at the farm of the *heemraad* Hendrik van der Merwe. After some discussion Barbier and his followers decided to keep the rendezvous, but, fearing an ambush by the landdrost and a commando, took the precaution of remaining well armed and in the open. Eventually they were persuaded to go to the farmhouse, where there were five or six *heemraden* present.[61]

According to Barbier's account of proceedings, Captain Jan Louw accused him of being a seducer of the common people. Barbier's supporters sprang quickly to his defence, saying: 'You are not a traitor, but in reality our good father, because you have helped us, and with justice; and you have opened our eyes to the truth; and without you we should all have been taken for scoundrels if you had not come to our rescue.'[62] Even if this speech was never actually made, it is a significant indication of the way in which Barbier viewed himself. A further point of interest is the way Barbier expressed ideal political relationships. His model was an essentially paternalistic one – and this he shared with his supporters – of a good father looking after his children. At various places in his writings he describes good rulers as being 'fathers' and appeals to them to protect their children. In this, as in many of his other actions, Barbier allowed hope to triumph over experience. Captain Jan Louw, however, was certainly no good father, for he had neglected to forward letters of complaint from the colonists. These letters had been given to Charl Marais, who had in turn given them to Louw, where they had stopped.

Barbier went on to castigate Louw and the other *heemraden* for having permitted Matthys Willemsz and Pieter de Bruyn to be arrested without cause. Warming to his theme, he then demanded to know why the government no longer paid each colonist who attended the compulsory annual military drill at Stellenbosch 3 rixdollars for expenses. Finally he returned to the question of the confiscated cattle, demanding their return. When Louw cautioned that only some of the cattle might be returned, Barbier launched into a blistering attack on the absent landdrost Lourensz and his chief henchman, Louw: 'You damned Piet Lourensz, you scoundrel: Why did you order my livestock to be stolen: My house to be burnt, my wife to be violated; with your damned brothers the Hottentots; and you would not give back all of my livestock; why have you allowed me to be robbed?' When Louw objected that he was not the landdrost and that Barbier should not speak so strongly against him, the reply was: 'If you are not the landdrost: in this case you are his principal; or you are the King of the Hottentots himself.'[63]

From this it may be seen that Barbier had a highly developed sense of the dramatic, casting himself as both champion of the people and public prosecutor. Though the account he gives of his own words and deeds may have been heightened for effect, there is good evidence that Barbier was indeed intemperate in his use of language. It may seem surprising that Barbier should delight in recording these outbursts of his, particularly since they are found in a letter (or book, so great is its length) written to Swellengrebel (who was appointed as Governor in April 1739), asking for pardon. The letter was probably written in August and its tone may be explained by Barbier's assumption that Swellengrebel would be ill disposed towards any of Van den Henghel's consorts – and, in Barbier's mind, landdrost Lourensz was 'King of those rogues'. By attacking the ex-Governor's cronies so vigorously, Barbier was counting on winning the new Governor's support. In addition, Barbier obviously found the exercise of writing down his case extremely cathartic. On paper, at least, he could shout down the corrupt traducers of the land, scoring great victories in debate, backed by the people's will and incontrovertible evidence.[64]

After lecturing the *heemraden* on their duties and suggesting that the landdrost had turned them into 'Hottentoten Heemraden', Barbier stated his demands: a free pardon for himself and his followers; the return of the stolen cattle or 8 rixdollars per head for those not returned; compensation payment for the inconvenience caused to those whose cattle had been confiscated; and the release of De Bruyn and Willemsz. If this was not done, threatened Barbier, he would burn them and their houses whilst sparing their women and children. Some of the *heemraden* seemed to be suitably chastened by Barbier's sermon and, in words which echoed the Bible, acknowledged that though he spoke the truth 'they who speak the truth, have no haven'. Barbier replied that though truth had no home in this country, he would take it to the Fatherland.[65] Charl Marais, who up to this point had backed Barbier's statements with the fervour of an acolyte, was suddenly accused by Barbier of being an 'idler' and of having paid ex-Governor De la Fontaine a hundred sheep in order to secure a loan farm. Marais acknowledged the fact and Barbier used this as evidence to illustrate the obstacles facing poor colonists who wished to acquire farms.[66]

The meeting ended with the *heemraden* promising to deliberate with the landdrost on 19 March. Once they had done so, the Council of Policy was informed of events. They decided, on 21 March, that there would be no pardon for Barbier. They realised, however, that it would be impossible to capture him or his followers, all perfect horsemen and shots, in an extensive country peopled with rebel sympathisers. Instead they offered a free pardon to anyone or any number of people, whether guilty of cattle thefts, barter or following Barbier, if they delivered him into the hands of justice. De Bruyn and Willemsz were released on condition that they helped to capture Barbier.[67]

It is an indication of Barbier's popularity that this offer did not result in his apprehension. Instead he continued his vendetta against officialdom by writing letters. Three of these were addressed to Swellengrebel and were dispatched on 6, 17 and 26 March. It would seem as though none of them reached their destination.[68] A fourth letter dated 22 March took the form of a 'public circulating letter'. In this, all 'Afrikaner brothers' were urged to disobey landdrost Lourensz. Indeed, if we are to believe Van den Henghel, Barbier threatened to evict him (Van den Henghel) from the Castle with armed force, having gone as far as procuring a scaling ladder for storming the walls![69]

For the time being, the Cape authorities faced a more serious problem than Barbier. The scale of Khoisan attacks on farms in the northern frontier regions was growing rapidly. It was particularly irritating that these attacks had been provoked by the same people who were now riding with Barbier, but the Council of Policy conceived of a plan to exploit this connection to their advantage. At a meeting on 28 April, the Council decided to placate the colonists by handing back to them the cattle which Counitz had confiscated. This meant, in effect, stripping the Namaqua of their recently returned livestock and disappointing the expectations of the aggrieved servants of the Orange River raiders.[70] By acting in this way, the authorities were acknowledging that they would rather deal with Khoisan aggression than a burgher rebellion. It was also an acknowledgement that unless they took rapid measures to defuse this rebellion, Barbier would go from strength to strength.

Quite naturally these arrangements led to an increase in Khoisan attacks, and the landdrost and *heemraden* of Stellenbosch realised that a commando would have to be raised in their district.[71] But something more was needed. The Council of Policy decided to accept the offer of the ex-burgher councillor Johannes Kruijwagen to lead a commando against the marauders. No doubt it was the scope, subtlety and economy of Kruijwagen's proposals that made them so attractive. He proposed that those people who had been guilty of bartering cattle from the Namaqua, as well as those who were, or had been, in any way involved with Estienne Barbier, should be given a free pardon on the condition that they joined his commando. By adopting Kruijwagen's proposals, the Company had the opportunity to appear to be punishing both the European and Khoisan malefactors. In reality all pretence of providing justice for the Khoisan was dropped and the expedient of using the initial instigators of the unrest to crush the uprising was an extremely cynical measure.[72]

Kruijwagen's commando set out on 10 May. It consisted of 36 men, at least ten of whom were desirous of receiving a pardon for their past misdeeds. The commando was not entirely successful – though its fortunes need not concern us here.[73] What is of greater relevance for our purposes is that in forming the commando, the government had separated Barbier from his followers. The farmers of the frontier, sympathetic though they were to Barbier and his aims, were gradually beginning to realise that the threat they faced from the Khoisan was greater than the threat of the Company. Even though the colonists had stirred up a hornet's nest, the Company had now demonstrated its willingness to support their claims rather than those of the Khoisan. It is possible to see this change in attitude as being one of the achievements of the Barbier rebellion. Barbier's supporters had, to some extent, got what they wanted. Their most pressing need was now to crush Khoisan opposition and reach an agreement with the Company. Unfortunately for Barbier, this meant the end of his dreams of an armed uprising. His followers, by joining Kruijwagen's commando, accepted the government's authority. Barbier had, once again, to substitute the pen for the sword. There was, however, a reason for optimism, for on 14 April, Swellengrebel had been appointed as Governor in Van den Henghel's place. Barbier had reason to believe that the new Governor would be far more sympathetic to his exposure of official corruption, and redoubled his efforts at letter writing.[74]

Not surprisingly, one of the new targets of Barbier's displeasure was Johannes Kruijwagen. This was not simply because Barbier wished to vent his spleen against the man who had taken away his armed followers. In fact, Barbier was showing commendable consistency in attacking one of the most powerful agrarian capitalists of the northwestern Cape frontier zone. Though Barbier was to wonder, sarcastically, how such a comic figure as Kruijwagen ever came to volunteer or be appointed as leader of a commando, Kruijwagen had the largest vested interests in restoring peace to the frontier. He was, without doubt, one of the wealthiest and most influential men in the colony. As one of the holders of the Company meat contract he had farms along the west coast and in the Gouritz River area of the southern Cape. By 1743 it is estimated that Kruijwagen was farming approximately 39,000 morgen of land in the vicinity of St Helena Bay.[75] This did not make him popular with less fortunate colonists but it did give him the authority, according to Barbier, of a second Governor. He had tremendous influence over the government by virtue of his control over the meat supply. He used this influence to determine the allocation of farms as well as the price to be set on land, livestock and the freedom of *knechts*. Nothing was achieved in the area without Kruijwagen saying 'Jaa, jaa' (Barbier portrays him as a clown) and receiving payment for his approval. A man who had more farms than twelve ordinary colonists together was, in Barbier's eyes, breaking the orders of the Heren XVII. These gentlemen had decreed, on 30 October 1706, that no single colonist should be granted land in an amount disproportionate to his fellows. Kruijwagen was therefore an enemy of the people whose sin was compounded by his making it impossible for others to sell their meat to the Company, for he, Kruijwagen, could supply all its needs.[76]

Quite obviously Barbier was reporting the grumblings of the poorer farmers and was, in this respect, continuing to champion their rights. He also busied himself by collecting letters of grievance from other colonists which he planned to forward to the Governor.[77] This helps to explain why the loss of his armed followers did not mean the end of his freedom. When Kruijwagen's commando returned at the end of May, Barbier's excomrades did not turn him in. A government edict of 2 June promised to pardon all Company deserters who returned within three months of the announcement but Barbier either did not learn of this or did not trust it.[78] At any rate, it is highly unlikely that the terms extended to include him, for he was not just a deserter but an outlaw as well.

The failure of Kruijwagen's commando had necessitated the organisation of a second one. The Council of Policy decided that this time the residents of Stellenbosch and Drakenstein should join the commando – as well as all those residents of the Cape district who had farms in the northwest.[79] The authorities had not, however, bargained on the less than enthusiastic support of the colonists, and the first attempts to implement these plans were a dismal failure. They no doubt believed that since the most rebellious of their subjects had already bowed to Company authority by fighting in Kruijwagen's commando, the meeker majority would follow suit. However, the two officers who had been chosen to round up men and supplies for the commando, Captain Theunis Boota and Lieutenant Johannes Louw, were obliged to report to their superiors on 23 June that they had had to return without being able to fulfil their mission. On reaching Vier en Twintig Rivieren, where they had expected to find men and supplies, they discovered that certain of the people from the Roode Zand were completely unwilling to support the commando or furnish it with supplies.[80] Once more the government's authority was being challenged by the colonists of the northern frontier, and the government, indeed the Governor himself, viewed the matter in a most serious light, ordering the landdrost, officers and the two *veldcorporaals* of the Roode Zand area, Jacobus Theron and Jan Coetsee, to report to him in person. These individuals were very roughly questioned by the Governor and Council of Policy. The *veldcorporaals* pleaded that the heavy rains, swollen rivers, lack of grazing and cold weather were all discouraging factors. In addition, it was the time for ploughing and sowing, and many farmers were reluctant to leave on a commando at that time. The *veldcorporaal* for the district beyond the Roode Zands Kloof, Jacobus Theron, explained that the men he had ordered out on commando had replied 'that they were quite willing to obey if those who had instigated the said Hottentots would also go without however mentioning names'.[81]

The government was far from pleased by this intelligence and reprimanded its appointed functionaries very severely for their lack of zeal. The Governor wanted the names of anyone who refused to co-operate but there was little alternative to postponing the proposed commando until September. In the meantime preparations were to be so thorough that Company control over the frontier would be assured. It was not forgotten that Barbier was still 'vagabondising' in the district and the landdrost was instructed to bring him in, dead or alive.[82] Though the opposition of the colonists to the proposed commando had not been inspired by Barbier – indeed, Barbier later offered to place his military skills at the disposal of an anti-Khoisan force[83] – it does suggest that his rebellion had had the effect of encouraging opposition to the government throughout the frontier district.

As preparations for the commando began, landdrost Lourensz received a report on 18 July that Barbier had been seen in the Roode Zand, and he lost no time in sending off his deputy, Counitz, to capture the outlaw. The unfortunate Counitz, though accompanied by two *veldwagters*, could not have relished the job, especially since he was the most unpopular man in the district. He reported back to Lourensz that one of the *veldwagters*, or assistants, had run away with his arms and provisions. The *veldwagter*, when traced, explained that he had merely been detained by going back to search for these items, which had fallen unobserved from his horse. Lourensz reported to Governor Swellengrebel that he suspected fear was the real reason for his substitute's return. As luck would have it, various complaints about Counitz reached the Governor at the same time. (Ironically many of these complaints had been penned with Barbier's help.) The Governor's response was to dismiss Counitz from his post and Barbier survived. Lourensz, meanwhile, asked for a new substitute.[84]

On 31 July Barbier circulated a second public letter to 'all the Afrikaner brothers'. There was more than a hint of desperation in this letter, for Barbier promised all who had had cattle stolen by the Khoisan, or who had been driven from their farms in the fighting, that he would repay them. He also assured his readers that he spoke in the name of the Heren XVII and the States General of the Netherlands. It is not known whether this letter attracted much public support but at least nobody betrayed him.[85]

On 20 August landdrost Lourensz reported to the Governor that he had sent his new substitute, Witstock, to the Roode Zand to investigate reports that Barbier had been seen in the homes of the widow of Joost Bevernagie and Arnoldus Basson. When Witstock went *incognito* to Basson's house, he could not find him there though he learnt afterwards that Barbier had been hiding under the bed at the time. His informant was the son of the widow Burgert at whose house Barbier had also stayed. Here he had struck the *knecht* of the widow Gobregts over the head for reasons which remain obscure. The *knecht*, Brand, said that Barbier had hit him 'because the widow Bevernagie had to pay a fine on his behalf and that the son of Burgert had sworn a false oath to this end, that he [Brand?] would wed the widow and wanted the fine again; he [Barbier] presented one of the pistols which he had to Brand and said "See here! Shoot me dead because I have deserved death" but seeing how Barbier was holding the muzzle against his body he did not dare hazard this.'[86]

Barbier was clearly beginning to despair, whilst a life filled with so many widows was obviously not without complications. Witstock had left instructions for the locals to hand him over to justice and set a Khoi spy to find out about his movements.[87]

On 9 September Barbier was arrested in the Roode Zand. According to him he was on his way to the Cape, on the wagon of Steven Fouché, to give himself up. According to Mentzel he was betrayed and set upon a horse with his feet tied beneath its belly. He reached Cape Town, via Stellenbosch, on 11 September, and the Governor ordered him to be placed in the 'Donker Gat'. Mentzel describes that 'Up till this time Barbier had been of good courage. He had laughed and jested over his captivity and had given it clearly to be understood that he had a letter of safe-conduct, on the production of which he would speedily be released from arrest, while Herr Allemann would be punished in his stead. He was taken off the horse by the Patrol-guard and went into the Castle on foot; when he had passed through the gate and come to the sergeant's guard-house he made as if to enter it, imagining that it would be his right as a sergeant to spend there his period of detention. He was ordered, however, to go on and was taken to the Donckle Gatt; when he realised that it in very truth was his destination he suddenly lost all his courage, became very cast down and began to weep.'[88]

This time Barbier was kept in the 'Donker Gat' for nine weeks. It was six weeks before he was even charged with anything, for, as Mentzel explains, this was the custom, producing an 'excellent effect' in the prisoner, who would then confess everything in order to gain a speedy death.[89] On 22 October Barbier's case began. The various documents which he had addressed to both the populace and the government were circulated for the consideration of the Council of Policy. Barbier had already been interrogated on 2 October by his old enemy, Van den Henghel, who was once again filling the office of fiscal.[90] A confession was hardly necessary. The Council had quite enough evidence to condemn Barbier and he did not deny any of the actions he had committed or retract any of the words he had said. All he could do was ask that his case be heard in Holland and that the Council show him mercy.[91]

The answer came on 12 November when sentence was passed. Barbier was found guilty of seven grave charges, most of which, since they were aimed at upsetting the political and civil order, were considered to be worthy of punishment by death. The incitement of armed rebellion amongst the people against their 'lawful authorities' was the key issue. Barbier had encouraged others to challenge the state's authority in the name of the States General. In the eyes of his judges, Barbier's crimes were enormous.[92]

He was sentenced to be bound on a cross and to have his right hand, then his head, chopped off. His body was to be quartered. His head and hand were to be raised on a stake and placed at the Roode Zands Kloof. The four quarters of his body were to be hung in four different places next to the busiest roads of the colony. In choosing to implement this atrocious execution the state was simply being true to its nature. As Michel Foucault has explained: 'The public execution is to be understood not only as a judicial, but also as a political ritual. It belongs, even in minor cases, to the ceremonies by which power is manifested.'[93]

The sentence was carried out on 14 November 1739. It was a Saturday and the crowd around the scaffold was so dense that Mentzel, who was present, could not get close enough to hear De Grandpreez reading the sentence. The words 'lands verrader' (traitor) occurred frequently in the indictment. After a short prayer Barbier was stripped, bound and put to death in the prescribed manner. His entrails were buried under the scaffold and the parts of his body distributed for public display along the high roads. 'Such was the melancholy end of a turbulent fellow,' says Mentzel.[94] But there was some indication that there was at least one person in the country who held Barbier in some esteem. The *knecht* of the pontoon holder on the Berg River reported to Lourensz that somebody at the crossing place had burnt down the pole on which one of Barbier's quarters was affixed. The landdrost, who had previously requested a gallows for Stellenbosch so that he could suspend slave suicides upside down, went personally to re-erect the pole.[95] The state was determined to implant the 'spectacle of the scaffold' in the countryside as well as in the town.[96] Arnoldus Basson, who had ridden with Barbier and sheltered him at his home, was banished to the Netherlands. He died at sea while trying to return to the Cape under an assumed name in 1742.[97]

From this account it may be seen that Barbier's rebellion meets the requirements of Hobsbawm in so far as social banditry is concerned. In the first place there is the character of Barbier: the lone wolf on the margins of society; the fugitive from the state who is protected by the people; the friend of widows and the poor who champions the oppressed whilst defying the oppressors. In the second place his rebellion conforms to Hobsbawm's idea of social banditry as a primitive form of social protest. It was, demonstrably, 'a cry for vengeance on the rich and the oppressors, a vague dream of some curb upon them'. Barbier went to some pains to demonstrate that the world he desired was one in which the traditional laws of the ultimate authorities (in this case the VOC and the States-General of the Netherlands) were respected. The rebellion was also, clearly, a reaction against the world of capitalism, in this case the powerful agrarian capitalism of the Cape gentry and their corrupt friends among the Company officials. Though the poor farmers who joined or protected Barbier were not 'traditional or pre-capitalist peasants', they did not have to be. As O'Malley has explained, the 'unified conflict consciousness' which they displayed in a terrain permeated by chronic class struggle is a more useful concept to employ than that of the 'traditional peasantry'.

Barbier's rebellion also satisfies Austen's stipulations about preconditions for social banditry. The state was very much present in both the town and countryside of the western Cape in the 1730s. It was determined to structure the social, political and economic life of the colonists to the best of its ability, for its hegemony was not to be flouted. It declared Barbier an outlaw and pursued him to the end. Significantly Barbier did not choose to slip beyond the colonial frontier altogether – like other deserters or escaped slaves – but stayed within the fringes of colonial society. It was no easy matter to abandon the protection of sympathetic supporters and exchange it for the arid inhospitability of the African interior. There was, in any case, a major war being fought between the Khoisan and the colonists along the northern frontier. (Besides, Barbier was not so much interested in running away as he was in justice and revenge.) Though the African colonial frontier and the 'primary resistance' of the Khoisan provided much of the background to the rebellion, they were not the same thing. Even though there was a strong connection between Barbier's followers and the origins of the frontier war of 1739, it is quite obvious that the Barbier rebellion was not a case of 'primary resistance'. It arose within colonial society and was conducted within colonial society.

To some extent the seriousness of the frontier war of 1739 contributed to the Company's success in containing Barbier's revolt. By appearing to take the colonists' side against the Khoisan, the authorities were able to detach Barbier's chief supporters from him.[98] With their farms being burnt and their cattle being stolen by Khoisan attackers, the majority of the frontier farmers had not time to join an anti-government revolt.

Ironically it was the government's very success in crushing Khoisan resistance in the war of 1739 – which it did in a series of commandos in August, September, October and November – that was to weaken its hold over the colonists in the long term. The defeat of the Khoisan in this region allowed the colonists to expand into the interior and satisfy their hunger for land, Khoi labour and livestock.[99] The result was decreasing state control, for as Austen says in another context, the life of the trekboers represented an institutionalised rebellion.[100]

Barbier remains something of an enigma. His rebellion was certainly typified by 'primitive goals' and archaic impulses. It was also 'inefficient in every way' and failed to make the transition to effective guerrilla warfare. However, one cannot but be impressed by the energy and consistency of Barbier's demands for justice. Against all odds, evidence and experience, he continued to believe that law and justice were synonymous. He also displayed a remarkable faith in the power of the written word, believing that both the people and the government would respond to his letters. There can have been few more literate sergeants in the eighteenth century,[101] and when one considers that Dutch was not his mother tongue, his achievements are even more remarkable. Our lasting impression of Barbier is of an unquenchable, intemperate sense of moral outrage. This he succeeded in conveying to both his supporters and adversaries, but his impact on the folk memory of South Africans has been surprisingly slight.[102]

In explaining this lack of mythic presence it is important to point out that Barbier's struggle for justice was limited to one particular section of Cape society alone and that it was, at the same time, a plea for injustice against the Khoisan. By the end of the eighteenth century it was the Khoisan who had been proletarianised whilst the position of the white farmers had improved at their expense. After 1740, the trekboers had little cause to complain that the authorities were not supporting their interests, for the influence of the state, where it was felt at all, was usually placed behind the commandos in their attempts to overcome Khoisan resistance.[103] In these circumstances, there was no need to appeal to the memory of Estienne Barbier. It was only when the frontier began to close, towards the end of the century, that state control began to prove irksome again and the burgher rebellions of this period, without invoking Barbier's name, echo some of the themes of his rebellion.[104] Whilst the Great Trek itself of the nineteenth century (which was in many ways a culmination of the burgher rebellions) may be interpreted as a flight from state control, it was also an attempt to create a new state which would be in greater sympathy with the aspirations of Afrikaners. But it was during this long and (ultimately) successful struggle by Afrikaner nationalists to capture state authority that the ambiguous contribution of Estienne Barbier – both anti-state and proto-nationalist – was forgotten.

4

The Beast of the Bokkeveld

The banishing of Carel Buijtendag, 1770–1780

On 20 January 1779, Carel Hendrik Buijtendag, burgher of Cape Town, was seized in his own home by the 'geweldiger', or sergeant, Hendrik Matthysen, and six 'caffers'.[1] Forcibly removed from the bosom of his family he was placed on board the VOC ship *Honkoop* bound for Batavia and, without trial, informed that he was to be banished from the Cape colony for life. On the shore, according to Buijtendag's supporters, his wife and children made a pitiful sight as one of his daughters cried out: 'Father, I will never leave you for as long as there is a drop of blood in me.'[2] But he was leaving her. What offence had Buijtendag committed?

On 5 or 6 January Buijtendag's wife, Maria Johanna, had approached the assistant fiscal, Timmer, and asked to be separated from her husband. Her request was taken to the Council of Policy and that body resolved, on 20 January, to banish Buijtendag. The independent fiscal, W.C. Boers, saw to it that the sentence was carried out that same day.[3]

It was at this stage that Buijtendag came to the attention of the group of Cape burghers that have been called the 'Kaapse Patriotte'.[4] These burghers saw in the treatment meted out to Buijtendag an example of the arbitrary and despotic character of the VOC government and, in particular, of the independent fiscal, Boers. Using Buijtendag as a potent symbol of the oppression which they believed they suffered under VOC rule, the 'Patriotte' petitioned the highest authorities in the Netherlands. So effective was their agitation that, within the year, Buijtendag was allowed to return to the Cape. He did not, however, survive the return voyage and died on board the *Stavenisse* on 13 November 1779,[5] thereby providing the 'Patriotte' with a martyr.

It is ironic that Carel Hendrik Buijtendag should have ended his days as the victim of oppression. This irony will be better appreciated in the light of his earlier life and, in particular, those events which led to his being in Cape Town in the first place. The dramatic circumstances of Buijtendag's banishment from the Cape colony have led historians to gloss over those of an earlier banishment – from the Koue Bokkeveld in 1776.[6] It was in that year that the landdrost of Stellenbosch sentenced him to be banished from the Cape as a 'pernicious subject' with instructions that he was never to be allowed to return to the magistracy of Stellenbosch, 'much less to be allowed to settle in the outlying districts'.[7] By this stage, the landdrost had 'five extraordinary secretarial statements' and 'nine original letters with an annexure attached'[8] complaining about Buijtendag. Clearly it was these offences and not so much Buijtendag's domestic squabbles that had moved the government to act so harshly, and it is with Buijtendag's activities in the 'outlying districts' rather than in Cape Town that this chapter is concerned.

These activities not only illuminate certain features of life in the northern Cape frontier zone in the eighteenth century, they also provide an excellent example of the processes at work on a 'closing frontier'. According to Hermann Giliomee, a closing frontier is a 'frontier zone' in a particular phase of development.[9] It is a frontier zone inasmuch as there is a process of colonisation or settlement taking place in a situation marked by weak political authority, and it is a closing frontier in that the process of colonisation or settlement is relatively far advanced. In contrast to an open frontier zone, where there is a rough balance of power between two or more societies competing for land or resources, a closing frontier zone is one in which the balance of power has tipped in favour of one of the societies rather than another. Processes of closure, particularly so far as the South African frontier is concerned, occur in different aspects; for instance economic closure, characterised by growing scarcity of land and resources, a shift from subsistence to commercial farming, and increasing control of the means of production by a specific class; growing social stratification as discrete 'races' or ethnic groups merged into a plural society with a given set of caste or class relationships; and political closure, in the imposition of a single source of authority.[10]

Though all the above processes of closure were at work in the Koue Bokkeveld and its environs during the period under consideration, it is the last of these processes, political closure, which is of particular relevance in the story of Buijtendag. When the authority of the colonial government was weak, as it was during the entire eighteenth century throughout the northern Cape, there was considerable scope for a fair degree of anarchy. Before the frontier could begin to close, it was up to the colonists to provide necessary force to conquer the land and subjugate its inhabitants. The institution which evolved to meet these requirements was the commando – 'the major institution of the open frontier zone'[11] – over which the colonial government exercised a far from perfect control. Once the commando had accomplished its task, the question still remained as to how to control or regulate relations between the colonists and the subjugated Khoisan,[12] between Boer and Boer, and between the colonists and the colonial government. In each of these cases, the details of Buijtendag's life provide edifying examples of the struggle between anarchy and authority. Before proceeding to study these details, however, it will be necessary to say something about the nature and extent of colonial penetration in the northern Cape prior to Buijtendag's arrival on the scene.

The first European settlers – as opposed to hunters, traders, raiders and explorers – had entered the Bokkeveld in about 1728,[13] and had little difficulty in acquiring the land, herds, flocks and labour of the Khoisan. The last major resistance to this process of colonisation in the area had been crushed between 1739 and 1740, and it is for this reason, as well as the fact that 1739 was the year of Buijtendag's birth, that this date marks the beginning of the period under discussion. Long before this date, though, the structure of the Khoisan societies in the area had been undermined by the combined effects of unequal trade exchanges, robbery and disease, which were concomitant with proximity to the colony.[14] In 1705 the landdrost of Stellenbosch, Johannes Starrenburg, led a Company-sponsored expedition as far as the present site of Klawer, north of the Olifants River, for the purpose of obtaining trek oxen. He noted with sorrow that in the twelve-day journey between the Berg River and Klawer 'I had found two kraals only, and these (although they included 12 Captains) so poorly provided with cattle. By this I have realised with regret how the whole country has been spoilt by the recent freedom of bartering, and the atrocities committed by the vagabonds,[15] since when the cattle of one kraal is carried off by the Dutch, they in turn go to rob others, and these again go to rob their neighbours, running off with the spoil into the mountains and feasting there until it is finished and then again seeking for more, and so from men who sustained themselves quietly by cattle-breeding, living in peace and contentment divided under their chiefs and kraals, they have nearly all become Bushmen, hunters and brigands, dispersed everywhere between and in the mountains.'[16]

This observation is interesting because it notes both the relative depopulation of the area and the process by which Khoi, or Hottentots, were apparently becoming like San, or Bushmen.[17] It is also interesting that the best-stocked Khoi kraals were those near present-day Tulbagh where their relative proximity to the colony protected them, to some extent, from the violent robberies to which those Khoi beyond the protective presence of the VOC government were subject. This well-being did not, however, survive the 1713 smallpox epidemic.[18]

Starrenburg did not venture into or beyond the mountains to the east of the Olifants River; had he done so, he is unlikely to have found the area densely populated. The river valleys were much better suited for pastoralists. In addition the Koue Bokkeveld area fell in a sort of no-man's-land between the Cochoqua, Chariguriqua, Chainouqua and Namaqua Khoi.[19] Because of the transhumant lifestyle of the Khoi pastoralists there were bound to be zones of disputed territory, and when such a zone coincided with a mountainous region it is safe to assume that San would have been a major presence. Of the Khoi, the Namaqua had been the strongest group and were encountered by colonists south of the Olifants River in 1661.[20] They seldom ventured south of the Kamiesberg after this date, however, and withdrew rapidly northwards when it became apparent to them what close contact with the colony entailed. The arid wilderness of the Knersvlakte (Knegsvlakte) between them and the colonists gave them better protection than the rest of the Khoi. So rapid was the disintegration of those Khoi groups closer to the Cape that, as early as the 1660s and 1670s, colonists who were desirous of trading or raiding Khoi cattle were being forced to journey to the 'cattle-rich' Namaqua. The result was an increasing number of both VOC and private (illegal) expeditions to the Namaqua, with a corresponding decline in their livestock holdings. One of these private expeditions, in 1738, was the first recorded visit of Europeans to the Great or Orange River,[21] and it succeeded in sparking off the most serious Khoisan resistance to the colonists thus far, the so-called Bushman War of 1739.[22]

It is not possible to go into the details of the war of 1739 in this chapter,[23] and it will have to suffice to give its results. These were the complete subjugation of the Khoisan who lived in or around the Bokkeveld, Piketberg and Sandveld, and the Olifants and Doorn rivers.

Over a hundred Khoisan were killed (compared to a handful of colonists) and much livestock, not all of it recovered booty, was taken from the survivors. The major fighting took place around the Langevlei, Meerhoff's Kasteel, Oorlogskloof, the Doorn River and the northern Bokkeveld. Doubtless many Khoisan fled, either to Namaqualand or to the Hantam and Roggeveld. Those who remained did so as a cowed and broken people in isolated kraals, their only hope of survival lying in their acceptance of Dutch overlordship (symbolised by the staff of office given by the VOC to the Khoi captains) and their promise to keep the peace.

As the colonists consolidated their hold over the land, its grazing and water resources, the chances of the Khoisan leading an independent existence diminished. Increasingly, and for a variety of reasons, Khoisan began to enter the service of the colonists. Those who had lost their means of subsistence naturally had a compelling reason to become servants but some who had retained livestock decided that they would benefit from the protection that an armed and mounted colonist could offer them against wild animals, thieves and the general insecurity of the frontier zone. In exchange they would tend their master's flocks and herds alongside their own and receive payment for their skills as herders or drovers. Some groups or kraals found it necessary to work for the colonists for only short periods, for example harvest time,[24] but others, as is evident from the testimony of those who worked for Buijtendag, had 'contracts' of a year or more. These 'contracts', being oral, were subject to abuse. In theory, at the end of the stipulated period of work the labourer could withdraw his service, his original stock, his wages (for instance, a heifer per year)[25] and his family. In practice, as the following details of the life of Buijtendag reveal, the options available to the Khoisan were governed by the availability of land, the prospects of employment, the attitude of one's employer and the power of the colonial authorities.

Carel Hendrik Buijtendag was the son of Carel Diedrik Buijtendag and Catherina Valk. His father, formerly of Berlin, served as a VOC soldier before becoming a burgher and, finally, brewer and tap-house owner in Cape Town. He obtained the licence for selling foreign liquors in 1738 and died in 1739.[26] Carel, one of his four children, was christened in the same year, two months after the remarriage of his mother to the burgher Johan Horn.[27] One may deduce, therefore, that his father died before his birth and that his mother, as a brewer's widow, was a highly eligible woman.

The next information available is that he hired the loan farm Vergunst in the Roode Zand in 1754.[28] In 1755 he hired the farm Rietvallei in the same district,[29] and the next year he married Maria Johanna Theron, daughter of a local farmer.[30] He was only 17 years old. The surprising thing is that one so young and with no parental backing should have made such an impressive beginning as a farmer.[31] In his tax returns for 1754 he is listed as owning nothing but a horse,[32] yet in the returns for 1755 he had one slave, 6 horses, 24 cattle and 150 sheep.[33] How he managed to accumulate so much so quickly is not recorded. The Roode Zand was prime farming land, ideal for wheat and on the right side of the mountain ranges to make transportation of produce to Cape Town feasible.

By the 1750s farms in the area must have been difficult to acquire. Even before the war of 1739 the open frontier had moved in a north-easterly direction, over the Cedarberg and Bokkeveld mountains to the Hantam and Roggeveld,[34] implying not only that the aridity of land to the north encouraged northeasterly expansion, but also that there was a shortage of farming land in the Roode Zand, where the first farms had been granted in 1720s.[35]

In 1760 Buijtendag took over Rietfontein, the vacated farm of Andries du Toit jun., in the Bokkeveld mountains on the other side of the Witzenberg – that is, in the Koue Bokkeveld. He did this with a partner, Willem Sterrenberg Pretorius.[36] This partnership was dissolved six years later, by which time Buijtendag was secure enough to renew his loan farms alone.[37] He was now owner of two farms, Rietvalley on one side of the mountains and Rietfontein on the other. This arrangement would have enabled him to move his stock down to the Roode Zand in winter to avoid the colder weather to which the Koue Bokkeveld, as its name suggests, is subject. An additional option also existed for Bokkeveld farmers to graze their stock in the Karoo between the Bokkeveld and the Roggeveld mountains.[38] Though sheep were his major farming interest it appears that Buijtendag specialised in trek oxen. In 1769 it is recorded that he paid 12 four-year-old oxen to the Company post at Klapmuts for three years' rental for the farm Rietfontein,[39] an interesting indication that loan-farm rental could be paid in cash or kine.[40]

In 1770 Buijtendag decided to consolidate his position by 'swapping' his farm Rietvalley in the Roode Zand for Jacobus Pienaar's farm Driefontein in the Koue Bokkeveld. The farms changed hands on the same day.[41] Of the two farms which he now owned in the Koue

Bokkeveld, and which were adjacent to each other,[42] Driefontein was to be his preferred residence between the years 1770 and 1775. Between 1768 and 1774 Buijtendag's tax returns are remarkably consistent, showing virtually no increase in the size of his holdings.[43] Of course he might not have been truthful in making his returns but the statistics contained in the records in no way single him out from other farmers. In terms of the property he possessed he was comfortably average. As a troublemaker, though, he was without equal.

The first complaints that reached the authorities about Buijtendag were those lodged by his neighbours in the Koue Bokkeveld in 1774. Most of these complaints were related to the way in which he treated his Khoi servants but there is good reason to suppose that they would never have reached the authorities had not Buijtendag succeeded in antagonising his neighbours and, in particular, the powerful Van der Merwe family. It is unlikely that mistreatment of Khoi servants would have been sufficient cause to expel Buijtendag from the Bokkeveld as there is ample evidence in the records that other colonists were guilty of similar offences without being punished for them. It was Buijtendag's misfortune, however, to clash with the most powerful man in the Bokkeveld, the *veldwagtmeester* Nicolaas van der Merwe, and with Van der Merwe's father, Izak.[44] By running foul of the *veldwagtmeester*, Buijtendag ensured that the authorities at Stellenbosch, the nearest magistracy, would be unable to ignore his behaviour. It should also be added that Buijtendag's attitude towards authority was so provocative as to present a challenge to even the mildest representative of the law, and Nicolaas van der Merwe was not mild.

Izak van der Merwe was, according to the tax returns of 1762, a wealthy man.[45] Nicolaas, one of three sons, obviously had some special qualities, for in 1774 he was appointed as one of the three *veldkommandants* of the General Commando.[46] As leader of the Bokkevelders in this commando he was at the head of 31 Dutch and 38 Khoi men. During the months of August, September and October 1774, he and his men succeeded in killing 142 Khoisan and capturing 89. Buijtendag, together with 63 other Dutchmen, 'stayed at home'.[47] Most of those captured were women and children, who were subsequently 'placed with the inhabitants'.[48] Before considering the charges brought against Buijtendag, it is worth mentioning that Nicolaas van der Merwe was accused by a fellow burgher of causing innocent blood to be spilt while on commando, that is killing wounded Khoisan women and children.[49]

Though Van der Merwe's actions were considered to have been quite reasonable by the landdrost and officers of Stellenbosch (so reasonable indeed that his accuser, A.G. Schombee, was fined 10 rixdollars for his pains), they do confirm that Buijtendag's antagonist was not a squeamish man. Buijtendag's own behaviour should be seen in the wider context of the violence of the so-called Bushman frontier,[50] for the idea that Khoisan life was fairly cheap must have been widespread at the time.

The trouble between Buijtendag and the Van der Merwes began early in 1774 when some of Buijtendag's Khoi servants ran away from him and sought refuge with other farmers, notably Izak van der Merwe. Buijtendag did not take this lying down. It seems that Izak was reluctant to return a Khoi woman called Janna, her daughter Caetjie and a child called Kleynebooij, to Buijtendag. Receiving no satisfaction from Izak, Buijtendag went to Nicolaas's farm. Nicolaas was away at Stellenbosch at the time, possibly discussing the preparations for the forthcoming General Commando. Quite why Buijtendag entered the house and grabbed the 'ouwe baster' (old Bastard) of the Van der Merwes by the neck is not recorded, but this he did and flung him from the stoep. The unfortunate man, who had been sent to Nicolaas's farm by Izak to help with the ploughing, was beaten up in the presence of Nicolaas's pregnant wife and his *knecht*.[51]

Piecing together the imperfect information contained in the letters received by the landdrost of Stellenbosch, we can say that Buijtendag was able to represent himself as being more sinned against than sinning and obtained a letter from the landdrost which ordered Izak van der Merwe to return Buijtendag's 'volk' immediately. By this stage, October, Nicolaas van der Merwe was away on commando and the man entrusted to carry out these instructions was the provisional *veldcorporaal*, Willem Janse van Rensburg. Van Rensburg went twice to the farm of Izak, the first time in the company of a Schalk van der Merwe and the second time in the company of a Petrus van der Merwe.[52] Izak, however, was unmoved and declared that he would sooner be struck dead than go to Buijtendag. Van Rensburg concluded that some more compelling force would be required to effect the return of Buijtendag's servants and humbly beseeched the landdrost not to expect him, Van Rensburg, to provide it.[53] Caught in the middle of the feud, Van Rensburg was quite powerless to command the Van der Merwes. Buijtendag meanwhile accused Van Rensburg of reluctance in carrying out his orders and threatened to go to Stellenbosch to complain in person. Finally, after two letters from the landdrost, Izak van der Merwe surrendered the Khoi to Buijtendag, denying that he had withheld them by force and explaining that ill health had prevented him from returning them. He told the landdrost that he had merely insisted that if Buijtendag came to his farm, he should be accompanied by some other men 'because you well know that he is a troublemaker'.[54] As for the allegation that the child (presumably Kleynebooij) of one of Buijtendag's Khoi was missing, Van der Merwe explained that the father himself had already taken him away with him.[55]

From the above it might appear that Buijtendag had legitimate grounds for complaint against the Van der Merwes. The question remains as to why his 'volk' had left him in the first place. Once back from leading the Bokkevelders of the General Commando in the Sak River region, Nicolaas van der Merwe and others began collecting evidence and witnesses prepared to testify against Buijtendag. The first of these was the Khoi captain Jan Abrahams.

Abrahams claimed that he had been hired by 'baas' Buijtendag to help him transport goods to the Cape. He had left Buijtendag, though, because the latter was too severe and had beaten him for no reason. Moreover, Buijtendag had taken the staff or copper cane which the Company had given Abrahams as a symbol that he was captain of a kraal, and had reduced it to solder. No action could have better demonstrated Buijtendag's contempt for both the Company and the Khoi.[56]

Abrahams was a good deal more fortunate than some others who entered Buijtendag's service. One such man was Engbert Dijkslag; he had been hired in 1773 to educate Buijtendag's children, who, by this date, numbered six – four daughters and two sons.[57] For his labours Dijkslag was to receive 15 guilders a month.[58] Obviously Buijtendag's views on education differed from those of the schoolteacher, who had only recently left the service of the Company. Dijkslag stuck the job for 14 months before leaving. Twice during this time he had been beaten by his employer, bearing this ill-treatment 'without retaliating and with patience'.[59] According to Dijkslag, Buijtendag had boasted to his half-brother Christiaan Horn that he did what he pleased with his schoolmaster, as with all in his service, hitting them whenever he pleased.[60]

It is interesting to note in passing that in 1771 Buijtendag had four slaves but in 1773 he had none.[61] Whether this meant that he no longer needed slaves as he began employing the Khoi whose testimony follows or whether he sold them because he needed extra money, or whether they died of natural or unnatural causes, is not known, but it is surely significant that the first complaints of his maltreating servants coincided with the departure of his slaves.

Boxing a teacher's ears was as nothing compared with the treatment reserved for Buijtendag's Khoi servants, namely Schalk, Booij and Kiewit. Kiewit had served Buijtendag for three years for the wages of one heifer per year.[62] After three years' work, when Kiewit wished to leave, Buijtendag informed him that, since he had allowed wild animals to eat some of his stock, his wages were forfeit. When Kiewit attempted to remove his own animals from Buijtendag's 'protection', namely twelve cows and three oxen, he was told that they were needed to replace those of Buijtendag's cattle which, he claimed, had been taken by Kiewit's wife and children. These cattle had actually died of 'tongsiekte' or been killed by predators. Furthermore, Kiewit was expected to pay for or buy back his own cattle with additional labour. This cheerless prospect caused Kiewit to leave Buijtendag, his wife managing to join him but being unable to take their two children with her.[63] Before he could escape, Kiewit and a young fellow labourer called Schalk were so severely beaten by Buijtendag that Schalk died.

This occurred when one day in 1774 Buijtendag decided to take his wagon and some oxen to the Cape. Schalk was sent from Driefontein to Rietfontein to round up the oxen. It so happened that Schalk's father, Booij, lived at Rietfontein: this may explain why it was that Schalk took longer to round up the oxen than Buijtendag thought permissible. That evening Buijtendag rode to Rietfontein himself and found Schalk visiting Booij. He tied one end of a thong around Schalk's neck and the other end to his horse and then rode back to Driefontein. On their return Buijtendag spread-eagled Schalk over a block of wood, binding his limbs with thongs, then beating him with a thong until he cried out, 'Ik heb genoeg.'[64] He then released Schalk but bound Kiewit to a tree and ordered Schalk to flog him. Schalk was unable to hit Kiewit hard enough for Buijtendag's taste, so Buijtendag continued the flogging himself with both sjambok and thong. Schalk was then returned to the block and flogged for 'nearly an hour' with the thong (an 'os riem') on the buttocks.[65] After this he was released but only to have the 'riem' tied tightly round his neck whilst Buijtendag punched and kicked him. He began bleeding from his mouth and nose. Finally, he died. Buijtendag then dragged the body to the slave house and then left, presumably to rest.[66]

The next day, at midday, Booij was summoned by Kiewit to help to bury Schalk, his son. The body, swollen and bloody, was buried on the orders of Buijtendag. Booij too had worked for Buijtendag and received much the same sort of treatment as Kiewit. After three years of service for the wages of a heifer a year, he tried to claim his dues and was told that he would first have to work to replace those of Buijtendag's animals which had been eaten by predators. Both Booij and Kiewit had complained twice to the landdrost about this and had been provided with letters to deliver to their master commanding him to give them their cattle. Buijtendag's only reaction had been to chase them away; when Booij proved to be persistent with his claims, Buijtendag tried to catch and bind him. Booij fled, leaving his wife and three children behind in Buijtendag's power.[67]

By 6 January 1775 both Booij and Kiewit had entered the service of Jacobus Joosten and had probably managed to retrieve most of their livestock, if not all of their family. One can only guess how many instructions Buijtendag ignored before satisfying both his ex-labourers and the authorities. No copies of the letters sent by the landdrost to Buijtendag survive. What is certain is that when Booij and Kiewit asked Nicolaas van der Merwe to fetch a cow, their children and Booij's wife, Buijtendag proved to be as stubborn as ever. Van der Merwe sent Jan Rasmus and Jan Joosten to Buijtendag to bring back the family members and the cow but they returned empty-handed with the message that in future the two of them need not bother to come to his house with messages from Nicolaas van der Merwe.[68]

Van der Merwe, exasperated by Buijtendag's contempt of his authority, wrote a strong letter to landdrost Bergh on 23 January complaining that all those of good name and standing in the Bokkeveld were anxious that Buijtendag be disciplined or reprimanded as soon as possible.[69] In accordance with instructions received from Bergh, Van der Merwe went to Buijtendag's farm a week later with three men and received the following reply from Buijtendag: 'That if you will repair the damage that the Hottentots did to him he will be obedient to the contents of your letter and if you've said your say, get off my property quickly.'[70]

By this time Driefontein and Rietfontein no longer belonged to Buijtendag as he had sold them to Johannes Claassen in December 1774.[71] Quite why Buijtendag decided to sell his farms, along with some other articles and livestock, is unknown. One can only suppose that the enmity of the Van der Merwes and the difficulty he must have been experiencing in acquiring labour had something to do with his decision to leave the Bokkeveld. At any rate Buijtendag sold out for the price of

10,000 guilders, a very good price for the time.[72] Claassen was not able to raise all this money at once, and an agreement was reached that he should complete payment by May 1776 as well as paying interest on the outstanding amount. Claassen took up residence at Driefontein on 5 January 1775 but Buijtendag requested that since he had not yet acquired a permanent dwelling in Cape Town, he and his family be allowed to stay at Driefontein for a while. Since Claassen still owed Buijtendag 100 rixdollars he was not in a strong position to deny Buijtendag, who liked getting his own way.[73]

During 1775 the landdrost was busy hearing and recording the statements of those who had been injured by Buijtendag. There do not seem to have been any new charges against him other than a fairly general complaint from yet another Van der Merwe, Schalk, who, when asked to testify against Buijtendag, painted his character in the blackest terms, saying that he thought it lamentable that someone should choose to quarrel with twenty of his neighbours rather than live in peace with ten of them.[74] It is probable that Buijtendag went to Stellenbosch in person to answer the charges against himself but what passed between him and the landdrost is not recorded.[75] In October Nicolaas van der Merwe was still reporting that Buijtendag was withholding Khoi children from their parents.[76]

In February 1776 Claassen planned a trip to the Cape and was warned by Buijtendag that unless he raised 1600 guilders to pay him, he, Buijtendag, would take back everything he had sold to him. Claassen said that he would try to raise a loan but that he was hampered by Buijtendag's refusal to allow him to take anything – cattle, horses, goods – away from the farm. Claassen had planned to take two wagon loads of wheat to the Cape but could now only take one load of five muids.[77] On the way to the Cape he borrowed a further six muids of wheat from Jan Theron of Roode Zand; this was not, however, sufficient. On his return to Driefontein Buijtendag greeted him with 'Well, Hannes Malabar, have you brought back money for me?'[78] Claassen could only reply that he had not brought any money and that Buijtendag should wait until the date of repayment before raising the subject.[79]

This was enough for Buijtendag to fly into a rage, which he vented, one might almost say characteristically, on the Khoi labourers. He seized a bamboo cane and began thrashing two of Claassen's servants. When Claassen, who was standing at the front door, asked him what he was doing with his 'volk', Buijtendag held up the cane for his contemplation and answered: 'Pas op! Jouw swarten neger jij sulx aanstands ook nat krijgent' (Look out, you black nigger, or you'll get it too).[80] He then stormed into the house and began chasing Claassen's Khoi servants outside, shouting that he didn't want any of them in the house and that they should 'Gaat in de Boschjis want jy konkeld maar met malkanderen' (Go into the bush because you are plotting together).[81] Buijtendag's wife, Maria Johanna, then threw the servants' belongings out of the kitchen and forbade them the use of the iron cooking pots which had been hers presumably before the sale. Buijtendag then retired to his room whilst Claassen wrote a letter which he gave to his servant Jantji to deliver to Willem Pretorius. What the contents of the letter were Claassen did not divulge, but Buijtendag believed that they concerned him, so he galloped after Jantji, caught him, took the letter from him and read it. He then returned, stick in hand, and proceeded to swear at Claassen and his wife, once more calling Claassen a 'Swart neger'. Buijtendag then went in search of the Khoi servants who had prudently fled the farm and were only to return three days later when Buijtendag was away. To add to Claassen's discomfort, Buijtendag took the key to the cellar and storeroom.[82]

This incident does more than simply illustrate the point that Buijtendag was an awkward house guest. It raises a lot of questions about race attitudes and racial prejudice on the frontier. Buijtendag's racist insults are perhaps less surprising than the fact that Claassen, the grandson of a Malabar slave, should have been able to farm in the Bokkeveld at all.[83] Neither Buijtendag nor Claassen was a typical frontier farmer and it may be asked whether they are representative of the extremes of racial prejudice and racial tolerance rather than the normal racial attitudes on the frontier. This may well be the case but the fact remains that, whatever processes or developments two such different men represented, they existed side by side in an obscure mountain valley in the Koue Bokkeveld.

The strain of this relationship told as much on Buijtendag as on Claassen, and Buijtendag decided to visit some like-minded neighbours in the vicinity. In January or February 1776 he and his family went to visit Daniel Pinard, or Pienaar, of the Koue Bokkeveld.[84] It is not clear from the reports whether this visit occurred before or after his violent outburst against Claassen but the latter is more probable.[85] At any rate, one Sunday whilst Buijtendag was staying at Daniel Pienaar's, they received a visit from Christiaan Horn, Buijtendag's half-brother.[86] A short while later the burghers Johannes Erasmus, Barend Forster and Pieter

Willems van Heerde arrived. After lunch Forster and Van Heerde left, but Horn and Erasmus were persuaded to stay. That evening during supper Pienaar and Horn began arguing over a span of tobacco that Pienaar alleged was owed to him by Horn. Horn denied this and the two began trading insults. ('Sward neger ape' and 'Hottentot koggelaar' featured in the catalogue.) Finally, after considerable provocation from Horn, Pienaar picked up a 'Noormans bankji'[87] and dealt him a mighty blow on the head and arm, knocking him, bleeding and senseless, to the ground. Whilst Pienaar's wife restrained her husband from further violence, Maria Buijtendag and her children carried Horn to a bed.

That night Buijtendag and Erasmus slept outside. In the morning Horn was found to be speechless with his bedclothes bloody. Seven days later Horn was still too badly injured to move and was transported in Buijtendag's wagon to Claassen at Driefontein. There his speech recovered sufficiently to enable him to complain of severe pain in his head. His arm appeared to be broken. He lay a further fourteen days in this condition, the last two of them speechless, 'pointing from time to time to his head above his right eye and to his chest. Also he could hardly see anything out of that eye.'[88] He died in the evening.

Now that he had lost his half-brother and probably the friendship of Pienaar, the Bokkeveld was fast becoming devoid of attractions for Buijtendag. He was still in the area on 26 March 1776, for on that date, according to Aletta Claassen, Claassen's wife, he entered the house when Johannes was absent and grabbed a small Khoi boy called Danser who had been sitting on the floor near to her. He began beating Danser with a sjambok even though Aletta rescued him three times from Buijtendag's grasp. Buijtendag then hit Danser's father Claas, and hurled a piece of wood at another boy, Jantji.[89]

Time was running out for Buijtendag, for the evidence against him was accumulating in Stellenbosch. On 6 May 1776, the landdrost banished him from the district.[90] On 13 June Buijtendag had to make a statement concerning the death of Horn, to which he had been a witness, and this was probably the last time he saw Stellenbosch. It appears that he appealed to the Governor against his original sentence, a sentence which banished him not only from the outlying districts but also from the Cape colony as a whole, and received permission to live in Cape Town with his wife and children on condition that he remained there and behaved decently.[91]

It was thus nearly two years after the authorities received the first complaints about Buijtendag that he was punished, albeit fairly mildly, for his brutalities. This long delay in the process of justice occurred despite the fact that the local government representative, the *veldwagtmeester* Nicolaas van der Merwe, had a personal interest in the affair. A *veldwagtmeester* in a frontier zone was almost by definition a proven commando leader and one whose authority was soundly based on local considerations such as wealth or an extensive family network. Despite the fact that Van der Merwe had all the attributes needed to enforce his commands, Buijtendag was still able to defy him for two years. One is left with the impression that had Buijtendag antagonised a lesser man he would never have been punished.

Governmental authority was only as real as the power of its local representative, and unless the personal interests of that man were involved there was little chance of intervention. On occasions, in different areas of the frontier, the *veldwagtmeester* himself might step outside the law and the people in his district would be powerless to restrain him.[92] What emerges from the Buijtendag affair is that there was a great deal of correspondence and information moving, fairly rapidly, between Stellenbosch and the Koue Bokkeveld. Letters were not enough to intimidate Buijtendag, though; he must have felt secure enough in his high sheltered valley to ignore them. The Bokkeveld was close enough to Stellenbosch for his Khoi servants to journey there, twice, in search of justice. It is significant that they both considered it worth their while to make such a trip and that their complaints were not sufficient in themselves to win them justice. Their initial complaints about Buijtendag were not recorded and one may assume that many such complaints of servants against their masters were not considered serious enough to record or act upon.

It would also seem that there was a shortage of labour in the Bokkeveld. This shortage is attested to by the desire for captured Khoisan women and children after a commando and the fact that Buijtendag's servants found employment with other farms quite readily. On the other hand, the acquisition and exchange of loan farms in the area suggest that there was a shortage of land, which would have compelled the Khoi to work for farmers if they wished to maintain flocks or herds of their own.

The unfortunate experiences of Claassen draw attention to the difficulty of commercial farming in the area. Claassen no doubt hoped to raise the money he owed to Buijtendag by selling produce and livestock at the Cape. Quite apart from the obstacles placed in his way by Buijtendag, this does not appear to have been a realistic expectation.

Claassen does not seem to have derived any benefit from Buijtendag's banishment and had to sell out to repay his debt. In April 1777 both Driefontein and Rietfontein had a new owner, Frans Joosten, and Claassen, who in the 1777 tax returns had 1000 sheep, 60 cattle and 20 horses, had nothing by 1778.[93]

Buijtendag is perhaps not the ideal type from which one may generalise about the violent or racist nature of inter-group relations on the frontier, for he is without doubt an extreme case.[94] There are reports of greater cruelty and violence concerning the treatment of servants by other frontier Boers,[95] but such reports would have to be balanced by the largely unrecorded details of everyday life – of which we catch but a glimpse in Claassen's kitchen before Buijtendag expels the Khoi from it – when master and servant lived on better terms with each other. The fate of Horn is a reminder that violent death was not the monopoly of the Khoisan and racism (though it influenced insults) not the only spur to rage.

In conclusion it remains to follow Buijtendag's career after his expulsion from the Bokkeveld. In February 1777 he bought a house and plot in Table Valley from a man called Spengelaar for 7400 guilders,[96] some of which money must have come from Claassen. After this purchase Buijtendag had enough money left to invest some capital in a partnership with a certain Jan Michiel Hatting, who was a stock farmer over the Bruintjes Hoogte on the eastern frontier.[97] This was not the wisest time to invest money in stock farming in Agter Bruintjes Hoogte but Buijtendag was not to live long enough to discover this fact. Instead it was his widow who had to listen to Hatting's account of devastating losses at the hands of the 'Bushmen' and 'Kaffers'.[98] The transition from Bokkeveld farmer to Cape Town burgher cannot have been an easy one for Buijtendag and he must have taken out some of his frustrations on his wife and children. So it was that in January 1779 Maria Johanna went to lodge her fateful request to be separated from her husband and brought about the final banishing of Carel Buijtendag.

5

Droster Gangs of the Bokkeveld and Roggeveld

1770–1800

BY THE second half of the eighteenth century, as colonial power advanced further into the Cape interior, the ranks of fugitive *droster* gangs became augmented by new recruits, Khoi and 'Bastaard-Hottentot' labourers who, in the eyes of their employers, had broken their contracts and left their places of work.[1] Though the word *droster* had occasionally been applied to runaway slaves as well as to absconding soldiers and sailors of the VOC before the 1750s, it came to have a new significance after this date.[2] The changed meaning of the word reflected a growing consciousness, amongst both colonists and their labourers, that there was little difference between the condition of being a slave and the condition of being a servant. The best way to explore this consciousness, and the experience behind it, is to make a detailed examination, concentrating on a particular case study, of the *droster* gangs of the late eighteenth century in the region where they were most active.

The mountains of the Cape interior had always seemed a haven to fugitives. At the core of these mountains – the Cape Fold Mountain System – lies the range now known as the Cedarberg, the geographical focus of this study. In the eighteenth century, however, the Cedarberg were considered to be part of the Bokkeveld, a vast and vague area used to describe the mountains which lie east of the Olifants River. It is, in fact, impossible to detach the Cedarberg from the wider environmental context of the Bokkeveld or, for that matter, from the Roggeveld further to the east. These regions are also, therefore, considered in this chapter.

We do not know when it was that fugitives first reached the Bokkeveld mountains. Perhaps those runaway slaves who are recorded as having reached the Chariguriqua Khoi in the 1680s were amongst the pioneers, for the Chariguriqua were, in the seventeenth century, sometimes to be found along the Olifants River.[3] In 1709 the slave Simon of Malabar reported that he, along with some other fugitives, crossed the Olifants River and entered the territory of the 'Cochemans', who then attacked them and forced them to retreat.[4] With the exception of the Chariguriqua this was, unfortunately, the usual response of Khoi societies towards colonial fugitives in the early years of the eighteenth century.[5] It should be appreciated that the Khoi were, in a sense, themselves fugitives from the colony, anxious to avoid the Company's reach by retreating further into the interior. As the colony expanded, however, it became increasingly difficult for the Khoi to isolate themselves from the shock waves emanating from the south-western Cape, particularly since they were, in turn, pursued by other colonial escapees. These runaways were mostly desperate, armed and ravenous, thus posing a direct threat to the lives and livestock of the indigenous populace.

Gradually, however, the situation changed. Hard on the heels of the fugitive pioneers of the turbulent frontier came the slightly more respectable stock farmers of the colony who, at least in the eyes of the Company, had a tenuous legality. But since their activities included the destruction of wild animals through uncontrolled hunting, the seizure of land and water resources, and the acquisition of Khoi livestock by fair means or foul, their impact on Khoi societies was far more destructive than that of their lawless precursors. Stripped of the means to continue an independent existence and devastated by the smallpox epidemic of 1713, the Khoi were obliged to become the servants of the ever-increasing number of colonists. The last overt Khoisan resistance to these processes in the Bokkeveld was crushed in 1739 and the creation of a common consciousness of oppression between slaves and Khoi labourers gathered momentum.[6]

A crucial stage in this process was associated with the creation of a new category of colonial subject, the 'Bastaard-Hottentot'. Those individuals who were deemed to fall within this category were children of mixed slave and Khoi parentage. As early as 1721 some free burghers of the Stellenbosch district had written to the government to ask for permission to bind in service, for a certain number of years, the offspring of slave and Khoi unions.[7] The issue seems to have lain dormant until 1775 when the landdrost and *heemraden* of Stellenbosch decreed that 'Bastaard-Hottentot' children should be bound to serve their masters until the age of 25. The only conditions of service were that such children should be well cared for and that their names, ages and parents' names should be recorded. It was but a short step from treating 'Bastaard-Hottentots' as slaves to treating Khoi labourers the same way. In 1781 a resolution was passed which declared that since runaway slaves were passing themselves off as Khoi, the names of local Khoi should be submitted annually to the authorities by the *veldwagtmeesters*. After 1787 an earlier suggestion, that 'Bastaard-Hottentots' should be made to carry passes, was implemented and extended to apply to the Khoi.[8]

Apart from these onerous laws the Khoi were, in theory, a free people. At the level of lived experience, however, there was increasingly little to distinguish their lives from those of other unfree labourers on colonial farms. One of the most important factors in determining their subservient status was the influence exerted over labour relations by the struggle taking place within the frontier zone. The victory of colonial commandos in 1739 had resulted in the subjugation of all the Khoisan south of Namaqualand and west of the Roggeveld. It had also enabled frontier farmers to advance beyond the forbidding immensity of the Cape Fold Mountains – for so long inhabited by unconquered Khoisan – and incorporate the entire winter rainfall region of the western Cape into the colony. One of the consequences of this was that the colonists now came into conflict with the Khoisan groups of the interior escarpment. By 1770 a life or death struggle had developed necessitating, for the colonists, the almost continuous mounting of commandos throughout the length and breadth of the frontier zone. But the commandos were not only used to crush enemies without; they were also used to control labourers within the colony. In 1774 it became virtually compulsory for 'Bastaards' and 'Bastaard-Hottentots' to serve in commandos whilst Khoi too were eligible for military service. It was in response to commando duties in particular that, from 1778 onwards, large numbers of Khoi and 'Bastaard-Hottentots' trekked beyond the boundaries of the colony to the Nama or to the Orange River.[9]

But not all *drosters* became Oorlams. Many dangerous days' journey lay between a fugitive and the distant haven of the Orange River.[10] Despite the fact that by 1740 the mountainous areas of the Cape interior were within, rather than beyond, the colonial frontier (thus providing a strong incentive for determined fugitives to flee even further northwards), they continued to attract runaways. Even if a *droster* had heard of the Oorlam societies of the Orange, he might not be prepared to run the gauntlet of roving commandos, hostile San, beasts of prey and the waterless wastes beyond the Bokkeveld. Fugitives continued to make for the mountains, and it is with these that this chapter is principally concerned.

In the beginning of the winter of 1793,[11] the slave Adam deserted his master, Jochem Scholtz the younger of the Roggeveld, and fled to the Ongens (or Ongeluks) River in the Tanqua Karoo.[12] The onset of the rainy season was, traditionally, a time of heightened mobility in the western Cape as the stock farmers of the Bokkeveld and Roggeveld mountain ranges moved their animals down to their loan farms on the warmer plains to avoid the freezing rain and snow.[13] For the colonists it was a period of enforced and welcome sociability when, in an area usually too arid to sustain their livestock, they met friends and relatives from remote regions. After the rains, for a brief period the grazing was good. So too was the hunting, and nineteenth-century descriptions of convivial camp fires and holiday spirits attending transhumance in the Tanqua Karoo can doubtless be extrapolated to the eighteenth century.[14] Nor were these seasonal upheavals without benefit for the slaves and servants of the trekboers. The long treks with livestock, the mingling and merging of people from different regions in an area where all were comparative strangers, provided the shepherds and drovers with circumstances that were most conducive to escape. They had legitimate mobility, partial anonymity and abundant resources of livestock or game close to hand.

The landscape too seemed to offer a place of refuge, for to the west of the Tanqua Karoo rose the brooding massif of the Cedarberg. To the north and south the mountains merged into the vast ridges of the Cape Fold Mountain System. The colonists were used to naming the entire mountain range the Bokkeveld though, strictly speaking, the district of that name began north of the Cedarberg. Conversely, the south-eastern ramparts of the range were known as the Zwarte Ruggens – a dark name for a grim place. Behind the Zwarte Ruggens, to the west, was the Koue Bokkeveld, an area of high mountains and secret valleys. The region was really the southern end of the Cedarberg and it was sometimes referred to as the Koue Bergen or Koue Veld, though its mountains were also called the Skurweberge. To the Khoi and 'Bastaard-Hottentots' who knew the region, the name 'Cedarberg' had a mildness which they rejected as incongruous and, in the mouths of the *drosters* who had lived there, the word underwent a bitter corruption, to 'Zuurbergen'.[15] But whatever the names given to the rugged mountains, they offered a broken wilderness of weathered sandstone, deep ravines and thick, fragrant fynbos. They were a good place to hide.

Adam, like others before and after him, used the favourable opportunities of time and place to desert. Once the standing water in the Ongeluks River began to dry up, they gravitated towards the western mountains. With him was a Khoi woman, Jannetje, whom he regarded as his wife. She too had worked for Jochem Scholtz. About twelve years before she had given birth to a boy, April, the son of Adam, and therefore a 'Bastaard-Hottentot'. April joined his parents in flight. But why had they fled? When Adam's subsequent interrogators asked him this question they must have thought that a man needed a specific, compelling reason to decide, suddenly, to reject enslavement. His answer cannot have satisfied them: he had run away because he had not been given any clothes.[16]

At this stage it may be instructive to say something about the milieu from which Adam and his family fled. Jochem Scholtz, his master, had the reputation of being one of the most notorious troublemakers in the Roggeveld; and not just because of his bulk. He was, as it happened, 'a man of immense size, so much so that he could not wear the usual articles of clothing; his daily dress was a night-gown and shirt.'[17] The field-cornet of the Roggeveld, Gerrit Maritz, described him as a 'groot sterk man' (big strong man) and a 'gewelt hebber in moet willige rust verstoorder' (tyrant and mischievous disturber of the peace) – an opinion based on painful personal experience.[18] By the 1790s Scholtz had registered three farms along the Riet River in the Roggeveld and at least one other in the Skurweberge.[19] His father had farmed in the district since 1756,[20] and his brother, Hermanus, was nearby to lend a hand.[21] Hermanus, in fact, was similar to Jochem in his treatment of labour. One day in the winter of 1792 he beat the heavily pregnant wife of his Khoi servant, Jan Swart. The woman, Sarmentje, ran away. Since Hermanus wanted to bind Jan for failing to slaughter a sheep quickly enough, he too ran away. The couple hid for a few days in the mountains not far from the farm before Jan's brother, Claas, joined them. Hermanus had wanted to beat Claas because he had not brought some oxen to the farm quickly enough. Claas's wife, Lena, and their one-year-old child were the next to join the group whilst the final adherent was Griet, the sister of the Swart brothers. The fugitives then moved to the Tanqua Karoo where the Scholtzes had a loan farm. Significantly, it was winter. The Swarts did not make their way to the west but tried to survive where they were. So scared of discovery was Claas that he ordered his wife to bash their baby's brains out on a rock to stop it from crying. Lena did so. Claas then went berserk and beat Lena to death with a kierie as well as inflicting serious wounds on his sister Griet. The rest of the group, cowed and shocked, were made to promise not to say anything. This was a necessary precaution because soon there was no food to be found in the veld and no livestock to steal. By summer the survivors were forced to return to the Scholtzes. Hunger and fear had defeated them.[22]

These events suggest that for some Khoi at least it was preferable to kill their own child rather than return to service under a harsh master. The Swarts' experiences also point to the difficulties of survival in the Tanqua Karoo, and it is possible that Adam learnt enough from their mistakes to head westward.[23]

He and his family were not the only fugitives in the landscape in the winter of 1793.[24] About a month after their flight they encountered the runaway slaves Africa and Cupido, who were in turn accompanied by two Khoi women and their children. These women, according to their own testimony,[25] had been forcibly abducted by Africa, the fugitive slave of the influential *veldwagtmeester* of the Hantam, Petrus Pienaar.[26] Africa had been at large for an unspecified period of time before he visited one of the Pienaar farms in the Hantam in the summer of 1792/3 and compelled Anna and her child to join him. At about the same time Africa also visited a farm of Christoffel Esterhuysen and forced Rosalijn and her child to go with him. It is not clear whether the children (girls called Roos and Klijne Flora) were Africa's, or what his relationship with the women had been prior to their abduction. It would seem, however, that part of Africa's concern to seize two women was to cater for his fellow *droster*, the slave Cupido of Malabar, who had fled from the burger Frans Joosten. At any rate, when Adam encountered this group, he thought the women to be the wives of the men.[27]

The slaves and their women were soon joined by some Khoi *drosters*: Steenbok, Lammert (Lambert) and Picqueur. It is not altogether clear why Steenbok and Lammert joined the *complot*,[28] where they came from or who they were, since their evidence was never recorded. We do, however, know something about Picqueur, for he was eventually captured and interrogated. He was about 18 years old and had been born on the farm of Jan Jacobs in the Bokkeveld. One day, whilst busy digging white lime for his boss (presumably Jacobs) on the farm of Frans Joosten (Cupido's boss) in the Bokkeveld, he was approached by Africa, who urged him to go with him. Picqueur was promised food and clothing but, in the end, claims to have accompanied him out of fear. It is quite likely that, since Picqueur and Cupido had both worked on Frans Joosten's farm, they already knew each other.[29] Africa, whose forceful recruiting methods are evidence of considerable strength of will, emerged as the leader of the group, which gradually made its way to the Winkelhaak Kloof in the Koue Bokkeveld.[30]

There is much uncertainty concerning the exact timing of the movements of the *droster* gang, just as there is a vagueness about where the constituent elements of the group met each other. But as the coldest days of winter receded and the multi-flowered spring arrived, the colonists left the Karoo and went back to their farms. The eastern sides of the mountain now became even less populated and the *drosters* felt both emboldened and compelled to move southwards.

Part of the reason for this compulsion was that there was a great deal of commando activity in the mountains of the Olifants River valley to the west and the Bokkeveld to the north during the spring of 1793. The *veldwagtmeesters* of these districts imagined that they had uncovered a conspiracy amongst the Khoi and 'oorlamse hottentots' of Swellendam, the Hex River and Namaqualand. This conspiracy, it was believed, would involve an attack by the 'schelm Donderbos Pokkebos' and 400 of his followers armed with guns. Donderbos was reported to have been seen in the Bidouw (the Pakhuis Pass area) and was believed to be trekking through the Bokkeveld in order to reach Namaqualand and raise his army. Further details concerning this fantasy need not detain us here.[31] It did, however, result in Johannes Lubbe, *veldwagtmeester* of the Olifants River, scouring the mountains of his district with commandos and declaring that ''t is hoogtyt om onse lant te behouden en swijgen voor de swarte nasie want 't schyn of sy alle op gemaakt is weest gewaapent en gereed' (it is high time we save our country and [not] to succumb to the black nation, for it seems as if they all have been incited; be armed and ready).[32] In such circumstances it made sense for the *drosters* to keep clear of the northern parts of the mountain range.

Another reason for the move to the Winkelhaak Kloof was that by doing so the *drosters* were ensuring that they kept within striking distance of isolated farms. All the *droster* groups of the western Cape were, to some extent, parasites who were obliged to live off the livestock of the farmers. In the harsh environment of the mountains and the Karoo, natural and seasonal resources like *veldkos* and game could not always be obtained in sufficient quantities to feed large groups of people. These scarcities were exacerbated by the fact that *drosters* did not have complete freedom to roam in search of supplies. The need for secrecy restricted their movements, making them inefficient hunters and gatherers. In consequence *drosters* became dependent on stealing livestock, thereby drawing attention to themselves and placing themselves in danger of discovery.[33]

Africa and Cupido had already managed to obtain some cattle before Adam and his family joined them. With Adam's help a further seven sheep were stolen from Rasmus Esterhuizen and seven from Hermanus Scholtz.[34] The resources and numbers of the group were also enlarged when the Meij brothers decided to throw in their lot with the *drosters*.

Rooi and Willem Meij were both about 20 years old and both worked for the burgher Jan Louw the elder. They were, in the parlance of the day, 'Bastaard-Hottentots' who worked on Louw's farm in the Bokkeveld. Louw himself lived at the Tijgerberg, near Cape Town, so the management of his farm, Pampoen Kraal, described as 'agter de Scheerfdenberg', was in the hands of a *knecht*. In the winter the livestock on this farm, like livestock throughout the Bokkeveld, was driven to the Karoo. It is likely that this task had been entrusted to the Meij brothers, for somewhere and sometime between the Bokkeveld and the Karoo Willem Meij fell victim to Africa's persuasive powers. It is not clear whether Willem had already decided to desert before meeting up with Africa's *complot* but it is unlikely that he needed much convincing. In his defence he did not say that he had been forced to desert but that he had done so 'om dat ik het daar slegt had en mijn verdiende loon mij onthouden wierd' (because I was treated badly and my wages I had earned were held back).[35] Strictly speaking, as a 'Bastaard-Hottentot' he was not entitled to a wage, but perhaps this is what rankled with him. We know that there were Khoi on Jan Louw's farm in 1793 who were receiving a wage of 12 rixdollars, one 'kirsaaije rok' (dress of coarsely woven fabric), two shirts and two pairs of trousers for a year's work.[36]

Rooi Meij, his brother, joined the others somewhat later, after having received permission from the *knecht* at Pampoen Kraal to go to Eylands Drift on the Doorn River in the Tanqua Karoo. Quite what his business was there is not known. Perhaps he had been dispatched to assist Willem and knew nothing of the *complot*, though this is unlikely. Whatever the reason, he met Willem and Africa near the Winkelhaak Kloof, surely no coincidence, particularly since Adam and Rooi had previously met. One of the Meij brothers had absconded with a musket belonging to Jan Louw, whilst the other *drosters* already had a gun. Jan Louw did not know it but he had also 'contributed' ten of his cattle to the *drosters*. It was, presumably, too risky to move about with any larger herd and further robberies could be – and were – committed when necessary.[37]

The *complot* now numbered fourteen men, women and children whose common bond was a desire to avoid discovery and capture. This ambition, it was felt, could best be realised in the vicinity of Eylands Drift. The attraction of this place probably lay in the fact that Willem Meij had legitimate business there – a useful alibi.[38] Besides, the robberies in the Winkelhaak area could not go unnoticed for ever.

Time had passed and it was summer as the *complot* made its way northwards, between the Skurweberge and the Zwarte Ruggens, possibly crossing the Katbakkies[39] to the Karoo, hugging the mountain fringes until it reached Eylands Drift under the Zuurbergen.[40] At the drift a Khoi by the name of Isaak (who was there with his family and who worked for Jan Kok) told them that the nearest people in the neighbourhood were Oude Rooij and his followers, a group of Khoi who had a kraal, Stille Kraal, further up Eylands Kloof. As luck would have it, one of Oude Rooij's oxen wandered in shortly afterwards, and it was promptly butchered and eaten. It was only after a good meal that the men began to wonder whether they had acted wisely. What if Oude Rooij reported the theft? Would it not be safest to silence him?

Oude Rooij, a Khoi, was known to his mother, Griet, as Jantje. In order, however, to distinguish him from his two sons, Klyn Jantje Rooij and Rooi Rooij, he was commonly known as Oude Rooij. In 1792 he, along with his mother, sons, his wife Mietje, and his daughter Griet, lived at Klip Fonteyn, the farm of the burgher Arnoldus Vlok in the Zwarte Ruggens. That year the family was visited by his elder brother, Wittebooij, and his brother's wife, Sara. Too much liquor was consumed and Oude Rooij, whilst under the influence of alcohol, hit his mother so hard on the head that she nearly died. For good measure he then stabbed her in the leg. Wittebooij, who was also drunk, took exception to this unfilial action and assisted his mother by stabbing Oude Rooij so deeply between the shoulder blades that the knife point protruded from his breast. Far from having a sobering effect, this thrust led him to stab his wife Sara in the left breast and then to slash her across the forehead. Although there were no fatalities, we must conclude that Oude Rooij's 1792 family reunion was not a success.

The very next year, however, undeterred by the unfortunate events which had accompanied his last visit to his brother, Wittebooij returned, bringing with him Sara and their children, Jan, Trijn and Leys. The two brothers proceeded to drink brandy and Wittebooij felt moved to thrash Leys with a bundle of reeds. Oude Rooij attempted to stop him but this made Wittebooij mad ('boos') and a fight ensued. Oude Rooij was flung to the ground and beaten so severely that his son Rooi intervened. He took his father's musket and shot Wittebooij above the left knee. An hour later his uncle bled to death. His mother, who had also had some brandy, was powerless to influence events and since Oude Rooij had temporarily lost the use of his arms and legs the assistance of some neighbouring Khoi was required in order to bury the body. Once Oude Rooij had recovered it became obvious to Sara that he planned to kill her and her children in order to prevent them from telling their story. They fled, hiding in an aardvark's hole to escape, and made their way to Sara's father, a man called Wissel Bockenveld.[41]

Shortly after the events described, Mietje, the wife of Oude Rooij, died. The cause of her death was not recorded but since Oude Rooij had a reputation for violence we may conclude that life alongside him had not been easy. Round about the beginning of the harvest time (November) in 1793 the surviving members of Oude Rooij's family journeyed to another of Arnoldus Vlok's farms, Eylands Drift, near the confluence of the Doorn and Tratra rivers in the Tanqua Karoo. Unfortunately for the Khoi family, Vlok then sold his farm to the burgher Hendrik Smit and the latter ordered them to move. This they did, establishing a kraal in one of the kloofs nearby.[42]

Oude Rooij was, however, desirous of female company other than that of his family. With this in mind he visited a kraal, about two days' journey away, belonging to a Khoi woman called Anna. He probably knew that Anna's daughter Flora was without her husband, Jan Swart Kees, who had been hired for the harvest time by the burgher Jacob Tas of Eselbank in the Cedarberg. Unfortunately this meant that Jan had to leave Anna, Flora and Flora's young brother, Marthinus, behind, but this suited Oude Rooij admirably. When he arrived at the kraal he told Flora that he was going to take her away and that if she resisted he would kill her. With no one to protect her, and with Oude Rooij's fearsome reputation to intimidate her, she was abducted.[43]

By the time the unwilling woman had been forced to Rooij's kraal – the ironically named Stille Kraal – some other visitors had arrived. They were Oude Rooij's daughter Griet, her husband Jurie Oortman, and a man called Claas Jager (who was also known as Claas Niegerman). Griet and Jurie had a baby girl called Leyn, who was about two years old, so the relationship had presumably been in existence for some time. Jurie worked for Gerrit Cloete, a burgher of the Olifants River area, and he was accompanied by his brother, Kleyne Donderbos.[44]

It was Christmas time.[45] Though it cannot be stated that the family visit had been specially timed to coincide with the holy day there was to be, in any event, little to celebrate. On the third night after Flora's arrival at Stille Kraal the dogs began to bark. Oude Rooij released them shouting 'Sa! Sa! Schiet er op!' in order to scare off any threatening presence. He suspected that there might well be *drosters* or predators about and he was right.[46] Although the dogs eventually stopped barking and the people returned to their slumbers they had been spied on by Lammert. He had been sent forward by Africa, who waited in hiding some distance away with the other men in his band. A decision had been reached earlier in the day to deal with Oude Rooij's kraal. The majority of the male *drosters* – the women were not privy to the discussion – were in favour of murdering the kraal's men. Those who took this hard line were Africa, Cupido, Steenbok, Lammert and Adam, with the others (the Meij brothers and Picqueur) reluctantly following suit.[47] Towards evening the men had left the women and cautiously approached Oude Rooij's kraal. Around midnight Lammert had crept up to try to gauge the number of people present but when the dogs detected him, the *drosters* decided to wait for daylight.

Next morning, before sunrise, Oude Rooij took his bow and his *koker* quiver full of arrows to scout about and try to find the cause of the previous night's disturbance. The kraal was situated on the bank of the Eylands River,[48] which at that particular point was not easily fordable. Oude Rooij crossed the river about a hundred paces from the kraal and began his search. He need not have gone looking for danger. Soon after his departure the *droster* men emerged on the bank opposite the kraal and shouted to Jurie Oortman to show them the way over the river. There were eight of them and since they had muskets, kieries and assegais they could not be denied. But it was Claas Jager who waded over to show them the crossing, since Jurie had an injured foot.

When it was established that Oude Rooij was missing, Africa sent Donderbos to go and fetch him. Oude Rooij's heart must have sunk to hear of the unwelcome visitors and, once he returned, his worst fears were confirmed. Whilst Adam and Lammert stood by menacingly with loaded muskets the hands of Oude Rooij, Jurie Oortman, Donderbos and Claas Jager were bound by the other *drosters*. The captive men were then forced to cross the river and walk away from the kraal up the kloof accompanied by Africa, Adam, Lammert, Willem Meij, Cupido and Steenbok. Picqueur and Rooi Meij stayed to guard Griet, Flora and Kleyn Leyn. What they did not know was that Oude Rooij's mother, Griet, had managed to hide herself and was observing the proceedings from nearby. About half an hour later the anxious woman heard a shot. Young Griet ran towards the clearing for her husband, but she was brought back by Picqueur and Rooi Meij. The elder Griet, however, crept through the bushes towards the sound. To her horror she saw her son, Oude Rooij, lying with his head smashed in. More shots rang out and Griet made sure she kept hidden. She fled when it was safe to do so and reached the kraal of a Khoi, Willem Fortuijn, by nightfall.[49]

What had happened? The exact details are hard to establish, for those men who were eyewitnesses to, or participants in, the crime, and who were later captured and questioned, had to convince their interrogators of their innocence. If one pieces together the contradictory evidence, it seems likely that Oude Rooij managed to free himself from his bonds and made a dash for freedom. Adam caught him and bashed his head with a rock, holding him still whilst Lammert shot him. Lammert also shot Claas Jager and then, with either Willem Meij or Adam, shot Jurie Oortman and Kleyne Donderbos. Africa employed his time by hitting the victims with a kierie whilst the others stood by. Willem Meij helped himself to Oude Rooij's hat for Rooij, by the standards of his deceased friends, was the best dressed. He was the only one in trousers (blue) and a jacket (red). The others wore karosses and Claas Jager had a hat but it was too bloodstained to wear.

The murderers returned to Picqueur, Rooi Meij and the women, telling them that they had shot the others. Willem Meij gave Picqueur his old hat whilst Africa gave Flora and Griet permission to see the bodies. They were escorted, by Cupido and Rooi Meij, to the site where they covered the bodies with branches. Back at Stille Kraal, Africa had discovered two knapsacks full of Oude Rooij's home-brewed honey beer.[50] Once this had been consumed, the pack oxen of Jurie Oortman and Claas Jager were laden with meat and karosses. The *drosters* then moved out, taking Flora and Griet with them, until, a short distance away, they were reunited with their own women. After staying a while in the vicinity they once more encountered Isaak, the shepherd, who told them he had heard that a commando was after them. With fearful urgency the group decided to head towards the Bokkeveld.

After two days of hurrying northwards Africa decided that their safety was jeopardised by the presence of Griet and, more specifically, her screaming infant Kleyn Leyn. He therefore drove them away from the group and threatened Flora with death if she ever breathed a word about the murder to the 'Christians'. On reaching the Bokkeveld mountains the group split up. Adam, April, Cupido and Jannetje wanted to go northwards, to Namaqualand. This was a virtually impossible journey in the summer because of the lack of water, and Adam, April and Jannetje did not persevere in the plan. The mother and her son eventually went to the farm of Pieter Langefontein whilst Adam, having run out of options, returned to the Scholtzes in the Roggeveld. His master, Jochem, was not at home but Jochem's brother Hermanus was. One of the Khoi servants, Anthony, had already heard of the evil deeds committed in Eylands Kloof and Adam could not deny that he had been amongst the *drosters*. He did, however, deny having done anything wrong, but this did not save him from arrest. He was taken to the Cape for trial. Cupido of Malabar was not recaptured and his fate is unknown.[51]

The rest of the group, under Africa's leadership, remained in the Bokkeveld. A craving for certain items of consumption seems to have influenced Africa's next series of commands, for he ordered Lammert, Steenbok and Rooi Meij to steal some spices and tobacco. Picqueur was sent to acquire some bread for the children whilst Africa, Willem Meij and the women and children went to see what they could find at the farm of Roelof van der Merwe. The dangerous game of robbing farm-houses had begun.

Meanwhile a commando had indeed been mobilised to find the *drosters*. At the end of December 1793 Gerrit Cloete had been informed of the murders by a Khoi servant of Hendrik Smit. Cloete had been left in charge of the Olifants River district by Lubbe, the *veldwagtmeester*, whilst the latter was absent in the Cape.[52] He therefore commanded Isaac Davel, the baptised 'bastaards' Carel van Rooijen and David Koopman, and some Khoi servants to accompany him. Griet, Oude Rooij's mother, had managed to tell her story. Since Cloete estimated that the murders had taken place on 28 or 29 December, the news had taken a mere two or three days to travel over the Cedarberg to him. The commando moved more slowly, taking eight days to reach Eylands Kloof, searching the mountains as they went but suspecting that the *drosters* had spies (like Isaak) who had warned them. At the scene of the crime all they found were two bloodstained, bullet-pierced karosses as well as a bloodstained hat which was identified as having been Claas Jager's. There were signs too that cattle had been slaughtered and cooked – but that was all. On the way back a horse and some cattle were found, some dead, some alive, and also an abandoned musket. Cloete identified it as Jan Louw's – the Meij brothers' boss.[53]

By 20 January 1794 the commando had returned, without any *drosters*, but with the news that 'die klyne hottentot' Picqueur had been captured. It was a Khoi servant of the burgher Willem du Toit who had caught him. The very next day Africa, Willem Meij, Anna and Flora were discovered and captured by two Khoi servants on the farm of Roelof van der Merwe. It was not, however, the end for Africa. Somehow he managed to break his bonds and escape. He was never recaptured.[54]

Rooi Meij and Lammert tried the farmhouse of the widow of Daniel van der Merwe. Steenbok was not with them as they crept into the garden at night. Realising that the house was empty they did not waste their time stealing fruit but broke open a window and took what they could find: two rolls of tobacco, a jacket, a pair of trousers and two women's dresses. Early next morning widow Van der Merwe's son, Erasmus, noticed the broken window and the missing items. He also noted footprints and quickly summoned two Khoi servants, Coert and Claas, to help him track down the thieves. That afternoon they found the two fugitives in the veld and called on them to stand still. Van der Merwe and his men were all armed with muskets but Lammert and Rooi Meij refused to surrender. Instead, they ran. Shots were fired and Lammert fell dead whilst Rooi Meij was wounded. To Van der Merwe's surprise, however, Rooi Meij continued running and escaped. The stolen goods were recovered.[55]

Four days later Joseph Joosten, who had a farm four hours away from the Van der Merwes, was informed by his Khoi servant Booij that a suspicious-looking 'Bastaard-Hottentot' was amongst his sheep. Rooi Meij obviously had a craving for tobacco, for he was sitting with the shepherd, a slave called Jephta, sharing a pipe. As Joosten rode up on his horse, he recognised Meij as the 'opgedroste Bastaard-Hottentot' of Jan Louw and called on him to halt. Joosten asked Rooi Meij where he thought he was going and the reply was 'to the Bokkeveld', whereupon Joosten accused Rooi of having stolen one of his sheep. This Rooi denied but Joosten began hitting him with the butt of his musket. As Rooi ran away Joosten fired at him. Seeing the *droster* drop and lie still, he dismounted to inspect what he hoped would be a corpse. But Rooi sprang up as he approached and Joosten felt obliged to hit him on the neck with his musket stock. Joosten then ordered Rooi to lie still and handed his musket to one of his servants for reloading. Before this task was accomplished, however, Rooi was on his feet again and running. Joosten followed, using his musket as a club, but Rooi managed to grasp the gun in one hand and stab Joosten with a knife which he kept in a knapsack tied to his arm. The burgher fell back with a wound in his right arm and the battered Rooi Meij made good his escape.[56]

After having been shot and clubbed, the seemingly indestructible Rooi Meij tried to steal a horse to carry his aching body to safety. Close to the widow Van der Merwe's farm was a farmer called Rasmus Erasmus. (Was it a coincidence that the widow's son was called Erasmus?) When one of his horses was found at the Van der Merwes, it seemed likely that it had been stolen. Erasmus van der Merwe enlisted the help of Daniel and Louw and together they tracked Rooi Meij to the Zoute River. This time he came quietly and was reunited with his brother in the custody of *veldwagtmeester* Jacobus Pienaar. From there the brothers were moved to *veldwagtmeester* Pieter Jacobs and finally, with Adam and Picqueur, stood trial in Cape Town.[57]

Steenbok was not captured; a later report that he was shot by a shepherd of Frans Joosten has to be weighed against other reports that he was still at large. The authorities could do little more than hope that the slaves Cupido and Africa might have encountered the same fate as Lammert whilst engaged in stock theft and met their just deserts. Statements were taken from Flora, Griet (Oude Rooij's mother), Anna, Rosalijn, Jannetje and April but these women and children were not held responsible for any crime. April and Jannetje were, however, returned to Jochem Scholtz, for he claimed, in 1800, that he had '1 baster genaamd April de welk door den agbaar Heer Fischall mijn als lijf eigenaar is gegeeven' (one 'Bastaard' named April who was given to me as serf by the honourable fiscal). He also listed a female Khoi, Jannetje, as a servant and noted that she was 'paired' with one of his slaves.[58] The other women, no doubt, returned to a life of servitude on the farms or to insecurity in their kraals in the mountain.

Adam lied desperately at his trial, claiming that he had not been at Oude Rooij's kraal when the murder took place but with the *drosters*' women and children. Nobody supported his story. Willem Meij, who had certainly gone up the kloof with the doomed men, denied having played an active role in their death. He was the only available eyewitness to events but Picqueur claimed that Lammert had told him that Willem had killed Jurie Oortman. Picqueur and Rooi Meij had several witnesses to attest to the fact that they had stood guard over the women and had therefore not played a part in the murder. In Picqueur's favour was his youth and the excuse that Africa had led him astray. Against Rooi Meij was the fact that he had stabbed a burgher (by accident he claimed), an action which could not be condoned. All of the men on trial were of course guilty, at the very least, of stock theft and desertion. Adam and Willem Meij were sentenced to be hanged, and their bodies to be suspended from the gallows until the birds and the air had cleansed their bones of flesh. Rooi Meij was to have a noose put round his neck, his body bound to a pole, and then to be whipped and branded. After this he would be chained and put to hard labour on the Company's works for life. Picqueur's sentence was similar to Rooi Meij's, except that he was given 25 years' hard labour and did not have to wear the hangman's noose around his neck.[59]

The events described above should be seen as helping to illustrate certain developments which were taking place in the lives of Khoi, 'Bastaard-Hottentots' and slaves in one region of the late-eighteenth-century Cape. The region in question was one which, by virtue of its mountainous remoteness and seasonal marginality, proved to be attractive to *droster* gangs. For the same reasons it proved to be attractive to those Khoi who were still desirous of living an independent life – independent, that is, from Dutch farmers. The extent to which this ambition was realisable may be partially gauged from the details of the lives of those Khoi connected to the nexus of relationships centred on Oude Rooij's kraal. We can see, for instance, that there was a high incidence of seasonal mobility as Khoi servants moved in response to the rhythms of transhumance or harvest time. It is obvious that some Khoi did not live on the farms of Dutch burghers all the year round but spent some time in independent kraals, tucked away in kloofs or secluded valleys, staying with friends or family. Sometimes a farmer might be fairly tolerant of the presence of a Khoi kraal on one of his remote farms, leaving them a large measure of independence and not demanding too much of them. Arnoldus Vlok does not, for instance, seem to have interfered too much in the lives of Oude Rooij and his family. At other times such a presence might be intolerable, and a kraal not closely tied into a farm's labour pool would be viewed as vagrants or unwanted consumers of environmental resources. This attitude is, perhaps, displayed in the eviction of Oude Rooij's kraal from Eylands Drift by Hendrik Smit when the farm changed hands.[60]

Living on the margins of Dutch farms had the obvious advantage of greater independence but it did not necessarily mean greater security. In the first place the land to which the Khoi had uncontested access was indeed marginal, meaning that it was hard to survive on it all year round. This necessitated a form of migrant labour, whereby the men would leave their kraals to help with the harvest or work short contracts. The dire consequences of leaving their families unprotected are clearly revealed in the example of Jan Swart Kees and his wife Flora. It was extremely dangerous to share the landscape with those other, and more desperate, fugitives from colonial control – the *drosters*.

There is a central paradox to be faced and it is one which historian Robert Ross was aware of when he wrote 'that, with certain exceptions, the steady reduction of the Khoisan to a position of bondage scarcely distinguishable from that of the slaves led to a slow growth of solidarity encompassing individuals from the two groups and to a slow diminution of . . . conflict between them.' He goes on to say that 'In the mid-eighteenth century the number of cases . . . in which slaves and Khoi took opposite sides, as it were, clearly outnumbered those in which they acted together. Fifty years later, the reverse is the case.'[61] What has to be explained, therefore, is why, though the oppressed were becoming more and more like each other and capable of uniting in common associations (the *droster* gangs),[62] this did not prevent them from preying on each other when necessary.

Unfortunately, in the harsh environment of the Cape mountains the twin imperatives of fugitives – to avoid discovery and to obtain food – could not both be met at the same time (or at least not for very long).[63] It was all too frequently necessary for *drosters* to rob in order to eat and to kill in order to remain unreported. Though farmhouses and farmers' livestock were stolen, this was a risky business and it was far easier to rob the more vulnerable outlying Khoi. Not all of these Khoi were unsympathetic to runaways (for example, Isaak at Eylands Drift) and some could actually be persuaded to join the ranks. But, on the whole, those Khoi who were permanent residents on colonial farms were far more likely to defend their masters' interests (and indirectly their own) by hunting down or shooting at *drosters*. All those of Africa's group who were captured or shot (except for Rooi Meij, who was, in any event, betrayed by Joosten's Khoi servant) had Khoi to thank for their misfortune. But we should not judge the servants over-harshly. After all, those who died at Oude Rooij's kraal were also part-time servants on Dutch farms.

It is clear that violence and brutality were not the monopoly of *droster* gangs or colonists. Khoi like Oude Rooij, Wittebooij and Claas Swart had themselves been brutalised by their harsh life. Oude Rooij, like others who existed in the peripheries of colonial space or endured gross ill-treatment from colonial masters, were subject to fits of uncontrollable rage. His homicidal family rows and his unchivalrous behaviour towards women were not simply inspired by lethal Cape brandy but were symptomatic of profound social disturbance. Though his sickening murder inspires pity and disgust, one cannot help feeling that this death was like his life – nasty, brutish and short. His killers had shared the same world of pain and fear, but some of them had had their inhumanity honed by a lifetime of enslavement.[64]

If anything, the position of Khoi women was even less enviable. In the two groups under consideration – Rooij's kraal and Africa's *drosters* – the women were little better than chattels, subject to rape, abduction and assault. At least they were valued highly enough to be kept alive, for both *drosters* and Khoi went to considerable trouble to add females to their groups. Though the women were threatened and forced into submission, this was, arguably, preferable to being killed.

An interesting feature of the events described is the importance of certain commodities and items of consumption to the people involved. Clothes were especially valued. Their non-provision could cause desertion (Adam's reason) whilst the prospect of them could win recruits (Africa's promise to Picqueur). Hats were extremely individualised items of fashion which changed heads only in exceptional circumstances (like the death of a wearer) and male robbers would not hesitate to steal dresses. Tobacco, spices and bread were items for which fugitives would take considerable risks, whilst brandy was available side by side with honey beer in Khoi kraals. Muskets, probably the most highly prized of all commodities, bore clear signs of their legitimate owner's identity. All of these little details indicate how thoroughly even the inhospitable mountains of the Cedarberg had been permeated by European commodities by the 1790s.

This raises another point: that though these regions seemed empty or sparsely populated, they were actually intersected by a network of human linkages which allowed for the extremely rapid dispersal of news. The landscape was not impervious to colonial power. A commando had a long reach, and once a group of *drosters* had rendered themselves visible by committing an anti-social act on 'independent' Khoi, it was only a matter of time before the noose was tightened.

Needless to say, Africa's *droster* gang was not the last group of fugitives to trouble the peace of the Bokkeveld and Roggeveld. Nor did the oppressive practices of bondage cease. For instance, two Khoi who had worked for nearly ten years for Willem Sterrenberg Pretorius in the Bokkeveld were prevented from leaving with their wages despite having received the landdrost's permission to do so. They were severely flogged and then fobbed off with a fraction of their earnings.[65] In March 1794 the authorities heard how a young Khoi boy, Jantje, had been taken from the side of his uncle no fewer than five times, beaten and chained by Willem Steenkamp of the Roggeveld.[66] That same year Toontje, who worked for Pieter Jooste of the Bokkeveld, wanted to leave and take his wife Else with him. Jooste informed him that Else was 'ingeboekt' or apprenticed (as a 'Bastaard-Hottentot') and could not leave. When Toontje took the trouble to confirm this with the landdrost he was informed that, indeed, Else had to stay with Jooste. Toontje, though, was free, so he tried to get a nearby farmer, Wessel Pretorius, to hire him. When Jooste heard of Toontje's insolent initiative he attempted to tie him up and, when he broke free, shot at him. Fortunately Pretorius deflected the gun but Jooste withheld twenty sheep and a horse that rightfully belonged to Toontje.[67] The list could be continued though, hopefully, sufficient evidence has been presented to explain why the Dutch farmers were plagued by the desertion of their labour.

A noteworthy trend of the 1790s was the increasing rapprochement between Khoi *drosters* and San north of the Roggeveld. In December 1791 *veldwagtmeester* Maritz had reported the desertion of a group of Khoi, from the colonists to the San, taking muskets with them.[68] In August 1795 Johannes Karstens reported from the Roggeveld that 'Bastaarts Hottentotten' were leaving, almost daily, to join the San and that no fewer than eleven had recently absconded with muskets.[69] Three years later Jacob Kruger reported from the same areas that he had sent a commando after a 'complot drossende Hottentots' in July, shooting one and capturing a woman and two children. In August he had been obliged to track down *drosters* who were stealing horses and riding away to the

Coup. He had also taken the precaution of putting 'de bosiman meyt' (the Bushman servant girl) of Gert Victor in chains to see if this would 'tame' her – the reason being that she had been responsible for the death of two Khoi whom, on separate occasions, she had persuaded to desert with her and who had then been shot dead.[70]

A further development of the late 1790s was that the arrival of groups of Xhosa in the northern frontier zone gave *drosters* a further option besides that of flight.[71] Typically, Jochem Scholtz was one of the first to be affected when, in late 1797, he noticed a slave amongst the followers of the Xhosa chief 'Brood'. Thinking that one of his slaves, who had escaped, might also be in the group, he decided to investigate, causing 'Brood' to fire at him with a musket. Fortunately for Scholtz, the gun misfired but he retreated forthwith to ask *veldwagtmeester* Visser for help.[72] We do not know whether Scholtz ever recaptured his slave but the incidents illustrate two points: that Khoi and 'Bastaard-Hottentots' were establishing a common ground with San; and that *drosters* from the Roggeveld were, increasingly, trying their luck to the north instead of the west.

This does not mean, however, that the Cedarberg had lost its attractions, for, as Johannes Hugo, the fieldcornet of 'de Kouwe Velt', reported of his district in August 1800, 'heet een conterijje is daar veel schelms sig op hout' (many rogues found themselves in this region).[73] The year before, he had reported the desertion of Khoi labourers from several farmers (himself included) with considerable stock theft. According to reliable reports these *drosters* had gone to the Zwarte Ruggens, which was full of 'schelmen', or rogues. He had also heard that Khoi from the Roggeveld were congregating in the Zwarte Ruggens whilst farmers in their winter loan farms in the Tanqua Karoo had been losing stock to thieves.[74]

As long as there were farmers like Jochem Scholtz the mountains would continue to be stocked with *drosters.* The exasperated landdrost of Stellenbosch wrote to him in January 1799, having received a complaint from Scholtz's ex-servant: 'I cannot content myself with the knowledge that there are men in the country ("in het veld") with you who have the idea that a Hottentot, once hired by somebody, is compelled to keep serving for a lifetime. The case of the Hottentot Cupido Jantje is another example of this. He has lived with you for 13 years and, now that he wants to leave, not only do you prevent him from doing so, but you also refuse to hand over his wife, children and livestock.'[75] It was indeed an unfortunate truth that, by the end of the century, the conditions of Khoi 'in het veld' were no better than that of a 'Bastaard-Hottentot' or a slave.

Notes

Introduction

1. This research forms the basis of my doctoral thesis, 'The Northern Cape Frontier Zone, 1700–*c*. 1815' (Ph.D. thesis, UCT, 1995).

2. The phrase 'exceptional normal' is Edoardo Grendi's and is quoted by Giovanni Levi in his chapter 'On Microhistory' in Peter Burke (ed.), *New Perspectives on Historical Writing* (Cambridge, 1994), p. 109.

3. The famous phrase of E.P. Thompson in *The Making of the English Working Class* (Harmondsworth, 1968), p. 13.

4. By microhistory I mean a historical narrative which is based on a reduced scale of observation, which is well detailed, which highlights the relationship between an individual and that individual's normative social structures, and which incorporates into the main body of the narrative some of the procedures of research itself. This definition is based on Levi's chapter 'On Microhistory' (see note 2 above) but the foremost practitioner of microhistory is Carlo Ginzburg. See especially his book *The Cheese and the Worms: The Cosmos of a Sixteenth-Century Miller* (London, 1980) and his article 'Microhistory: Two or Three Things That I Know About It', *Critical Inquiry*, 20 (1993).

5. Studies which have highlighted the role of slavery in the Cape's economy are R. Ross, *Cape of Torments: Slavery and Resistance in South Africa* (London, 1983) and R. Ross, 'The Rise of the Cape Gentry', *Journal of Southern African Studies,* 2 (1983); N. Worden, *Slavery in Dutch South Africa* (Cambridge, 1985); and L. Guelke and R. Shell, 'An Early Colonial Landed Gentry: Land and Wealth in the Cape Colony (1652-1731)', *Journal of Historical Geography*, 9 (1983).

6. See R. Elphick and R. Shell, 'Intergroup Relations: Khoikhoi, Settlers, Slaves and Freeblacks, 1652–1795', in R. Elphick and H. Giliomee (eds.), *The Shaping of South African Society*, 2nd edition (Cape Town, 1989).

7. This is an issue which Robert Shell began to explore in 'The Family and Slavery at the Cape, 1680–1808', in W. James and M. Simons (eds.), *The Angry Divide: Social and Economic History of the Western Cape* (Cape Town, 1989). See also his later work *Children of Bondage: A Social History of the Slave Society at the Cape of Good Hope, 1652–1838* (Hanover, NH, 1994).

8. Different positions in the debate are occupied by Ross and Worden on the one hand, who argue that conditions at the Cape made it extremely difficult for a distinctive slave culture to emerge before the abolition of the slave trade in 1807, and by Shell, on the other hand, who argues that a slave creole culture was evolving at a much earlier date. See works cited in foot-

notes 5 and 7 above.

9. My understanding of the connection between narrative and the human apprehension of time has been informed by Paul Ricoeur, *Time and Narrative*, 3 vols. (Chicago, 1983). 'Time becomes human to the extent that it is articulated through a narrative mode'. Ricoeur, Vol. 1, p. 52.

10. An important article here is Norman Stone's 'The Revival of Narrative: Reflections on a New Old History', *Past and Present*, 85 (1979). See also Peter Burke, 'History of Events and the Revival of Narrative', in Peter Burke (ed.), *New Perspectives on Historical Writing* (London, 1991). Commentators have pointed out, however, that those who argue for a return to narrative have not really noticed that historians have never really departed from it. See Joyce Appleby, Lynn Hunt and Margaret Jacob, *Telling the Truth About History* (New York, 1994).

11. For Hayden White's work on the relationship between history and fiction see *The Content of the Form*, especially the chapter 'Narrative in Contemporary Historical Theory' (Baltimore, 1987); *Tropics of Discourse* (Baltimore, 1978) and *Metahistory* (Baltimore, 1973). See also Lloyd S. Kramer, 'Literature, Criticism, and Historical Imagination: The Literary Challenge of Hayden White and Dominick La Capra', in Lynn Hunt (ed.), *The New Cultural History* (Berkeley, 1989).

12. 'Thick description' is a technique described by Clifford Geertz in 'Thick Description: Towards an Interpretive Theory of Culture', in C. Geertz, *The Interpretation of Culture* (New York, 1973). For an example of how cultural historians use thick description see Robert Darnton's 'The Great Cat Massacre', in R. Darnton, *The Great Cat Massacre* (London, 1984). The connections between thick description and microhistory are discussed by Giovanni Levi in 'On Microhistory'. See note 4 above.

13. Carlo Ginzburg has given us several perceptive accounts of the historical use of criminal records in his 'Witchcraft and Popular Piety: Notes on a Modenese Trial of 1519' in *Clues, Myths and the Historical Method* (Baltimore, 1989), pp. 1-16 and in *The Worm and the Cheese* (London, 1980).

14. Individuals gain self-knowledge by recounting their lives and we can understand past actors not only by recognising the stories they have made of their lives but also by emplotting their stories for them. This is a point which David Carr develops in his article 'Narrative and the Real World: An Argument for Continuity', in *History and Theory*, 25 (1986), pp. 117–31.

15. Natalie Zemon Davis's book *Fiction in the Archives* (Cambridge, 1987) contains a discussion of the way in which popular narrative forms influenced the presentation of legal evidence in early modern France. Her book *The Return of Martin Guerre* (Harvard, 1983) is a good example of narrative history based on the narratives of court records.

16. This is a viewpoint of Dominick La Capra, who would add the qualification that the context itself is a text of sorts which calls for a reading that respects its intertextuality. He would also add that not knowing where the text ends and the context begins, or the exact nature of the relationship between them, should be a cause for celebration among intellectual historians. See Dominick La Capra, *History and Criticism* (Ithaca, 1985); *Rethinking Intellectual History: Texts, Contexts, Language* (Ithaca, 1983); and Lloyd S. Kramer's article on White and La Capra cited in footnote 11.

1 The Fatal Passion of Brewer Menssink

1. The principal sources of information from which the above narrative have been constructed are the court records concerning the trial of Trijntje and three other slaves for certain 'vuijle abominabel crimen'. They are contained in the Cape Archives Depot (CA), CJ 5, Original Rolls and Minutes (Criminal and Civil); CJ 317, Crimineel Processtukken 1713, pp. 219–406; and VC 20, Journal of Cape Governors, 1711–1714, pp. 42–74. H.F. Heese has published the sentence of Trijntje in *Reg en Onreg: Kaapse Regspraak in die Agtiende Eeu* (Bellville, 1994), pp. 113–21.

2. See A.J. Böeseken, *Slaves and Free Blacks at the Cape 1658–1700* (Cape Town, 1977), pp. 176 and 72 for references to Trijntje and *De Soldaat.*

3. Table Valley was the name that eighteenth-century Capetonians gave to what twentieth-century estate agents call the City Bowl.

4. Masulipatam is a town on the Coromandel coast of India.

5. Rutgert Messink was originally from the town of Bathmen. He married Gerbregt Berdenis, a widow, on 13 January 1660, an event recorded in the register of the Reformed church of Deventer. The Berdenis family was of fairly high status, a Dr Theodorus Berdenis acting as a member of Deventer's town council between 1655 and 1667. Rutgert was himself probably of patrician or semi-patrician status, enjoying full burgher rights in Deventer (an honour which cost 300 golden guilders), and attaining the rank of lieutenant in the militia. The couple had three sons: Willem, born 29 June 1665; Herman, born 23 November 1670; and Jan, born 28 June 1672. I am grateful to Anna Hesselink of Deventer for this information.

6. H.C.V. Leibbrandt, *Precis of the Archives of the Cape of Good Hope. Letters Despatched, 1696–1708*, No. 20: To the Seventeen at Middelburg, 1 Aug. 1696, p. 21. See also A.J. Böeseken (ed.), *Resolusies van die Politieke Raad, Vol. 3, 1681–1707* (Cape Town, 1961), 21 Aug. 1696, note 22, p. 304.

7. O.F. Mentzel, *A Complete and Authentic Geographical and Topographical Description of the Famous and All Things Considered Remarkable African Cape of Good Hope*, 3 vols. Translated by G.V. Marais and J. Hoge. Revised and edited with an introduction by H.J. Mandelbrote (Cape Town, 1921, 1925, 1944), Vol. 2, p. 53. Mentzel makes the mistake of stating that the name of the first brewer was Willem Menssink (or Menzings), believing father and son to have shared the same first name. Peter Kolb, another German visitor to the Cape in the first decade of the eighteenth century, also got the brewer's name wrong, stating that the brewer who was transported to the Cape at the Company's expense in order to introduce the Deventer method of brewing was called Jacob Lonwen. Peter Kolb, *The Present State of the Cape of Good Hope* (London, 1731), Vol. 2, p. 5.

8. Leibbrandt, *Letters Despatched, 1696–1708*, No. 20, 1 Aug. 1696, p. 21.

9. In August 1696 the Cape authorities asked the Heren XVII what price they were to charge for the massive kettles, which weighed 1190 and 972 pounds respectively. Leibbrandt, *Letters Despatched*, 1 Aug. 1696, p. 21. Payment for the kettles did not become an issue until later, however.

10. See Simon Schama, *The Embarrassment of Riches* (London, 1987), pp. 199, 190 for the significance of beer in Dutch society.

11. Jonathan Israel, *The Rise and Fall of the Dutch Republic* (Oxford, 1995), pp. 1008–9.

12. Khoisan societies knew how to make an intoxicating liquor out of fermented honey and kanna roots. See D. Gordon, 'From Rituals of Rapture to Dependence: The Political Economy of Khoikhoi Narcotic Consumption', *South African Historical Journal*, 35 (1996).

13. M. Whiting Spilhaus, *The First South Africans and the Laws Which Governed Them* (Cape Town, 1949), p. 107. Given the centrality of beer in Dutch society and the importance of beer at the Cape, it is noteworthy that the Cape beer industry has not received the same sort of attention from historians as that which has been lavished on the Cape wine industry. The reasons for this neglect are no doubt complex but, at the heart of the matter, lies the unpalatable truth that it was easier to make bad wine than good beer in the Cape Colony.

14. G.C. de Wet, *Die Vryliede en Vryswartes in die Kaapse Nedersetting 1657–1707* (Cape Town, 1981), p. 92.

15. Böeseken (ed.), *Resolusies van die Politieke Raad, Vol. 3*, 14 July 1694, pp. 283–4.

16. Spilhaus, *First South Africans*, p. 106.

17. Leibbrandt, *Letters Despatched*, 1 Aug. 1696, p. 21.

18. An aum, or aam, was a measure of liquid volume, approximately 155 litres.

19. Böeseken (ed.), *Resolusies van die Politieke Raad, Vol. 3*, 11 Feb. 1697, pp. 309–10.

20. Leibbrandt, *Letters Despatched*, 30 June 1697, p. 46.

21. Ibid., 8 and 9 March 1698, p. 68.

22. H.C.V. Leibbrandt, *Precis of the Archives of the Cape of Good Hope. Journal, 1699–1732* (Cape Town, 1896), 25 Aug. 1699, p. 12; Böeseken, *Resolusies van die Politieke Raad, Vol. 3*, 25 Aug. 1699, p. 350.

23. Leibbrandt, *Journal*, 1 Oct. 1699, p. 14; Leibbrandt, *Letters Despatched*, 18 March 1699, p. 103; Böeseken (ed.), *Resolusies van die Politieke Raad, Vol. 3*, 1 Oct. 1699, p. 351.

24. C.C. de Villiers and C. Pama, *Geslagsregisters van die ou Kaapse Families* (Cape Town, 1981), Vol. 1, p. 553.

25. Ibid., Vol. 2, pp. 966–7. For the Tas and Lindenhovius family trees see J.L.M. Franken, 'Adam Tas en sy Familie', *Die Huisgenoot*, 24 Sept. 1926, pp. 39–41. See also L. Fouché (ed.), *Dagboek van Adam Tas 1705–1706* (Cape Town, 1970), p. 34, n. 4.

26. Böeseken, *Slaves and Free Blacks*, pp. 172, 179, 188, 193 and 190.

27. Böeseken (ed.), *Resolusies van die Politieke Raad, Vol. 3*, 29 Dec. 1699, p. 357; 5 Nov. 1699, p. 352; 13 Dec. 1697, p. 321; Leibbrandt, *Journal*, 5 Nov. 1699, p. 16.

28. De Villiers and Pama, *Geslagsregisters*, Vol. 1, p. 553.

29. De Wet, *Vryliede en Vryswartes*, p. 99; De Villiers and Pama, *Geslagsregisters*, Vol. 1, p. 553. De Wet lists David Lingelbach as dying, or leaving the Cape, in 1703. It is clear, however, from the testimony of David Lingelbach's daughter, Elizabeth, that he died at the Cape in 1705 or 1706. See CA, CJ 317, pp. 334–5.

30. Leibbrandt, *Journal*, 30 Dec. 1701, p. 45.

31. Ibid., 30 Aug. 1700, p. 31; Böeseken (ed.), *Resolusies van die Politieke Raad, Vol. 3*, 30 Aug. 1700. p. 374.

32. Leibbrandt, *Journal*, 29 Aug. 1701, p. 40; Böeseken (ed.), *Resolusies van die Politieke Raad, Vol. 3*, 29 Aug. 1701, p. 383.

33. CA, CJ 317, Elizabeth Lingelbach's testimony, 16 Nov. 1712, p. 329.

34. Ibid., p. 330.

35. Ibid., pp. 330–1.

36. Ibid., pp. 331–2.

37. The institution of marriage was not legally recognised among slaves although some slaves, particularly those in the Company slave lodge, were able to establish stable unions with slaves of the opposite sex. See James C. Armstrong and Nigel A. Worden, 'The Slaves, 1652–1834', in R. Elphick and H. Giliomee (eds.), *The Shaping of South African Society, 1652–1840* (Cape Town, 1989), pp. 122–49. Also Robert C.H. Shell, *Children of Bondage*, pp. 201–2.

38. CA, CJ 317, pp. 332–3.

39. See p. 66 below.

40. Genesis 16: 2.

41. Barbara Bush, 'White "Ladies," Coloured "Favourites" and Black "Wenches": Some Considerations on Sex, Race and Class Factors in the Social Relations in White Creole Society in the British Caribbean', *Slavery and Abolition*, 2, 3 (1981), p. 246.

42. Mentzel, *Description*, Vol. 2, pp. 109–10.

43. Spilhaus, *First South Africans*, pp. 127, 130.

44. H.B. Fine, 'The Administration of Criminal Justice at the Cape of Good Hope, 1795–1828' (D.Phil., Faculty of Law, UCT, 1991), Vol. 2, pp. 554–5. For a detailed investigation into the incidence of marriage between free slave women and white males at the Cape at this time see H.F. Heese, *Groep sonder Grense: Die Rol en Status van die gemengde Bevolking aan die Kaap, 1652–1795* (Bellville, 1984).

45. CA, CJ 317, p. 337.

46. Ibid., p. 333; Fouché (ed.), *Adam Tas*, p. 34, n. 4.

47. De Wet, *Vryliede en Vryswartes*, p. 159.

48. This letter has not been preserved in the archives but it is referred to in Elizabeth Lingelbach's testimony in CA, CJ 137, p. 333.

49. Ibid., pp. 333–4.

50. Ibid., pp. 334–5.

51. Leibbrandt, *Journal*, 29 Aug. 1705, p. 79.

52. Ibid., 27 July 1706, p. 96; Böeseken (ed.), *Resolusies van die Politieke Raad, Vol. 3*, 27 July 1706, p. 444.

53. Fouché, *Adam Tas*, pp. 241–3. Fouché's remains the best account of the opposition to W.A. van der Stel. The time has come, however, for a reinterpretation of the circumstances of the controversial Governor's period of rule.

54. The research of Van Duin and Ross on the Cape economy in the eighteenth century has shown that the Cape economy was less static and oversupplied than previously believed. They argue for constant growth in the production of all major agricultural produce, with a substantial and ever-increasing internal market based on demographic increase. Despite these findings, the fact remains that, at the beginning of the eighteenth century, the colonists were restricted by limited access to a restricted market. See Pieter van Duin and Robert Ross, *The Economy of the Cape Colony in the Eighteenth Century* (Leiden, 1987).

55. Fouché, *Adam Tas*, p. 152.

56. Ibid., p. 135.

57. Ibid., pp. 247–9.

58. Algemeen Rijksarchief (ARA), 4057 (Brieven en Papieren van de Caap de Bonne Esperance overgekomen in 1707), Brief en request van de brouweresse aan de Caep van 20 April 1707 herwaerts geschreven, p. 1017.

59. Ibid.

60. Fouché, *Adam Tas*, pp. 185–6.

61. Ibid., pp. 38, n. 4 and 169, n. 246.

62. A.M. Hugo states that De Waarburg is today known as Matjieskuil. See n. 91 in Fouché, *Adam Tas*, p. 72. See also n. 246 on pp. 168–9. A brief glimpse of Menssink's farming activities may be had in Adam Tas's diary. On 16 December 1705 Tas recorded that 'This morning a slave of brother Menssink came with 6 muids of rye and the same quantity of wheat, and told me that he had been to the mill, but that the miller had told him that he could not oblige him these 8 days as there was no water and a large quantity of corn waiting to be milled'. Ibid., p. 123.

63. Ibid., p. 72, n. 91 and p. 34, n. 4.

64. ARA 4054 (Brieven en Papieren van de Caap de Bonne Esperance overgekomen in 1706), 3 March 1706 and 9 April 1706. For details of Meyer and Van Zevenhoven's interrogation see Fouché, *Adam Tas*, pp. 287–91.

65. ARA 4054. For Van Brakel's relationship to Tas see Fouché, *Adam Tas*, p. 5.

66. ARA 4057 (Brieven en Papieren van de Caap de Bonne Esperance overgekomen in 1707), Vol. 3, pp. 866 and 872; Böeseken (ed.), *Resolusies van die Politieke Raad, Vol. 3*, 14 Sept. 1706, pp. 448–9; Leibbrandt, *Journal*, 31 Aug. 1706, p. 98. Jan Mijndertsz Kruijwagen was the son of Mijndertsz Kruijwagen, Trijntje's first owner.

67. ARA 4057, p. 866.

68. Böeseken (ed.), *Resolusies van die Politieke Raad, Vol. 3*, 14 Sept. 1706, pp. 448–9.

69. ARA 4057, 11 Sept. 1706, p. 879.

70. Böeseken (ed.), *Resolusies van die Politieke Raad, Vol. 3*, 14 Sept. 1706, pp. 448–9.

71. ARA 4057, pp. 882–4; Böeseken (ed.), *Resolusies van die Politieke Raad, Vol. 3*, 17 Sept. 1706, pp. 449–51.

72. ARA 4057, pp. 882–5; Böeseken (ed.), *Resolusies van die Politieke Raad, Vol. 3*, 17 Sept. 1706, pp. 449–51; Leibbrandt, *Journal*, 17 Sept. 1705, p. 99.

73. Leibbrandt, *Letters Despatched*, 15 April 1707, p. 316.

74. ARA 4057, p. 885; Böeseken (ed.), *Resolusies van die Politieke Raad, Vol. 3*, 17 Sept. 1706, p. 450.

75. Böeseken, *Resolusies van die Politieke Raad, Vol. 3*, 17 Nov. 1706, pp. 452–3; Leibbrandt, *Journal*, 17 Nov. 1706, pp. 109–110.

76. The petition may be read in ARA 4057, pp. 1015–22.

77. A.J. Böeseken, 'The Settlement under the Van der Stels', in C.F.J. Muller (ed.), *500 Years: A History of South Africa* (Cape Town, 1969), p. 48; H.C.V. Leibbrandt, *Precis of the Archives of the Cape of Good Hope. Letters Received, 1695–1708* (Cape Town, 1896), 30 Oct. 1706, pp. 432–6.

78. Kruijwagen was, in fact, found guilty of theft in 1712. Böeseken (ed.), *Resolusies van die Politieke Raad, Vol. 3*, p. 448, n. 47.

79. ARA 4057, pp. 1015–22.

80. Leibbrandt, *Journal*, 31 Aug. 1707, p. 135.

81. Ibid., 30 Aug. 1708, p. 172; Böeseken (ed.), *Resolusies van die Politieke Raad, Vol. 4, 1707–1715* (Cape Town, 1962), 30 Aug. 1708, p. 70.

82. Böeseken (ed.), *Resolusies van die Politieke Raad, Vol. 4*, 3 Jan. 1708, p. 42; Leibbrandt, *Journal*, 3 Jan. 1708, p. 150.

83. See Moorrees, *Die Nederduitse Gereformeerde Kerk*, pp. 121–33 for details of Le Boucq's dispute with D'Ableing.

84. Leibbrandt, *Letters Despatched*, 18 April 1708, p. 374.

85. Included amongst the signatories were Maria Lindenhovius's niece, Sara Tas (now married to the wealthy burgher Claas Diepenauw); her nephew, Adam Tas; Tas's wife, Elizabeth van Brakel; Elizabeth's sister, Maria van Brakel; Jacobus van der Heiden (one of the principal leaders of the opposition and a very wealthy man) and his wife, Abigel Vroom.

86. Leibbrandt, *Journal*, 3 Jan. 1708, p. 150; Böeseken (ed.), *Resolusies van die Politieke Raad, Vol. 4*, p. 42.

87. Leibbrandt, *Journal*, 10 Jan. 1708, p. 153; Böeseken (ed.), *Resolusies van die Politieke Raad, Vol. 4*, 10 Jan. 1708, pp. 44–6.

88. Ibid.

89. Böeseken (ed.), *Resolusies van die Politieke Raad, Vol. 4*, 27 Aug. 1709, p. 107; Leibbrandt, *Journal*, 27 Aug. 1709, p. 198.

90. Böeseken (ed.), *Resolusies van die Politieke Raad, Vol. 4*, 19 Aug. 1710, pp. 170–1; Leibbrandt, *Journal*, 19 Aug. 1710, p. 240.

91. Böeseken (ed.), *Resolusies van die Politieke Raad, Vol. 4*, 26 Aug. 1710, pp. 171–2; Leibbrandt, *Journal*, 26 Aug. 1710, p. 241.

92. Böeseken (ed.), *Resolusies van die Politieke Raad, Vol. 4*, 13 April 1711, p. 220; Leibbrandt, *Journal*, 13 April 1711, p. 249.

93. Böeseken (ed.), *Resolusies van die Politieke Raad, Vol. 4*, 23 and 30 Aug. 1712, pp. 282–3.

94. Ibid., 15 Dec. 1711, p. 249.

95. CA, CJ 317, pp. 335–6.

96. Ibid. To sell a slave 'buijten' was to sell that slave to an outlying rural area, where life would usually be less pleasant than in Cape Town, with harder work and fewer opportunities for socialising with other slaves.

97. Tutucorijn or Tuticorin is in the south of India.

98. Henricus Brouwer, *De Jure Connubiorum*, 2 vols. (2nd edn, Delphis, 1704). Translated into Afrikaans by P. van Warmelo and F.J. Bosman as *Oor die Huweliksreg*, 2 vols. (Johannesburg, 1967).

99. Brouwer, *De Jure Connubiorum*, Vol. 2, pp. 156–62.

100. Leonard Blussé, *Strange Company: Chinese Settlers, Mestizo Women and the Dutch in VOC Batavia* (Dordrecht, 1986), pp. 162–71, 207–10.

101. Ibid., p. 210. Blussé's essay in this book, 'Butterfly or Mantis? The Life and Times of Cornelia van Nijenroode', pp. 172–259, is a particularly interesting case study of a feuding couple in seventeenth-century Batavia and throws much light on Dutch laws of marriage at that time.

102. 'Social control through ecclesiastical discipline was one of the corner-stones of early Batavian colonial society.' Blussé, *Strange Company*, p. 256.

103. See Moorrees, *Die Nederduitse Gereformeerde Kerk*, pp. 121–34; J.N. Gerstner, 'A Christian Monopoly: The Reformed Church and Colonial Society under Dutch Rule', in R. Elphick and R. Davenport (eds.), *Christianity in South Africa: A Political, Social and Cultural History* (Cape Town, 1997), p. 20.

104. Blussé, *Strange Company*, p. 172.

105. Brouwer, *De Jure Connubiorum*, p. 163.

106. CA, CJ 317, pp. 336–8. D'Ableing arrived at the Cape to assume his duties on 6 May 1707. He seems to have been separated from his wife and this may have coloured his judgment and made him reluctant to grant to other people what he did not himself possess, i.e. a divorce. Böeseken (ed.), *Resolusies van die Politieke Raad, Vol. 3*, 2 May 1707, n. 29, p. 465.

107. CA, CJ 317, pp. 338–9.

108. Ludovico Ariosto's *Orlando Furioso* was an immensely popular work, first published in Italian in 1532. We do not know in what language Menssink had read the epic but we do know that he was a book lover and probably had an edition in his library. The quotation is taken from Sir Paul Harvey (ed.), *The Oxford Companion to English Literature*, 4th edn (Oxford, 1969), p. 908.

109. Menssink may, on the other hand, have been removing Cupido because he did not want any males – apart from himself – in his wife's household.

110. CA, CJ 317, pp. 339.

111. CA, VC 20, pp. 46–7; CA CJ 317, pp. 340–1.

112. It was not uncommon for female slaves to sleep in the house of their owners but in spacious houses they usually slept in the kitchen rather than the bedroom. See Shell, *Children of Bondage*, pp. 251–62.

113. CA, VC 20, pp. 47–8; CA, CJ 317, pp. 340–1.

114. CA, VC 20, pp. 48–9; CA, CJ 317, pp. 341–2.

115. CA, VC 20, pp. 49–50; CA, CJ 317, pp. 342–3.

116. CA, VC 20, pp. 50–1.

117. Bush, 'White "Ladies," Coloured "Favourites" and Black "Wenches,"' p. 246. Bush is citing M. Foucault, *The History of Sexuality*, Vol. 1 (London, 1978), p. 102.

118. Elizabeth's situation may remind readers of that of the heroine of Jean Rhys's *The Wide Sargasso Sea*.

119. Bush, 'White "Ladies," Coloured "Favourites" and Black "Wenches,"' p. 246.

120. CA, VC 20, pp. 52–3.

121. 'As die eggenoot 'n moordenaar of 'n gifmenger is, of iemand is wat heiligskennend is of 'n rower of 'n onderhouer van rowers, of 'n veedief of 'n menserower of koppelaar van sy vrou of dogters, of poog om dit te wees, of iets onderneem in stryd met die gesag, of aan die Franse siekte ly, sodat daar 'n vermoede van gepleegde owerspel bestaan, of hy van die misdaad van vervalsing veroordeel is, dan bestaan daar 'n parate aksie vir die eggenote vir skeiding van bed en tafel.' Brouwer, *De Jure Connubiorum*, Vol. 2, p. 157.

122. CA, VC 20, pp. 53–4.

123. Ibid., p. 54; CA, CJ 317, pp. 343–4.

124. Ibid.

125. CA, CJ 317, p. 344; CA, VC 20, p. 55.

126. It is interesting to note that even today visitors to Deventer's town square may admire a pair of scales which, in less enlightened times, was used to test the weight of people suspected of being witches. If the scales moved in a certain direction the person was pronounced guilty. This is, at the very least, an indication that citizens (or ex-citizens) of Deventer came from a society where witchcraft was regarded as a reality.

127. CA, CJ 317, pp. 244–5.

128. Ibid., p. 344.

129. See for instance Barbara Bush, *Slave Women in Caribbean Society* (London, 1990), pp. 52–63.

130. Ibid., p. 147.

131. CA, VC 20, pp. 56–7.

132. Ibid., pp 61–2. According to Gerrit, Menssink brought him the hand still fresh from the brewery. He could not see whether it was a white or black hand because of the darkness. CA, CJ 317, p. 406.

133. See Keith Thomas, *Religion and the Decline of Magic* (London, 1971), pp. 597–606. On the magical power of the hands of hanged men see Peter Linebaugh. 'The Tyburn Riot Against the Surgeons', in D. Hay, P. Linebaugh, J. Rule, E.P. Thompson and C. Winslow, *Albion's Fatal Tree: Crime and Society in Eighteenth Century England* (London, 1975), pp. 65–117. Linebaugh writes (p. 109): 'Despite regional and class differences a single rule may be said to have governed the folklore, ritual and superstition surrounding death and burial; meticulous attention to the proper forms of burial was required to ensure the peaceful departure of the dead. When death was violent and moreover willed by society, as in deaths by hanging, something of a corollary to this rule existed. Believing that the corpse possessed therapeutic powers, able to cure sickness and heal wounds, it appeared that even this most terrible of society's sanctions against wrong-doers was qualified in popular belief by the ability of the corpse to confer by magic some marvellous sign of health to society.'

134. Executed criminals in the Cape often had their right hand cut off as part of their sentence. Thus the slave Corydon of Madras, who attacked his mistress with a crowbar, 'was to be brought to the place of execution; his right hand cut off, and then broken from his lower extremities upwards until death followed (after having previously been half strangled). After that he was to be taken to the outside place of execution and left there on a grating, with the hand and crowbar above his head until destroyed by the birds of the air. Leibbrandt, *Journal*, 22 Sept. 1708, p. 174. See also *Journal*, 7 Feb. 1714, p. 258; and 9 Sept. 1719, p. 279; and 23 Nov. 1719, p. 279.

135. See Florike Egmond, *Underworlds: Organized Crime in the Netherlands 1650–1800* (Cambridge, 1993), p. 55, and pp. 209–10, n. 17. Egmond makes the following comment: 'Perhaps it is significant that such statements were apparently only made by women and children. Was this the kind of secret trade knowledge never spoken about by the men in front of the authorities, or were women and children the only ones to believe in such customs?'

136. CA, VC 20, p. 58.

137. Ibid., pp. 62–3.

138. Ibid., p. 59; CA, CJ 317, p. 245.

139. CA, CJ 317, pp. 345–6. The records state 'Hendrik Kruijwagen' but there is no record of a person of this name in the colony at the time and Jan Mijndertsz is probably meant.

140. Van Assenburgh was himself a notorious womaniser whose loose conduct drew unfavourable comments from Johanna van Riebeeck, granddaughter of Jan van Riebeeck, when she visited the Cape in 1710. He further scandalised the devout by inviting officials, councillors and officers to witness a fight between dogs and bulls on the parade ground in front of the Castle one Sunday after church. Moorrees, *Nederduitse Gereformeerde Kerk*, p. 142.

141. CA, VC 20, p. 60; Böeseken (ed.), *Resolusies van die Politieke Raad, Vol. 4*, 2 Dec. 1711, p. 250.

142. CA, VC 20, pp. 63–8.

143. Ibid., p. 64.

144. Ibid., pp. 65–8.

145. Ibid., pp. 60–1.

146. Ibid., p. 61.

147. CA, CJ 317, p. 355.

148. Ibid., p. 233.

149. Ibid., p. 220.

150. Böeseken (ed.), *Resolusies van die Politieke Raad, Vol. 4*, 13 Dec. 1712, pp. 296–7.

151. CA, CJ 5, 1 Dec. 1712, pp. 86, 89.

152. C.G. Botha, *History of Law, Medicine and Place Names in the Cape of Good Hope* (Cape

Town, 1962), p. 57.

153. Ibid., p. 57.

154. Leibbrandt, *Journal*, 1 Sept. 1714, p. 260.

155. 'The slave Titus, mentioned above, died about midday, having lived in his misery about 48 hours; something horrible to think of, to say nothing of personally beholding the misery. It is said that 4 hours after his empalement he received a bottle of arrack from which he drank freely and heartily. When advised not to take too much lest he should get drunk, he answered that it did not matter, as he sat fast enough, and that there was no fear of his falling. It is true that whilst sitting in that deplorable state, he often joked, and scoffingly said that he would never again believe a woman. A way of dying lauded by the Romans, but damnable among the Christians.' Leibbrandt, *Journal*, 3 Sept. 1714, p. 260–1.

156. Fine, 'Administration of Criminal Justice', Vol. 2, p. 551.

157. CA, CJ 5, 16 Nov. 1713, p. 80.

158. The sexual preferences of Menssink were obviously even more embarrassing for the Government Archivist of 1896 than for the authorities of 1713. When H.C.V. Leibbrandt came to make his precis of the *Dagboek* of the Castle he decided to leave out the record of the Menssink case that may be found in the original.

159. Fouché, *Adam Tas*, p. 169.

160. Böeseken (ed.), *Resolusies van die Politieke Raad, Vol. 4*, 29 May 1714, pp. 387–9; 31 May 1714, pp. 389–91; 1 July 1714, pp. 392–3; 10 Jan. 1715, pp. 431–2.

161. Ibid., 13 Dec. 1712, pp. 296–7.

162. CA, VC 20, pp. 71–2.

163. CA, CJ 317, p. 223.

164. Ibid., p. 73.

165. CA, VC 20, pp. 73–4.

166. Ibid.

167. CA, CJ 5, 2 March 1713, p. 17.

168. Böeseken (ed.), *Resolusies van die Politieke Raad, Vol. 4*, 13 Dec. 1712, pp. 296–7; 12 Sept. 1713, p. 359.

169. CA, CJ 5, 9 March 1713, pp. 21, 25.

170. Ibid., 23 March 1713, p. 28.

171. CA, VC 20, 18 April 1713, p. 109; 26 April 1713, p. 114; 3 May 1713, p. 119; 6 May 1713, p. 121; 7 May 1713, p. 122; 10 May 1713, p. 125; 12–15 May 1713, pp. 126–7; 19 May 1713, pp. 129–30; 31 May 1713, p. 139; 13 June 1713, p. 146; 24 June 1713, p. 157; 2 Aug. 1713, p. 185; 26 Aug. 1713, p. 198; 28 Nov. 1713, p. 296; 17 Dec. 1713, p. 313.

172. CA, CJ 5, 30 March 1713, p. 29; 5 May 1713, pp. 30, 90.

173. Brouwer, *De Jure Connubiorum*.

174. CA, CJ 5, 26 Oct. 1713, p. 71.

175. Ibid., 2 Nov. 1713, p. 76; 9 Nov. 1713, p. 82.

176. Fouché, *Adam Tas*, pp. 72, n. 91; 168–9, n. 246.

177. An interesting fact, which may have some bearing on the case, is that Hercules van Loon had been the bookkeeper of Willem Menssink in 1697. CA, C 361 (Memorie der families die repatrieren), Batavia, Jan. 1697, pp. 25–7. (I am grateful to Ad Biewenga for this reference.) On his death his papers were left in chaos and it is logical to suppose that his widow, Maria, would have looked through them. This may have been the source of the detailed and privileged information which Maria and her new husband, Helot, had about the financial foundations of the Menssink estate.

178. CA, CJ 5, 16 Nov. 1713, p. 80; 30 Nov. 1713, p. 97; 7 Dec. 1713, p. 101.

179. CA, CJ 2916 (Vendu Rollen, 1696–1727), pp. 25–32, 51–5.

180. Ibid, pp. 33–6, 38–40.

181. Diepenauw had been the Company's meat contractor, a member of the Burgher Council and master of the Orphan Chamber. Sara was his second wife. He died a very wealthy

man owning three farms and a piece of land 'onder de Wintberg'. See Böeseken (ed.), *Resolusies van die Politieke Raad, Vol. 3*, 8 Sept. 1693, p. 275, n. 42. Also *Vol. 4*, 20 Dec. 1707, p. 37; 31 Dec. 1707, p. 41; 30 Jan. 1708, p. 49; 15 Dec. 1711, p. 249.

182. CA, CJ 2916, pp. 47–50, 33–6, 25–8.

183. Franken, 'Adam Tas en sy Familie', *Die Huisgenoot*, 1 Oct. 1926, p. 32. The records sometimes refer to one of the Menssink farms as Joostenbergh instead of Hercules Pilaar at Joostenberg.

184. CA, MOOC 3/1/5 (Inkomende Briewe Weeskamer), 24 April 1722.

185. Ibid., Sara Tas to Willem Menssink, 24 April 1722: 'het sal voor mijn wel droevig zijn als mijn Mittjen weg is'.

186. Fouché, *Adam Tas*, p. 34, n. 4; Franken, 'Adam Tas en sy Familie', *Die Huisgenoot*, 24 Sept. 1926, p. 39.

187. CA, MOOC 3/1/5, Margarieta Maria Menssink to Willem Menssink, 24 April 1722.

188. Ibid.

189. Franken, 'Adam Tas en sy Familie', *Die Huisgenoot*, 24 Sept. 1926, p. 43 and 1 Oct. 1926, p. 31.

190. CA, 1/STB 12/82 (Generale Opneem tot Ontvangst van Schapen en Bestengeld en Leeuwen en Tijgergeld), 1716.

191. CA, CJ 2916, p. 46.

192. CA, CJ 5, 17 May 1714, p. 44; 24 May 1714, p. 49.

193. CA, 1/STB 18/157, 28 Sept. 1716.

194. Menssink had had a great deal of trouble with slave runaways in the past. In 1713 he told the Court of Justice that he had had three runaways that year and that four others had been missing for over a year. CA, CJ 2916, p. 46. Some of these slaves had been called to join a *droster* gang by Jacob van Ceilon and Ary of Bengal in 1709. These slaves stole three firearms from the brewer and took to the mountains in an attempt to reach 'Caffersland'. The *drosters* broke up in disunity after several weeks. Not all were recaptured. CA, VC 19, Verbatim Copy, Dagboek, 1709–1710, 21 Sept. 1709, pp. 299–306.

195. CA, 1/STB 18/157, 28 Sept. 1716.

196. CA, CJ 5, 17 May 1714, p. 43.

197. Ibid., 24 May 1714, p. 46.

198. Ibid., p. 48.

199. Ibid., 31 May 1714, p. 52; 7 June 1714, p. 54.

200. Ibid., 22 June 1714, pp. 67–9.

201. CA, CJ 2916, pp. 42–3.

202. CA, CJ 5, 7 June 1714, p. 56; 14 June 1714, p. 59; 21 June 1714, p. 64.

203. CA, 1/STB 18/156, 30 Oct. 1714.

204. Franken, 'Adam Tas en sy Familie', *Die Huisgenoot*, 1 Oct. 1926, p. 32.

205. Quite why Tas's second marriage was unhappy is not recorded but that it was unhappy is attested to by no less a person than his sister, Sara Diepenauw.

206. CA, MOOC 7/1/3, No. 23, 10 April 1721. Valentijn was also to be given 25 guilders.

207. Franken, 'Adam Tas en sy Familie', *Die Huisgenoot*, 24 Sept. 1926, p. 39.

208. CA, CJ 2651, No. 31, 1 April 1718.

209. CA, MOOC 7/1/3, No. 23, 10 April 1721. When Tas himself died in 1722 there were 23 lots of books at the auction of his goods and a further 12 lots were auctioned in 1726. Some of these would doubtless have been given to him by Menssink. Fouché, *Adam Tas*, p. 72, n. 91.

210. See CA, MOOC 3/1/5 (Inkomende Briewe Weeskamer, 1722–1732). Franken has published copies of these letters in 'Adam Tas en sy Familie', *Die Huisgenoot*, 24 Sept. 1926, pp. 39, 41, 43, 63 and 1 Oct. 1926, pp. 31, 32, 33.

211. Franken, 'Adam Tas en sy Familie', *Die Huisgenoot*, 24 Sept. 1926, p. 39.

212. CA, MOOC 3/1/5, Gerard Tas to Willem Menssink, 17 April 1722; Sara Tas to Willem Menssink, 24 April 1722.

213. Ibid., Sara Tas to Willem Menssink, 24 April 1722.

214. Ibid.

215. Ibid.

216. I could not find Margarieta Menssink's letter in the MOOC 3/1/5 file along with the others, so have used Franken's copy in *Die Huisgenoot*, 1 Oct. 1926, p. 31.

217. CA, MOOC 3/1/5, Sara Tas to Willem Menssink, 24 April 1722.

218. Ibid., Gerard Tas to Willem Menssink, 17 April 1722.

219. Franken, 'Adam Tas en sy Familie', *Die Huisgenoot*, 24 Sept. 1926, p. 43; 1 Oct. 1926, p. 32.

220. Franken, 'Adam Tas en sy Familie', *Die Huisgenoot*, 1 Oct. 1926, p. 32; Fouché, *Adam Tas*, p. 17.

2 Fugitives on the Cape Frontier

1. For a further discussion of these issues, particularly after 1770, see Chapter 5 below.

2. Studies which deal with fugitive slaves and their relationship with other societies at the Cape are R. Ross, *Cape of Torments* and N. Worden, *Slavery in Dutch South Africa.*

3. Böeseken (ed.), *Resolusies van die Politieke Raad, Vol. 3, 1681–1707*, 20 July 1686, p. 140.

4. CA, LM 10, Council of Policy, Précis of Letters Despatched, 1699–1708, 10 Oct. 1702, pp. 763–4.

5. Böeseken (ed.), *Resolusies van die Politieke Raad, Vol. 4, 1707–1715*, 1 June 1711, p. 227.

6. Böeseken (ed.), *Resolusies van die Politieke Raad, Vol. 3*, 13 Dec. 1696, p. 307.

7. See for instance the evidence of the fugitive slaves Sato of Macassar, Jan of Malabar and Jacob of Malabar in CA, VC 19, 7 May 1709, pp. 145–153.

8. See Ross, *Cape of Torments*, pp. 64–6. In March 1736 it was thought that a severe fire in Cape Town might have been caused by slave or European *drosters* who were hiding out on Table Mountain. G.C. de Wet (ed.), *Resolusies van die Politieke Raad, Vol. 9* (Pretoria, 1981), 20 March 1736, p. 59.

9. On 30 June 1697 the Cape authorities reported to the Heren XVII that they had managed to take two of the Griqua hostage, thanks to the Cochoqua having captured them, and questioned them about harbouring slaves. The Griqua claimed to have killed some 15 or 16 slaves but admitted to having a few still living with them. One of the Griqua captives was released with instructions to tell his fellows that the other Griqua would only be freed once all slaves were restored. 'Hitherto, however, no further news has been received.' Leibbrandt, *Letters Despatched*, 30 June 1697, pp. 46–7.

10. CA, VC 18, 1707–1708, 5 Nov. 1707, pp 348–55.

11. CA, VC 17, 1705–1706, 5 Oct. 1706, p. 678. It is more than likely that the present-day Hoedjies Bay (the northern end of Saldanha Bay) is named after Hoeties Kraal and not, as Raper suggests, after the Dutch family name Oetgens van Waveren. P.E. Raper, *The Dictionary of Southern African Place Names* (Johannesburg, 1987), p. 215.

12. CA, LM 18, Letters Received 1709–1718, 16 Jan. 1712.

13. 'Some fugitive Javanese and Macassaren slaves having been followed up and only one caught, it was considered that the fugitives might do a great deal of harm – they were therefore followed on horseback by 10 men, and a reward of 3 Rds. was offered to the surrounding Hottentots for everyone caught by them. 15 were captured and brought to the Castle and punished, the rest were, it is said, killed in a fight with the Hottentots, amongst them the ringleader, an Oriental exile sent hither last year.' CA, LM 21, Letters Despatched 3 Jan. 1707–31 Dec. 1720, 4 April 1713, p. 29. See also CA, LM 21, 22 Oct. 1712.

14. Mentzel, *Description of the Cape*, Vol. 3, p. 300.

15. See Ross, *Cape of Torments*, p. 48.

16. CA, VC 20, 1711–1714, 24 Jan. 1713, pp. 7–23.

17. A point made by Ross in *Cape of Torments*, p. 22.

18. CA, VC 19, 1709–1710, 25 June 1709, pp. 221–7.

19. CA, VC 20, 16 July 1712, pp. 121–39.

20. The hill called 'Drosterskop' outside present day Durbanville is evidence of the attraction this area used to have for *drosters*.

21. CA, VC 20, 16 July 1712, pp. 121–39.

22. Ibid. 'Tabee' was a common form of greeting in the colony and is thought to derive from the Dutch word for tobacco, *tabak*, since the first words that most non-Europeans addressed to a pipe-smoking Dutchman were invariably a request for tobacco.

23. CA, VC 20, 16 July 1712, pp. 121–39.

24. Ibid.

25. CA, LM 23, Letters Despatched 1723–1725, 23 Oct. 1724, p. 170.

26. CA, LM 20, Letters Received 1726–1732, 10 Oct. 1730.

27. Leibbrandt, *Journal*, 17 Dec. 1707, p. 144.

28. Ibid., p. 145.

29. *Hotnotsvy*, ghaukum or *carpobrotus edulis*. The fruits of this succulent are large and yellow when ripe with an edible, jelly-like sweet pulp. See C.A. Smith, *Common Names of South African Plants* (Pretoria, 1966), pp. 251–2.

30. Leibbrandt, *Journal*, 17 Dec. 1707, p. 146.

31. G.C. de Wet (ed.), *Resolusies van die Politieke Raad, Vol. 5, 1716–1719* (Cape Town, 1964), 22 Dec. 1716, p. 120; 5 Jan. 1717, p. 128.

32. CA, LM 21, Letters Despatched 1707–1720, 11 Jan. 1717, p. 69.

33. Leibbrandt, *Journal*, 9 May 1717, pp. 272–3.

34. CA, LM 19, Letters Received 1717–1726, 25 May 1719.

35. Leibbrandt, *Journal*, 7 Nov. 1714, p. 263.

36. CA, LM 18, Letters Received 1709–1718, 6 Jan. 1714.

37. One of Menssink's runaway slaves, a Madagascan, survived six years as a fugitive before being recaptured and broken on the wheel. Leibbrandt, *Journal*, 17 August 1719, p. 278.

38. CA, LM 23, Letters Despatched 1723–1725, 12 May 1724, p. 148.

39. Ibid., 6 Feb. 1725, p. 200.

40. CA, LM 24, Letters Despatched 1726–1728, 24 Jan. 1726; LM 19, Letters Received 1717–1726, 26 Jan. 1726, 31 Jan. 1726.

41. CA, LM 24, Letters Despatched 1726–1728, 20 April 1726, pp. 65-6.

42. CA, LM 21, Letters Despatched 1707–1720, 31 July 1719, p. 112.

43. R. Slotkin, *Regeneration Through Violence: The Mythology of the American Frontier 1600–1860* (Middletown, 1973), p. 34.

44. CA, VC 15, 7 Oct. 1701, p. 1007.

45. CA, LM 21, Letters Despatched 1707–1720, 3 Nov. 1717, p. 78. Five other vagabonds are named in this letter.

46. CA, LM 23, Letters Despatched 1723–1725, 5 Feb. 1725, p. 199.

47. CA, LM 25, Letters Despatched 1728–1732, 22 June 1730, p. 349; LM 20, Letters Received 1726–1732, 21 June 1730.

48. CA, LM 24, Letters Despatched 1726–1728, 18 Aug. 1727, p. 147; LM 20, Letters Received 1726–1732, 19 Aug. 1727, 22 Aug. 1727.

49. CA, LM 25, Letters Despatched 1728–1732, 3 April 1729, 7 April 1729; LM 20, Letters Received 1726–1732, 3 April 1729, 5 April 1729.

50. A great deal of work still has to be done on the subject of *knechts* but see R. Shell, 'Land, Labour and Cape Families: The Introduction of Slavery and Serfdom' (unpublished paper), pp. 20–42.

51. See CA, 1/STB 13/31, Alphabetiese Lyst van Persone wat op Veldtogten zyn uijt gegaan, beginnende met Nov. 1737 (1736-1744). In January 1735 the landdrost and *heemraden* of Stellenbosch resolved that in future all those going inland would have to give their names to the secretary and report back once they had returned. CA, C 650, Dag Register van

Stellenbosch en Drakenstein 1729–1736, 16 Jan. 1735.

52. Böeseken (ed.), *Resolusies van die Politieke Raad, Vol. 3*, 25 Dec. 1687, p. 181.

53. Leibbrandt, *Journal*, 18 June 1709, p. 194.

54. CA, LM 25, Letters Despatched 1728–1732, 28 March 1729, p. 278.

55. De Wet (ed.), *Resolusies van die Politieke Raad, Vol. 9*, 3 Dec. 1737, pp. 168–9.

56. Ibid.

57. The case of Estienne Barbier (in Chapter 3) is a good example of the type of hospitality that personable fugitives could expect from widows.

58. CA, LM 18, Letters Received 1709–1718, 17 April 1715.

59. For the impact of the expansion of the colonial frontier on Khoisan societies between 1700 and 1740 see Penn, 'The Northern Cape Frontier Zone', pp. 49–139.

60. Leibbrandt, *Journal*, 24 March 1732 and 4 April 1732, p. 333.

61. De Wet (ed.), *Resolusies van die Politieke Raad, Vol. 9*, 17 Aug. 1738, p. 220.

62. CA, LM 20, Letters Received 1726–1732, 12 Nov. 1728.

63. CA, C 457, Inkomende Briewe, April 1740–Dec. 1740, 16 Feb. 1742.

64. CA, C 650, Dag Register van Stellenbosch en Drakenstein, 1729–1736, 10 Sept. 1731, 12 Sept. 1731; LM 20, Letters Received 1726–1732, 11 Sept. 1731.

65. CA, C 650, 12 Sept. 1731.

66. CA, LM 20, Letters Received 1726–1732, 13 Nov. 1731.

67. CA, C 650, 12 March 1736.

68. For the frontier war of 1739 see Chapter 3 below; also Penn, 'Northern Cape Frontier Zone', pp. 91–139, and Penn, 'The Frontier in the Western Cape, 1700–1740' in J. Parkington and M. Hall (eds.), *Papers in the Prehistory of the Western Cape, South Africa* (Oxford, 1987).

69. CA, LM 58, Resolutions of the Council of Policy 1743–1745, 19 Oct. 1745.

70. CA, C 652, 26 July 1743.

71. CA, 1/STB 3/10, Criminal Records 1749–1758, 19 Nov. 1755.

72. CA, 1/STB 3/11, Criminal Records 1759–1782, 8 May 1775. Eastern slaves, who came from a culture where 'running amok' was a ritualised form of violence against a hopeless situation, often ran amok as a form of resistance (invariably suicidal) against slavery at the Cape. See Edna Bradlow, 'Running Amok and its Historical Significance', *Cabo*, 5, 1 (1990), pp. 8–11. For other examples, see the Constantia slave uprising of 1713 (CA, VC 20, 24 Jan. 1713, pp. 7–23) and the uprising of *bandieten* on Robben Island in 1751 (CA, CJ 359, Criminele Processtukken 1751, pp. 319–71) and N. Penn, 'From Penguins to Prisoners: Robben Island, 1488–1805' in N. Penn, H. Deacon and N. Alexander, *Robben Island: The Politics of Rock and Sand* (Cape Town, 1992), pp. 26–7.

73. CA, 1/STB 3/11, 8 May 1775.

74. See Chapter 5 below for a consideration of fugitive groups in the second half of the eighteenth century.

75. See Penn, 'Northern Cape Frontier Zone', pp. 169–210.

76. A notable exception to this trend was Hendrik Wikar, a Swede in Company employment, who deserted from service in April 1775 and made his way northwards to the Orange River. He travelled extensively along the river and kept a journal. So valuable was his knowledge that the Company decided to pardon him in 1779. E.E. Mossop, *The Journal of Hendrik Jacob Wikar (1779) and the Journal of Jacobus Coetsé (1760) and Willem van Reenen (1791)* (Cape Town, 1935).

77. See Chapter 5 below for the *drosters* of the Cedarberg.

78. For the role of 'Bastaards' and 'Bastaard-Hottentots' in the eighteenth-century Cape frontier zone, see Penn, 'Northern Cape Frontier Zone' and Penn, 'The Orange River Frontier Zone, *c.*1700–1805' in A.B. Smith (ed.), *Einiqualand: Studies of the Orange River Frontier* (Cape Town, 1995), pp. 21–109.

79. For a discussion of the word 'Bastaard' see M. Legassick, 'The Northern Frontier to *c.*1840: The Rise and Decline of the Griqua People' in Elphick and Giliomee (eds.), *The Shaping of South African Society, 1652–1820* (Cape Town, 1979) pp. 69–70. See also G. Nienaber,

Khoekhoense Stamname (Pretoria, 1989), pp. 170–9.

80. For a discussion of race, class and social status in eighteenth-century Cape society see R. Elphick and R. Shell, 'Intergroup Relations: Khoikhoi, Settlers, Slaves and Free Blacks, 1652–1795' in Elphick and Giliomee (eds.), *The Shaping of South African Society,* pp. 184–239; Heese, *Groep sonder Grense*; W.M. Freund, 'Race in the Social Structure of South Africa 1652–1836' in *Race and Class,* 17 (1976); H. Giliomee, 'Eighteenth Century Cape Society and its Historiography: Culture, Race and Class', *Social Dynamics*, 9 (1983).

81. See sources cited in footnote 78 above. See also J. S. Marais, *The Cape Coloured People, 1652–1937* (London, 1939), pp. 10–13.

82. Elphick and Shell, 'Intergroup Relations', p. 199.

83. Ibid., p. 199.

84. G.C. de Wet (ed.), *Resolusies van die Politieke Raad, Vol.10 1740–1743* (Pretoria, 1984), 14 Feb. 1743, p. 226.

85. See Chapter 3.

86. See Penn, 'Northern Cape Frontier Zone', pp. 281–95.

87. J.A. Heese, 'Onderwys in Namakwaland 1750–1940' (D.Ed., University of Stellenbosch, 1942), p. 80.

88. H. Lichtenstein, *Travels in Southern Africa in the Years 1803, 1804, 1805 and 1806* (reprinted, Cape Town, 1965), Vol. 2, p. 303.

89. Ibid., p 304.

90. A. Böeseken (ed.), *Resolusies van die Politieke Raad, Vol. 6, 1720–1723* (Cape Town, 1965), 2 Sept. 1721, pp. 128–9.

91. CA, C 655, Dag Register van Stellenbosch en Drakenstein, 1771–1779, 28 Dec. 1773.

92. For a discussion of Oorlams see J. de Bruyn, 'The Oorlams Afrikaners: From Dependence to Dominance, *c.*1760–1823' (paper delivered to the South African Historical Society, Durban, July 1981), and Nienaber, *Stamname*, pp. 794–803.

93. For Oorlam gangs see Penn, 'Northern Cape Frontier Zone', pp. 281–384 and Penn, 'The Orange River Frontier Zone', pp. 34–93.

94. Legassick believes that the word was applied by extra-colonial Khoikhoi to those Khoikhoi who had been in colonial service and that the latter group came to accept the designation. See Legassick, 'The Northern Frontier to 1840', p. 410 n. 49.

95. Ibid., pp. 368–9.

96. De Bruyn, 'Oorlams', p. 2.

97. CA, 1/STB 13/31, Alphabetiese Lyst van Persone wat op Veldtogten zyn uijt gegaan (1736–1740).

98. CA, 1/STB 3/10, Criminal Records 1749–1758, 21 Feb. 1749.

99. Ibid., 13 March 1749, 11 April 1749, 21 April 1749.

100. My analysis has been informed by Mary Douglas, *Purity and Danger: An Analysis of the Concepts of Pollution and Taboo* (London, reprint 1989); R. Buijtenhuis, *Essays on the Mau Mau,* (London, 1992); Eric Leed, *No Man's Land: Combat and Identity in World War One* (Cambridge, 1979).

101. L. Guelke, 'The Making of Two Frontier Communities: Cape Colony in the Eighteenth Century', *Historical Reflections*, 12 (1985), p. 419.

102. Ibid., p. 434.

103. For the concept of an open and closed frontier zone see H. Giliomee, 'Processes in the Development of the Southern African Frontier', in H. Lamar and L. Thompson (eds.), *The Frontier in History* (New Haven, 1981).

3 Estienne Barbier

1. Apart from archival records the work I have relied on most heavily in preparing this chapter is the doctoral thesis of Professor Roy Henry Pheiffer. In his thesis, 'Die Gebroke

Nederlands van Franssprekendes aan die Kaap in die eerste Helfte van die agtiende Eeu' (University of the Witwatersrand, 1976), Professor Pheiffer has collected together the most important documents written by or pertaining to Estienne Barbier. He has also subjected them to a linguistic and historical analysis, providing the first accurate outline of Barbier's life. I have preferred to use his clear typescripts of the Barbier documents rather than the originals. Where I quote from Professor Pheiffer's collection I shall cite his thesis pagination. (This thesis has been published, under the same title, in Cape Town, 1980.) Where I quote from the fruits of my own archival labours, only the archival references shall be given.

2. A recent account of the Barbier rebellion is in Gerrit Schutte's chapter 'Company and Colonists at the Cape' in Elphick and Giliomee (eds.), *The Shaping of South African Society* (Cape Town, 1979). Following the lead of various other authorities he puts the date of Barbier's capture as 17 March 1739, whereas it was actually 9 September 1739. Apart from this error the rebellion simply deserves more space than most accounts give it.

3. Professor Pheiffer gives an account of these scholars in the introduction to his thesis.

4. D. Crummey (ed.), *Banditry, Rebellion and Social Protest in Africa* (London, 1986).

5. R. Austen, 'Social Bandits and Other Heroic Criminals: Western Models of Resistance and their Relevance for Africa', in ibid.

6. There are, to my knowledge, two other possible contenders for the ranks of social banditry in early South African history. The first is the brutal runaway slave, Leander Bugis, described by Robert Ross in *Cape of Torments*, chapter 5. Ross himself admits that Bugis and his followers, who were active near Cape Hanglip in 1735–6, were far more like bandits than social bandits (p. 61). V.C. Malherbe has described the other candidates in her article 'Hermanus and his Sons: Khoi Bandits and Conspirators in the Post-Rebellion Period (1803–1818)', *African Studies*, 41, 2 (1982), pp. 189–202. As with many other Khoisan rebels, it is difficult to determine where 'primary resistance' ends and banditry begins.

7. E.J. Hobsbawm, *Primitive Rebels* (Manchester, 1959), p. 5.

8. Ibid., pp. 19–20.

9. Ibid..

10. Ibid., p.3.

11. For a discussion see Crummey's 'Introduction' to *Banditry, Rebellion and Social Protest in Africa.*

12. A. Blok, 'The Peasant and the Brigand: Social Banditry Reconsidered', *Comparative Studies in Society and History*, 14, 4 (1972), pp. 494–505.

13. Or hardly anything. There is a reference to Ghanaian cocoa smugglers in the preface to the Penguin edition of E. Hobsbawm, *Bandits* (London, 1972).

14. Austen, 'Social Bandits', p. 89.

15. Ibid., p. 91.

16. P. O'Malley, 'Social Bandits, Modern Capitalism and the Traditional Peasantry: A Critique of Hobsbawm', *Journal of Peasant Studies* 6, 4 (1979), pp. 489–99.

17. Hobsbawm, 'Peasants and Politics', *Journal of Peasant Studies*, 1 (1973), pp. 3–22.

18. O'Malley, 'Social Bandits', p. 492.

19. P. Corrigan, 'On the Politics of Production: A Comment on "Peasants and Politics" by Eric Hobsbawm', *Journal of Peasant Studies,* 2 (1975), pp. 341–9.

20. O'Malley, 'Social Bandits', p. 492.

21. Pheiffer, 'Gebroke Nederlands', Vol. 1, p. 14.

22. O.F. Mentzel, *Life at the Cape in Mid-Eighteenth Century: The Biography of Rudolf Siegfried Allemann, Captain of the Military Forces and Commander of the Castle in the Service of the Dutch East India Company at the Cape of Good Hope* (Cape Town, reprint 1919).

23. Pheiffer, 'Gebroke Nederlands', Vol. 1, pp. 16–17.

24. Ibid., pp. 17–18.

25. Ibid., pp. 18–19.

26. Ibid., pp. 19–20.

27. Mentzel, *Allemann*, p. 37.

28. Pheiffer, 'Gebroke Nederlands', Vol. 1, pp. 21–2.

29. From the notes of M. Greenlees and K.M. Jeffreys on pp. 119–120 of Mentzel, *Allemann*. These notes contain an account of the case of *Allemann* vs *Barbier*.

30. Ibid., p. 74.

31. Ibid., p. 114.

32. Ibid., p. 106 and M.W. Spilhaus, *South Africa in the Making, 1652–1806* (Cape Town, 1966), p. 106.

33. Mentzel, *Allemann*, p. 107.

34. Pheiffer, 'Gebroke Nederlands', Vol. 1, p. 23; Vol. 2, p. 89–93.

35. Ibid., Vol. 1, p. 24.

36. Ibid., Vol. 1, p. 24 and Vol. 2, pp. 98–101, 112–18.

37. Ibid., Vol. 1, pp. 25–7; Vol. 2, pp. 12–14. An interesting aspect of Barbier's life at the Cape was the support he received from widows of French descent. Pheiffer has noted how the widow Elizabeth Joubert had been willing to give evidence for Barbier against Sergeant Kok (Vol. 2, p. 90). She had been born in Provence in 1668. Widow Celliers had been born in Orleans in 1676. Her maiden name was Elisabeth Couvret. She married Josué Celliers of Orleans and arrived at the Cape in 1700 along with her husband and her brother Paul. Paul's wife, Anné Falleté, was from the same village as Barbier – Bazoches. When Paul Couvret returned to Europe in 1712 with his wife and four children, it is not inconceivable that they went back to Bazoches or Orleans. Perhaps Barbier, then aged 13 or 14, knew the family. See Pheiffer, 'Gebroke Nederlands', Vol. 2, note on p. 77. See also De Villiers and Pama, *Geslagsregisters*, pp. 135 and 160.

38. Pheiffer, 'Gebroke Nederlands', Vol. 2, p. 14.

39. Hobsbawm has noted the high prevalence of soldiers, deserters and ex-servicemen amongst social bandits in *Bandits*, pp. 33–4.

40. See Penn, 'The Northern Cape Frontier Zone', pp. 91–8 for the background to these events. Also Penn, 'The Frontier in the Western Cape, 1700–1740'. The expedition was first noted in De Wet (ed.), *Resolusies van die Politieke Raad, Vol. 9*, 13 March 1739, pp. 256–7.

41. It is interesting to note that Van Wyk's mother, Agnita Campher, was the daughter of the slave woman Ansela of the Cape and her husband Lourens Campher of 'Muratie'. Van Wyk's uncle was Cornelis Campher and Frans Campher was thus his cousin. Willem van Wyk's brother Gerrit was married to his cousin Sophia Campher whilst Willem himself was married to Anna Campher, the pre-marital daughter of Cornelis Campher's wife Dorothea Oelofse (herself of slave descent). Lodewyk Pulter, or Putter, was married to one of Agnita's daughters by a previous marriage. See Helena Sheffler, 'The History of the Historic Wine Estate Muratie, 1699–1991' (Stellenbosch, unpublished, no date), pp. 5–34. I am grateful to the Melck family for letting me read this work.

42. Popular opinion is that Jacobus Coetzee was the first European to reach the Orange River in 1760. See for instance J.M. Coetzee, *Dusklands* (Johannesburg, 1991), p. 115 and *Reader's Digest Atlas of Southern Africa* (n.p., 1984), p. 29. The records of the Council of Policy are, however, quite explicit: 'Capn. Gaaren verhaald wijders dat over een geruijmen tijd geleeden eenige Europeanen, voorsien met wagens en verseld met andere Hottentotten, bij zijn vaders coraal, geleegen bij de soogenaamde Groote Rivier, sijn gekoomen ...' De Wet (ed.), *Resolusies van die Politieke Raad, Vol. 9*, 13 March 1739, p. 258.

43. De Wet (ed.), *Resolusies van die Politieke Raad, Vol. 9*, 13 March 1739, p. 257.

44. Ibid. Van Wyk underwent a Namaqua initiation ceremony ('t Kammi) to make him a member of the tribe. This is described by H. Cloete in a letter to Hendrik Swellengrebel, jnr. Since the ceremony involved being urinated upon, Van Wyk became quite famous in the colony and at the time of his death, in 1777, was known as Willem Namaqua. See G.J. Schutte, *Briefwisseling van Hendrik Swellengrebel Jr oor Kaapse Sake 1778–1792* (Cape Town, 1982).

45. De Wet (ed.), *Resolusies van die Politieke Raad, Vol. 9*, 13 March 1739, pp. 257–9.

46. Ibid.

47. For Khoisan resistance during this phase of frontier expansion see N. Penn, 'Northern Cape Frontier Zone', pp. 91–139 and 'The Frontier in the Western Cape, 1700–1740'.

48. CA, LM 49, Res. 19 Jan. 1740, p. 99.

49. Pheiffer, 'Gebroke Nederlands', Vol. 2, p. 15; Vol. 1, p. 28.

50. Ibid., Vol. 1, p. 29.

51. The names of those who went on the expedition to the Orange River were Willem van Wyk, Lodewyk Putter, Hendrik Ras, Matthys Willemsz, Jacob Swart, Frans Campher, Andries van der Walde, Sybrand van Dyk, Augustus Lourens and Jan Gous. Pieter de Bruyn had preceded them. CA, LM 49, Res. 13 March 1739, p. 261. The names of those who accompanied Barbier to the church were Hendrik Kruger (whose servants had gone on the expedition), Lodewyk Putter, Frans Campher, Arnoldus Basson, Hendrik Ras, Jan Olivier, Sybrand van Dyk and Johannes Ras. See G.M. Theal, *Belangrijke Historische Dokumenten*, Parts 1 and 2. *Verscheidene Dokumenten betrekking hebbende tot den Oproermaker Estienne Barbier* (Cape Town, 1896), p. 5.

52. A copy of the avis is to be found in Pheiffer, 'Gebroke Nederlands', Vol. 2, pp. 26–29.

53. Ibid.

54. See pages 118 and 119 below for further instances of 'deposits' on loan farms.

55. R. Ross has commented on the high growth rate of the free population of the Cape Colony, which was largely due to the low age at first marriage of women, in 'Capitalism, Expansion and Incorporation on the Southern African Frontier', in H. Lamar and L. Thompson (eds.), *The Frontier in History* (New Haven, 1981), pp. 217–18.

56. This observation is based on a study of the Oude Wildschut Boeke (RLR) in the archives. I am grateful to Professor L. Guelke for making his notes on the RLR available to me.

57. For some of the expenses facing frontier farmers see L. Guelke, 'Freehold Farmers and Frontier Settlers, 1657–1780' in Elphick and Giliomee (eds.), *The Shaping of South African Society*. For the creation of the Cape gentry see Guelke and Shell, 'An Early Colonial Landed Gentry' and Ross, 'The Rise of the Cape Gentry'.

58. Theal, *Belangrijke Historische Dokumenten*, p. 5.

59. CA, LM 49, Res. 21 March 1739, pp. 236–9.

60. Pheiffer, 'Gebroke Nederlands', Vol. 2, p. 65.

61. Ibid., pp. 67–70. At a later date Barbier's prosecutors were to make a great deal out of the words he uttered whilst going to this meeting when his followers feared an ambush: 'Neen kinderen; het en is geen swaerigheijd; want wij ben goed gewaep' (No children; that is no problem; because we are well armed).

62. Ibid., 2, p. 70.

63. Ibid., pp. 73–4.

64. For the idea that Barbier was trying to exploit ill-feeling between Van den Henghel and Swellengrebel see Mentzel, p. 107 and Pheiffer, 'Gebroke Nederlands', Vol. 2, p. 107.

65. Pheiffer, 'Gebroke Nederlands', Vol. 2, p. 77.

66. Ibid., p. 78.

67. CA, LM 49, Res. 21 March 1739, pp. 236–39.

68. Pheiffer, 'Gebroke Nederlands', p. 33.

69. Ibid., p. 21.

70. Penn, 'Northern Cape Frontier Zone', p. 117; 'Frontier in the Western Cape', p. 480.

71. Penn, 'Northern Cape Frontier Zone', pp. 118–19; CA, C 651, 20 April 1739.

72. Penn, 'Northern Cape Frontier Zone', p. 119; De Wet (ed.), *Resolusies van die Politieke Raad, Vol. 9*, 28 April 1739, pp. 265–6.

73. Penn, 'Northern Cape Frontier Zone', pp. 119–21; 'Frontier in the Western Cape', pp. 482–3.

74. See note 24 above.

75. M.H.D. Smith, *Boerepioniers van die Sandveld* (Pretoria, 1985), pp. 58–9.

76. Pheiffer, 'Gebroke Nederlands', Vol. 2, pp. 84–8.

77. Ibid., pp. 50–4.

78. Ibid., Vol. 1, p. 34. Barbier was later to argue that he would have turned himself in had he but heard of the edict in time, or had he dared to appear in the open when the *veldwagters* had been instructed to kill him. Ibid., Vol. 2, p. 24.

79. Penn, 'Northern Cape Frontier Zone', p. 121; De Wet (ed.), *Resolusies van die Politieke Raad, Vol. 9*, 2 June 1739, pp. 277–9.

80. CA, I/STB 13/4, 23 June 1739; C 651, 22 June 1739.

81. CA, C 651, 29 June 1739; De Wet (ed.), *Resolusies van die Politieke Raad, Vol. 9,* 7 July 1739, pp. 280–1.

82. CA, LM 49, Res. 7 July 1739, pp. 64–5.

83. Pheiffer, 'Gebroke Nederlands', Vol. 2, p. 88.

84. CA, C 455, Lourensz to Swellengrebel, 23 July 1739; C 1101, 24 July, 1739, p. 14; C 524, Vergaande Briewe, 24 July 1739, pp. 410–11.

85. Pheiffer, 'Gebroke Nederlands', Vol. 2, p. 31.

86. CA, C 455, Lourensz to Swellengrebel, 3 Dec. 1739.

87. Ibid. The words of Mr. Weller to his son, Sam, come to mind: 'Take example by your father, my boy, and be very careful o' vidders all your life.'

88. Mentzel, *Allemann*, pp. 115–16.

89. Ibid.

90. Pheiffer, 'Gebroke Nederlands', Vol. 2, pp. 12–24.

91. Ibid.

92. Theal, *Belangrijke Historische Documenten*, pp. 6–12.

93. M. Foucault, *Discipline and Punish* (London, 1979), p. 47. 'In the "excesses" of torture, a whole economy of power is invested', p. 35.

94. Mentzel, *Allemann*, pp. 116–17.

95. CA, C 455, Lourensz to Swellengrebel, 3 Dec. 1739; C 455, Lourensz to Swellengrebel, 8 Dec. 1739. There are several letters from Lourensz to the Governor in which he describes the vigour with which he drags the corpses of slaves who committed suicide to deposit them in porcupine holes. LM 20, Letters Rec. 1726–1732, Lourensz to Governor, 12 Feb. 1729.

96. The phrase is Foucault's. I think Hobsbawm is quite wrong to say that the ritual of public execution belongs to the myth of urban crime rather than to social banditry. Hobsbawm, *Bandits*, p. 128.

97. De Wet (ed.), *Resolusies van die Politieke Raad, Vol. 9*, 21 March 1739, p. 260, n. 105.

98. Actually the government never returned the confiscated cattle to the colonists. As soon as the frontier war and the rebellion were over, the cattle were sold to pay for the costs of the commandos. CA, LM 49, 19 Jan. 1740, p. 100.

99. Penn, 'Northern Cape Frontier Zone', pp. 137–9, 169–210; N. Penn, 'Labour, Land and Livestock in the Western Cape during the Eighteenth Century: The Khoisan and the Colonists', in W.G. James and M. Simons (eds.), *The Angry Divide: Social and Economic History of the Western Cape* (Cape Town, 1989).

100. R. Austen, *African Economic History* (London, 1987), p. 161.

101. Only Robert Graves's Sergeant Lamb is a serious rival!

102. There is an Afrikaans novel for children by Dan Sleigh called *'n Man om te hardloop* which features Estienne Barbier (Cape Town, 1973). After this chapter was first published as an article in *Social Dynamics* in 1988 it was read by André Brink. It stimulated him to read more about Barbier and to write the novel *On the Contrary* (London, 1993). Barbier's mythic presence is growing.

103. See Penn, 'Northern Cape Frontier Zone', pp. 169–278.

104. H. Giliomee, 'The Eastern Frontier, 1770–1812' in Elphick and Giliomee (eds.), *The Shaping of South African Society*.

4 The Beast of the Bokkeveld

1. 'Caffers' were the servants of the *fiscaal* (prosecutor), 'convicts from the East Indies who were thus in effect slaves and who doubled as hangman's assistants'. Ross, *Cape of Torments,* pp. 33–5. See Shell, *Children of Bondage*, pp. 189–90 for the etymology of the word.

2. Quoted by C. Beyers from the Burgher Memorial of 1779. C. Beyers, *Die Kaapse Patriotte* (Pretoria, 1967), p. 166.

3. Ibid., p. 166. According to Beyers, husband and wife had already reconciled their differences.

4. Ibid.

5. CA, MOOC (Master of the Supreme Court, Section Deceased Estates 1670–1834) 'Bylae by Boedel Rekeninge', 1780–1782, Vol. 11, No. 16.

6. Though Beyers is aware of this occurrence he does not investigate it. G.M. Theal is not very informative either in his *History of South Africa before 1795*, Vol. 4 (Cape Town 1964), p. 178. Buijtendag's biographer in *The Standard Encyclopaedia of Southern Africa* (Cape Town, 1970), pp. 635–4, states simply that he was guilty of maltreating his family.

7. CA, C 655, Dag Register van Stellenbosch en Drakenstein, 1771–1779, 6 May 1776.

8. Ibid.

9. Giliomee, 'Processes'. See M. Legassick, 'The Griqua, the Sotho–Tswana, and the Missionaries, 1780–1840: The Politics of a Frontier Zone' (Ph.D. thesis, University of California, 1969), pp. 1–22, for the concept of a frontier zone.

10. Giliomee, 'Processes', p. 79.

11. M. Legassick, 'The Northern Frontier to 1820', p. 247.

12. See note 17.

13. Penn, 'The Northern Cape Frontier Zone', pp. 49–139 for a detailed account of this process.

14. Ibid.

15. Prominent among these vagabonds was one 'Dronke Gerrit' who 'was come to their kraal [Hannibal's Kraal, three miles north of Verloren Vlei] a few years previously, accompanied by some others and without any parley fired on it from all sides, chased out the Hottentots, set fire to their huts, and took away all their cattle, without their knowing for what reason, since they had never harmed any of the Dutch.' See F. Valentyn, *Description of the Cape of Good Hope with the Matters Concerning It*, Vol. 2 (Cape Town, 1971), p. 41.

16. Ibid.

17. The surest use of the words 'Khoi' and 'San' is when they are used to describe people whose principal means of subsistence is based either on pastoralism or on hunting and gathering. These activities were never completely mutually exclusive and would tend to overlap even in 'normal' times especially in an area like the Western Cape coastal belt between the Atlantic and the Bokkeveld mountains. Here, in a narrow area of land with a variety of terrain, contact between pastoralists and hunter-gatherers had been occurring for at least 1500 years before the arrival of Europeans. In 'abnormal times', such as the period under consideration, which was a time of 'primitive accumulation' ('The historical process of divorcing the producer from the means of production', according to Marx) when the original pastoralists and hunter-gatherers were being deprived of their means of subsistence, the categories 'Khoi' and 'San' would become even more blurred. This problem is reflected in the growing tendency of eighteenth-century colonists to use the blanket term 'Boesjesmans Hottentotten' to describe those whose livelihood they were threatening. 'Khoisan' is simply a more polite, but no more accurate, equivalent for 'Boesjesmans'. See Shula Marks, 'Khoisan Resistance to the Dutch in the Seventeenth and Eighteenth Centuries', *Journal of African History*, 13 (1972), pp. 55–80.

18. Penn, 'Northern Cape Frontier Zone', pp. 49–139.

19. I. Schapera, *The Khoisan Peoples of South Africa* (London, 1930), p. 45 and maps.

20. Heese, 'Onderwys in Namakwaland 1750–1940', p. 2.

21. See Chapter 3.

22. P.L. Scholtz, 'Die Historiese Ontwikkeling van die Onder-Olifantsrivier 1660–1902', *Archives Year Book for South African History*, 1966, Part 2, p. 35.

23. See Penn, 'The Frontier in the Western Cape, 1700–1740'.

24. See for instance the evidence of Pilatus of Bengal who 'with the help of the Hottentots Hani Goeijeman and Couragie, who had been hired by his "baas" to help harvest and clean the wheat' was a slave at a Piketberg farm. CA, 1/STB 3/9, Jan. 1744.

25. Statement of 'Hottentot Kiewit', 23 June 1775, CA, 1/STB 3/11. The wages of one heifer per year seem to be a widespread and enduring payment – see for instance Gudrun Dahl, 'Ecology and Equality', in *Pastoral Production and Society* (Cambridge, 1979), p. 272: 'In Northern Kenya the traditional salary of a herdsman employed to look after cattle was one heifer per year. This norm was accepted by both Somalie and Boranna.' For further details of Khoi–colonial labour contracts, see Penn, 'Labour, Land and Livestock in the Western Cape'.

26. De Villiers and Pama, *Geslagsregisters,* p. 118; CA, LM 49, Res. 21 Oct. 1738 and Res. 9 Dec. 1738.

27. De Villiers and Pama, *Geslagsregisters*, Vol. 1, p. 333. It does not seem that Horn was a very successful licensed victualler for he found himself owing 8000 guilders in arrears for licence fees as lessee of the Cape wine licence by September 1739 and being sued by the fiscal for the sum of 7450 guilders. CA, LM 49, Res. 3 Sept. 1739.

28. CA, RLR (Receiver of Land Revenue – Oude Wildschut Boek) 14/1, p. 29.

29. CA, RLR 14/1, p. 167.

30. De Villiers and Pama, *Geslagsregisters*, Vol. 1, p. 118.

31. According to the 'opgaaf rollen' neither Christiaan Horn, Buijtendag's half-brother, nor Buijtendag's other brother owned anything more than a horse and firearm for years. The failure of Buijtendag's stepfather is recorded in note 27.

32. CA, J 197 (Opgaaf Rollen – Census Rolls), 1/5.

33. CA, J 198.

34. P.J. van der Merwe, *Noordwaartse Beweging van die Boere voor die Groot Trek* (The Hague, 1937), pp. 2–7.

35. C,G. Botha, *Place Names in the Cape Province* (Cape Town, 1926), pp. 104–7.

36. CA, RLR 16/1, p. 39.

37. CA, RLR 19/2, p. 249.

38. P.J. van der Merwe, *Trek: Studies oor die Mobiliteit van die Pioniersbevolking aan die Kaap* (Cape Town, 1945), pp. 120–3.

39. CA, MOOC 14/51.

40. See for instance CA, LM 49, Res. 10 Aug. 1728.

41. CA, RLR 21/1, pp. 61 and 63.

42. On visiting the farm Driefontein I was shown a map dating from the 1930s which shows that Driefontein and Rietfontein were adjacent. There is no Rietfontein in the neighbourhood today.

43. CA, J 203–207. For instance, 1768: 1 son, 3 daughters, 3 slaves, 20 horses, 30 cattle, 300 sheep. 1771: 1 son, 4 daughters, 3 slaves, 1 female slave, 30 horses, 30 cattle, 300 sheep. 1773: 2 sons, 4 daughters, no slaves, 20 horses, 30 cattle, 300 sheep. It is possible that Buijtendag used his favourable position near the Karoopoort, the gateway to the Roggeveld, to sell items to farmers from the interior.

44. The glossary of Elphick and Giliomee, *Shaping of South African Society*, p. 392, defines a *veldwagtmeester* as a 'free burgher militia officer in rural areas; also responsible for some civil administrative duties in the division to which he was appointed'.

45. CA, J 201. Izak van der Merwe had 3 sons, 2 daughters, 1 *knecht*, 8 slaves, 1 female slave, 2 girl slaves, 8 horses, 60 cattle, 500 sheep.

46. The General Commando was the biggest commando ever organised. Its purpose was to crush Khoisan resistance along the length and breadth of the frontier, from the Hantam to the

Sneeuberg and beyond the Roggeveld and Nieuweveld. It killed 503 and captured 241 Khoisan. See D. Moodie, *The Record* (Cape Town, 1960), Part 3, p. 40. See also Penn, 'Northern Cape Frontier Zone', pp. 169–278.

47. Moodie, *The Record*, Part 3, pp. 35–7.

48. Ibid., p. 46.

49. Ibid., pp. 41–2.

50. Called this by J.S. Marais, *The Cape Coloured People 1652–1937* (London, 1939), p. 17. See also N. Penn, '"Fated to Perish": The Destruction of the Cape San' in P. Skotnes (ed.), *Miscast: Negotiating the Presence of the Bushmen* (Cape Town, 1996).

51. CA, 1/STB 10/166: N. van der Merwe to Landdrost Bergh, 27 May 1774; Willem Janse van Rensburg to Bergh, 3 Oct. 1774; I. v.d. Merwe to Bergh, two letters, undated; N. van der Merwe to Bergh, 17 or 27 May 1774; Buijtendag to Van Rensburg, 2 Nov. 1774. A *knecht*, according to the glossary of Elphick and Giliomee, *Shaping of South African Society*, p. 391, was 'a released Company servant or more rarely a free black in the service of a freeburgher; on farms, often an overseer of Khoikhoi and slave labour'. Nicolaas's wife was delivered of a daughter, Cecilia, in 1774. De Villiers and Pama, *Geslagsregisters*, Vol. 2, p. 563.

52. Even with the help of De Villiers and Pama it is no easy task to discover the exact relationship of all the Van der Merwes, who were already a large family by 1774.

53. The events described in this paragraph are reconstructed from the letters listed in note 51.

54. CA, 1/STB 10/166, I. van der Merwe to Bergh, undated.

55. Ibid.

56. CA, 1/STB 10/166, Statement of Captain Jan Abrahams, undated.

57. CA, J 207.

58. CA, MOOC 14/51.

59. CA, 1/STB 3/11, Statement of Engbert Dijkslag, 14 June 1775.

60. Ibid. It was Dijkslag who gave evidence in N. van der Merwe's favour when the latter was facing charges of cruelty.

61. CA, J 205, 206, 207.

62. CA, 1/STB 3/11, Statement of 'Hottentot Kiewit', 23 June 1775. See note 25.

63. Ibid.

64. Statements of Kiewit and Dijkslag.

65. Ibid.

66. Ibid.

67. CA, 1/STB 3/11, Statement of 'Hottentot' Booij, 23 June 1775.

68. CA, 1/STB 10/166, N. van der Merwe to Bergh, 6 Jan. 1775.

69. CA, 1/STB 10/166, N. van der Merwe to Bergh, 23 Jan. 1775.

70. CA, 1/STB 10/166, N. van der Merwe to Bergh, 30 Jan. 1775.

71. CA, 1/STB 3/11, Evidence of Johannes Claassen, 15 April 1776.

72. L. Guelke in 'The White Settlers, 1652–1780', in Elphick and Giliomee (eds.), *Shaping of South African Society* (Cape Town, 1979), p. 64, states that 'The cost of an "opstal" (fixed improvements) in areas suitable for stock farming was usually considerably lower than the cost of an arable freehold farm. The average value of an opstal ranged from 300 to 500 guilders compared with 6,000 to 10,000 guilders for a freehold farm. In some areas an opstal could be purchased for as little as 100 guilders while a good arable farm could cost as much as 20,000 guilders.' Given the fact that Driefontein and Rietfontein were loan farms, they were expensive.

73. CA, 1/STB 3/11, Evidence of Johannes Claassen, 15 April 1776.

74. CA, 1/STB 10/166, Schalk van der Merwe to Bergh, 8 June 1775.

75. Schalk van der Merwe wrote that he was sure that Carel Buijtendag 'op het tapyt is gekoomen om tegens syn Buuren weedrom een nieuwe schaderslag te slaan'.

76. CA, 1/STB 10/166, N. van der Merwe to Bergh, 29 Oct. 1775.

77. CA, 1/STB 3/11, Evidence of Johannes Claassen, 15 April 1776. It is interesting that Buijtendag's 'opgaaf' never mentions wheat. A mudden or muid was 'a dry measure roughly equivalent to one hectolitre'.

78. CA, 1/STB 3/11, Evidence of Johannes Claassen, 15 April 1776. This greeting of Buijtendag's alludes to Claassen's ancestry: Johannes Claassen, born 1724, son of Johannes Claassen or Claasz, son of Claas of Malabar, who married Johanna de Ryk, daughter of Constantia of Bengal, 1725. De Villiers and Pama, *Geslagsregisters*, Vol. 1, p. 138.

79. CA, 1/STB 3/11, Evidence of Johannes Claassen, 15 April 1776.

80. Ibid.

81. Ibid.

82. Ibid.

83. See note 78.

84. CA, 1/STB 1/11, Evidence of Johannes Erasmus, 28 May 1776, evidence of Carel Hendrik Buijtendag, 13 June 1776, evidence of Johannes Claassen, 25 May 1776.

85. Ibid. Claassen said February, Erasmus and Buijtendag said January.

86. Horn owned nothing but a horse in 1773. CA, J 207.

87. Evidence of Erasmus, Buijtendag and Claassen. See note 84. J. du P. Scholtz in his *Afrikaans-Hollands in die agtiende Eeu* (Cape Town, 1970), pp. 147–8, says the meaning of 'Noormans bankji' is obscure.

88. CA, 1/STB 3/11, Evidence of Claassen, 25 May 1776.

89. CA, 1/STB 3/11, Evidence of Aletta Booijsen, wife of Johannes Claassen, 15 April 1776.

90. CA, C 655, Dag Register van Stellenbosch en Drakenstein, 6 May 1776.

91. Ibid., 5 Aug. 1776.

92. For example the *veldwagtmeester* Petrus Pienaar of the Hantam.

93. CA, RLR 25/1, pp. 141 and 151; also J 207. In 1792 the Koue Bokkevelders petitioned the Council of Policy to request that the roads and passes to their district be improved as the difficulties in transporting their produce to Cape Town made this economically unviable. C 207, p. 204, 18 Sept. 1792. See also Van der Merwe, *Die Trekboer in die Geskiedenis van die Kaapkolonie* (Cape Town, 1938), p. 196.

94. When Lichtenstein and De Mist visited the Koue Bokkeveld in 1803 they remarked that the colonists they encountered there were far more civilised than the Roggevelders. E.C. Godée-Molsbergen (ed.), *Reizen in Zuid-Afrika in de Hollandse Tijd* (The Hague, 1916–32), Vol. 2, pp. 187–8.

95. See for example the case of Jan Otto Dideriks of the Roggeveld who killed his Khoi servant Klynveld by beating him and pulling out his fingernails with a pair of pliers. CA, 1/STB 3/11, Statement of Hottentot Danser, 2 Nov. 1763; statement of Hottentot Coridon, 2 Nov. 1763; statement of slave Jacob of Mallabaar, 24 Nov. 1763,.

96. CA, MOOC 14/51.

97. Ibid.

98. Ibid.

5 Droster Gangs of the Bokkeveld and Roggeveld

1. See Chapter 2 above for the origins of *droster* gangs.

2. My approach has been shaped by the belief that language plays an important role in the content of meaning. The signifier is essential to our understanding of the signified. For a succinct summary of a vast literature on this subject see P. Schöttler, 'Historians and Discourse Analysis', *History Workshop Journal*, 27 (Spring 1989), pp. 37–65. Before the late eighteenth century the words 'fugitives' or 'het weglopen sijns slaavs', 'deserteerden slave' or 'gefugeerde slaaven en andere landloopende vagebonden' were far more common than 'droster'. We should also note that whilst slaves and deserters of European origin sometimes joined together in flight

before 1720, this was extremely rare thereafter.

3. Böeseken (ed.), *Resolusies van die Politieke Raad, Vol. 3,* 13 Dec. 1696, pp. 307–8; Ross, *Cape of Torments*, pp. 40–1.

4. CA, VC 19, 1709–1710, 25 June 1709.

5. See Chapter 2 above.

6. See Penn, 'The Frontier in the Western Cape, 1700–1740'.

7. Böeseken (ed.), *Resolusies van die Politieke Raad, Vol. 6,* 2 Sept. 1721, pp. 128–9.

8. For a more detailed discussion of these processes see Penn, 'Labour, Land and Livestock in the Western Cape'. There is some doubt as to whether Khoi had to carry passes. A resolution passed by the Council of Policy on 20 November 1787 said that they ought to. But in January 1797 the landdrost of Stellenbosch wrote to Floris Visser of the Roggeveld saying: 'I also cannot help expressing my surprise to you about where such an order came from that a Hottentot must have a pass, I do not understand that at all; they are free, and my wish is that, if they have served their time, they should (be allowed to) go wherever they wish). CA, 1/STB 20/30, Uitgaande Briewe van Landdros v.d. Riet to Visser, 10 Jan. 1799.

9. Penn, 'Labour, Land and Livestock', pp. 13–29. On the origin of Oorlam groups see De Bruyn, 'The Oorlams Afrikaners'. See also Legassick, 'The Northern Frontier'.

10. For the Oorlam groups of the Orange River, see Penn, 'The Orange River Frontier Zone'.

11. Many of the details which follow have been taken from the documents concerning the trial of Willem Meij, Adam, Rooi Meij and Picqueur. My interpretation of events is often a synthesis of scattered and contradictory evidence. It would be tedious to cite all the page references of the separate pieces of the puzzle and I have therefore kept references to a minimum. The trial is to be found in CA, CJ 454, 1795, pp. 193–397.

12. The Tanqua Karoo, between the Bokkeveld and the Roggeveld, is known by many names: the Ceres Karoo, the Onder Karoo and the Bokkeveld Karoo are some alternatives.

13. See Van der Merwe, *Trek,* pp. 121–46 for a thorough account of this practice.

14. Ibid., pp. 142–3.

15. CA, CJ 454, p. 345.

16. Adam's interrogation is in CA, CJ 454, pp. 367–90.

17. The recollections of Petrus Borchardus Borcherds who encountered Scholtz whilst travelling through the Skurweberg in March 1802. P.B. Borcherds, *An Autobiographical Memoir* (Cape Town, 1861), p. 107.

18. CA, 1/STB 10/153, Maritz to Landdrost, 16 Feb. 1801. Scholtz had struck Maritz whilst the unfortunate fieldcornet was investigating charges against him.

19. Scholtz's farms were 'de Eende Kuijl – agter de Roggeveld aan de Riet Rivier' (CA, RLR 34, 28 Feb. 1786, p. 154), 'de Elandsberg – agter de Roggeveld aan de Riet Rivier' (CA, RLR 34, 24 July 1785) and 'de Baviaans Drift – agter op de Roggeveld aan de Riet Rivier' (CA, RLR 34, 24 July 1785) and 'de Baviaans Drift – agter op de Roggeveld aan de Riet River' (CA, RLR 36, 6 July 1790, p. 232). Elandsberg and Eende Kuijl were taken over by the Olivier family in 1787 and 1788. Borcherds describes Scholtz's farmhouse in the Skurweberg in 1802 (see note 20).

20. Scholtz was known as Jochem (or Joachim) Scholtz the younger since his father, Jan Joachim, was also called Jochem. Jochem senior registered Roggecloof in the Roggeveld on 9 Sept. 1756 (CA, RLR 14, p. 180). It is probable that he retired from farming in 1784 when his current farm, Drooge Land, was taken over by Dan Jacobse (CA, RLR 31, p. 86). See De Villiers and Pama, *Geslagsregisters*, Vol. 2, p. 856 for the Scholtz family genealogy.

21. Hermanus registered 'de Matjes Cloof aan de Klipfontein geleegend in Middelste Roggeveld' in 1776 (CA, RLR 24, p. 75). He was eight years older than Jochem.

22. CA, 1/STB 3/12, Verklarings, Pleidooie en Interrogatorien (Krimineel), 1786–1793, Relaas van Hottentot Jan Swart, 22 June 1793.

23. It was possible to go northwards but one had to be on good terms with the San and

know how to cross the almost waterless expanse of Bushmanland in order to reach safety. A group of four slaves were discovered living with a Khoi shepherd over the Renoster River behind the Roggeveld in 1791. CA, 1/STB 10/162, Maritz to Landdrost, 26 Dec. 1791.

24. See also the lament of Pieter Jacobs of the Roggeveld concerning his worthless, wandering and light-fingered servants. CA, 1/STB 10/162, 25 May 1793.

25. Anna's statement is in CA, CJ 454, pp. 287–9; Rosalijn's is on pp. 291–3.

26. For Petrus Pienaar, see Penn, 'Orange River Frontier Zone', pp. 58–76.

27. CA, CJ 454, pp. 363–90. Picqueur, at a later stage, said that he had been sent to steal bread for Africa's children.

28. *Complot*, meaning a plot, was often used as a collective noun for a group of drosters.

29. Picqueur's interrogation is in CA, CJ 454, pp. 303–22.

30. The Winkelhaak Kloof is close to two other areas of the Koue Bokkeveld that have an interesting history as far as labour relations are concerned. See chapter 4 on the banishing of Carel Buijtendag for the farm Driefontein. Robert Ross has written of the slave revolt on 'Houd den beke' in *Cape of Torments*, Chapter 8.

31. Penn, 'Labour, Land and Livestock', pp. 28–9; also Penn, 'Northern Cape Frontier Zone', pp. 349–52.

32. CA, 1/STB 10/162, letter from Johannes Lubbe, 16 Sept. 1793. The Olifants River Mountains, forming part of the western Bokkeveld Mountains, had long been favourite haunts of *drosters*. In 1802 Willem Burger, fieldcornet of the district, was in charge of a commando that tracked down five runaway slaves. Two were shot dead and three captured. One of those shot dead had been at large for 13 years (to the best of Burger's knowledge), but those who were captured said he had been a *droster* for 25 years in the district with a 'gekonkkel onder de slave en hottentotte so dat mijn hem nooijt hep kenne kreijge'! CA, 1/STB 10/151, Burger to Landdrost, 2 Aug. 1802. Another group of four *droster* slaves were caught in the mountains over the Olifants River in February 1776; two escaped. CA, 1/STB 3/11, Schalk Burger to Landdrost, 21 Feb. 1776.

33. A partial exception to this rule was the runaway slave Fortuijn, of Cornelis Coetze Cornelius in the Middel Roggeveld. Fortuijn was managing to support himself with a flock of goats (supplemented with food from the slave of Hendrik Olivier) in the Roggeveld Mountains when, unfortunately, Gerrit Maritz encountered him and shot him. CA, 1/STB 3/11, Verklarings, Pleidooie en Interrogatorien (Krimineel) 1759–1782, Relaas van Gerrit Maritz, 8 June 1775.

34. Presumably Hermanus Scholtz, a Roggeveld farmer, had his sheep stolen when they were in the Karoo.

35. Willem Meij's interrogation is in CA, CJ 454, pp. 343–62.

36. CA, 1/STB 3/12, Relaas van Hottentot Piet Claas, 2 April 1793.

37. Rooi Meij's interrogation is in CA, CJ 454, pp. 323–42. Cornelis Jooste also had cattle stolen from him.

38. It is also possible that Africa, ex-slave of Petrus Pienaar, knew the area well, for in April 1779 the farm had been registered in Pienaar's name. CA, RLR 26, p. 58.

39. The present owner of Winkelhaak, Mr Pohl, assured me that this route had been a popular one for reaching the Karoo. It was not necessary for people with livestock or wagons to go via Karoo Poort.

40. On the Doorn River. Jan Kok farmed at 'de Vogelfontein – aan de Oosterkand van 't Olifants Rivier in 't gebergte'. CA, RLR 34, p. 131, 20 Dec. 1785.

41. CA, 1/STB 3/13, Crimineele Verklaaringen, 1793–1796, Relaas van Hottentottine Griet, 14 March 1794; Relaas van Hottentottine Sara, 7 March 1794; CJ 454, pp. 271–5. A letter from Jasper Cloete in 1795 reported that Wissel Bokkevelt had come to him to report that all the other Khoi with him had been murdered by 'de vreemde nasie'. CA, 1/STB 10/163, 28 June 1795.

42. There is no Elands River or Elands Kloof marked on the map near Eylands Drift so it

is difficult to place the site.

43. CA, 1/STB 3/13, Relaas van Hottentottine Flora, 14 Feb. 1794; CJ 454, pp. 259–69.

44. CA, CJ 454, pp. 271–5; 255–7.

45. Ibid., pp. 237–8.

46. It is significant that even Rooi and his followers spoke of *drosters.* CA, 1/STB 3/13, Relaas van Flora, 14 Feb. 1794; CA, CJ 454, p. 339.

47. CA, CJ 454, pp. 303–90. Naturally those who were captured claimed to have had no part in planning the murder.

48. See note 43.

49. CA, 1/STB 3/13, Relaas van Griet, 14 March 1794; CA, CJ 454, pp. 271–5. For Willem Fortuijn see note 64.

50. Joshua Penny, a deserted sailor who took refuge amongst the farmers of the Koue Bokkeveld in 1795, describes how this honey beer was made: 'While among the Hottentots I had learned their method of making a very pleasant beverage resembling metheglin. I was fortunate enough to find an old hollow tree, which I cut off with my knife and seized a green hide on one for a bottom. Into this tub honey and water was put to stand twenty-four hours; then was added some pounded root to make it ferment. This root, in use among the frontier Hottentots, does not resemble any of my acquaintance in America, but makes an excellent drink in this preparation.' J. Penny, *The Life and Adventures of Joshua Penny* (New York, 1815; reprinted Cape Town, 1982), p. 33. Penny's experiences, incidentally, reveal that white deserters did not join *droster* gangs since they were assured of refuge amongst the frontier farmers. This had probably been the case since about the 1720s.

51. CA, CJ 454, pp. 363ff; 202.

52. Frans Lubbe was actually *veldwagtmeester* of the Bidouw (now spelt Biedou) area and not the same Lubbe as Johannes. This area, and the Cedarberg in general, was well known as a reservoir of 'Bastaards'. On 23 July 1790 W.A. Nel of the Hantam was going to write to Frans Lubbe of 'de Bidouw om de bastaards en hottentots die in de Kouwe bergen woont' to call them out on commando. CA, 1/STB 10/162, 23 July 1790. In about 1795 there were 22 men eligible for commando duty in the Bidouw valley and 16 of them were 'Bastaards'. CA, 1/STB 10/163, undated letter from Johannes Spanneberg. See also Penn, 'Labour, Land and Livestock', p. 29, footnotes.

53. CA, CJ 454, pp. 237–40; CA, 1/STB /13, Relaas van de gedoopte bastaard hottentotte Carel van Rooijen en David Koopman, 7 March 1794; Relaas van Gerrit Cloete, 5 March 1794.

54. CA, CJ 454, pp. 229–35.

55. Ibid., pp. 279–81, 323–42.

56. Ibid., pp. 283–5, 323–42.

57. Ibid., pp. 279–81.

58. CA, 1/STB 10/153, Jochem Scholtz to Van der Riet, 4 May 1800; CA, CJ 454, pp. 194–227. At one stage it was suggested that the women serve four months' detention in the Company slave lodge. CA, CJ 76, 31 July 1794.

59. CA, CJ 454, pp. 194–229; CJ 76, pp. 445–52; CJ 77, p. 50.

60. A more radical proposal was that of *veldwagtmeester* Gerrit Maritz and 30 other colonists of the Roggeveld who had requested in 1787 that no Khoi kraals at all be permitted between the Middle and Klein Roggeveld in the Bokkeveld [*sic*] and that all Khoi should be deprived of their guns. CA, 1/STB 10/162, 3 March 1787.

61. Ross, *Cape of Torments,* pp. 48–9.

62. The composition of Africa's *droster* gang is, in itself, an indication that, by the 1790s, different categories of unfree labour were being united by a common consciousness of oppression. There were three slave men, three Khoi men, two 'Bastaard-Hottentot' men and one boy, three Khoi women and two little girls (who, if Africa was their father, would have been classified 'Bastaard-Hottentot').

63. One slave who managed to stay free in the mountains for over 20 years was a certain Reijner. He ran away from his master in Drakenstein in about 1727 and lived in the mountains behind the Berg River until 1749 when he was recaptured. CA, 1/STB 3/8, 8 and 9 Jan. 1749.

64. An illuminating example of Khoi violence to Khoi is found on Jan Louw's Bokkeveld farm (the Meij brothers' home) in February 1793. There were at least four Khoi labourers, three Khoi women and a slave at the farm. One of the Khoi, Klein Booij, had acted as overseer but once he left Geduld, the slave became a *mandoor.* Willem Fortuijn, one of the labourers, accused Piet Claas of sleeping with his wife and of handling oxen badly. The two men fought whilst harvesting dagga flowers. Claas hit Fortuijn with a kierie but Fortuijn stabbed Claas with the harvesting knife. He was helped up by a certain Willem Stompie and nursed back to health by a slave of the widow Frans Jooste. Perhaps this is the same Willem Fortuijn to whom Griet fled after Oude Rooij's murder. CA, 1/STB 3/12, Relaas van Hottentot Piet Claas, 2 April 1793.

65. CA, 1/STB 3/13, Relaas van Hottentots Wildschut en Fredrik Platje, 5 March 1794.

66. Ibid., Relaas van Hottentot Jantje, 24 March 1794.

67. Ibid., Relaas van Hottentot Toontje, 24 Nov. 1794.

68. CA, 1/STB 10/162, Maritz to Landdrost, 26 Dec. 1791.

69. CA, 1/STB 10/151, Karstens to Landdrost, 15 Aug. 1795.

70. CA, 1/STB 10/165, Kriger to Landdrost, 18 Aug. 1798.

71. On the Xhosa see P. Kallaway, 'Danster and the Xhosa of the Gariep: Towards a Political Economy of the Cape Frontier 1790–1820', *African Studies*, 41, 1 (1982), pp. 143–60 and E. Anderson, *A History of the Xhosas of the Northern Cape 1795–1987* (Cape Town, 1985).

72. CA, 1/STB 10/65, Visser to Landdrost, 17 Nov. 1797.

73. CA, 1/STB 10/150, Hugo to Landdrost, 1 Aug. 1800.

74. CA, 1/STB 10/152, Hugo to Landdrost, 24 Aug. 1799. This picture was confirmed by Jacob Kriger in the Klein Roggeveld who wrote in the same month that 'hier de inloopende Hottentots beginnen balstoorig te worden, en kop te toonen; ook als hun wort niet aanstaal, van hunne Baassen wegloopen'. CA, 1/STB 10/152, Kriger to Landdrost, 27 Aug. 1799.

75. CA, 1/STB 20/30, Van der Riet to Jochem Scholtz, 10 Jan. 1799.

Index